CULT HEROES

NEWCASTLE UNITED

CULT HEROES
NEWCASTLE UNITED

Dylan Younger

This edition first published by Pitch Publishing 2012

Pitch Publishing
A2 Yeoman Gate
Yeoman Way
Durrington
BN13 3QZ
www.pitchpublishing.co.uk

A CIP catalogue record is available for this book
from the British Library

ISBN 978-1-9080516-2-2

Typesetting and origination by Pitch Publishing.

Printed in Great Britain by TJ International.

Contents

Acknowledgements

THANKS FIRST OF all to my family - my mother Lorna for encouraging me to write, my partner Karen and my children Cai and Tegan for rescuing me from the study as and when necessary (even if it didn't seem so at the time!).

Many thanks to my publisher Simon Lowe for giving me the opportunity to write the book, and giving me so much freedom to write what I wanted to write.

I remain grateful to Malcolm Macdonald - one of the most glittering stars in Newcastle's history - for his foreword.

Thanks one and all to:

- The boys - or is that old men? - on the *Sunday Sun* sports and in particular Neil Farrington - a first-class journalist and a good friend.

- The *Newcastle Chronicle & Journal* Library staff - Ann Dixon, Keith Clark and Christine Dixon.

- All the fanatical supporters herein, young and old, who gladly shared their memories with me.

- All the friends, especially Nigel Good, Colin Mitcheson, David Quinn and Steve Hargraves, who have helped me debate the points in this book a touch too long and a bit too hard.

Finally, thanks to all the sportswriters past and present who have provided such a massive bibliography on Newcastle United.

Five men in particular have provided a huge backdrop of knowledge and research on past Magpies stars - official club historian Paul Joannou and lifetime sports journalists Ken McKenzie, John Gibson, Alan Oliver and Paul Tully.

This is not a facts-and-figures book, but without the work done by these men, and many others over the decades, the task of drawing comparisons between heroes from different eras would be all the more daunting.

Foreword

by Malcolm Macdonald

Whenever I am approached by a member of the Geordie public, it is invariably for that individual to regale me with their memory of a goal I scored many years back whilst wearing the famous black and white stripes of NUFC.

It would be easy to go, "Yeah, Yeah" and walk on, but, that would be to miss the very important nub of what has just happened. That recollection being spoken of is that very important moment of sharing a past memory together.

Never having met before, but, strangers no longer. For that person is saying to me, "I was there, I was scoring it with you", and few were the televised games then, so, I know they really were there.

That shared recollection becoming that most human of necessities, connection. How easy the conversation then starts to flow. To other goals, matches, to team mates, some still with us, some not.

On departing each is left with a rejuvenation from a long-past moment of thrill, even ecstasy. Certainly... excitement.

A million good memories in the sands of time are honed into one all-powerful memory encapsulated by one particular goal selected from hundreds.

That person before me is telling me how he saw my five years on Tyneside all in one strike.

What a wonderful honour it is to be remembered so, you see, nobody has ever come to me and said, "Do you remember that miss?"

Geordies, although appreciative of any silverware that might come their way, don't make it the be-all-and-end-all of their lives, unlike many football supporters, and, perhaps, that's not such a bad thing considering.

Instead, they are much happier to make their focal point the players, those striving to win silverware. You see, they are a peoples'people.

Introduction

Welcome to the refuge. Here, you can forget, for a while, that the club you love has relentlessly broken your heart for more than three decades.

No domestic trophy wins for 57 years, no major silverware of any kind for 43 and no league title for 85 years.

But forget your increasingly bitter hope for a while – within these pages are reminders aplenty why Newcastle United is still one of the greatest of all football clubs . . .

Some of the most captivating characters the game has ever known – some of the most outrageously talented players the world has seen – have worn the black and white shirt.

Indeed, heroes in black and white are writ larger on Tyneside than perhaps anywhere else on the British football map.

The £16m purchase of Michael Owen in late summer 2005 continued a long-held tradition of providing an idol for the Gallowgate crowd, at a time when more sober souls reflected on various weaknesses elsewhere in the squad.

Individual idolatry – and a slavish devotion to attacking football – always seem higher on the black and white agenda than all-round team-building.

Was it not ever thus?

Not in the days when Newcastle United really did rule the football world, winning three league titles and an FA Cup in the first decade of the last century.

That side, built on a tight defence and playing a possession football that was the very epitome of teamwork, was full of heroes too – and three of those epic Edwardian figures stand proudly in this book as proof positive that Newcastle's footballing gods CAN also be winners.

But there are so many different types herein . . .

Six Geordies, four Scots, four Yorkshiremen, an Irishman, a Welshman, a Midlander, a Cockney, a Lancastrian and a South American . . .

Eleven strikers (naturally), four central midfielders, two inside-forwards, two defenders and a winger . .

We have drinkers, womanisers, gamblers, brawlers, playboys, hermits and tee-totallers ... wise-cracking egotists and painfully shy recluses, handsome braggarts and awkward introverts, model professionals and hot-to-handle rogues, on-pitch gentlemen and battle-hardened warriors.

There is the tormented genius of Hughie Gallacher and Paul Gascoigne and the mature, willed determination of Alan Shearer.

Some, such as charismatic self-publicists Malcolm Macdonald and Kevin Keegan, took to heroic status as if it was their birthright, natural stars on and off the pitch.

Others – quiet men like Len White, Tony Green and Andy Cole – never quite came to terms with the peculiar ferocity of hero worship on Tyneside.

A few – Gallacher, Shackleton, Gascoigne – can lay claim to the title of genius while others (Harvey, Brennan) have been celebrated for their tenacity or, like Colin Veitch and in particular, Bill McCracken, their tactical mind.

Two men – Harvey and Keegan – have earned their place in the pantheon at least partly because of their impressive achievements as Newcastle manager.

There are, of course, many omissions, among them:

Jock Peddie, Bill Appleyard, Jimmy Lawrence, Peter McWilliam, Tom McDonald, Andy Aitken, Frank Hudspeth, Neil Harris, Stan Seymour, Jack Hill, Roy Bentley, Tommy Pearson, Charlie Wayman, Ernie Taylor, Jack Fairbrother, Ronnie Simpson, George Eastham, Ivor Allchurch, Bobby Moncur, Terry Hibbit, David Craig, Frank Clark, Jimmy Smith, Chris Waddle, Micky Quinn, Robert Lee, Les Ferdinand, David Ginola, Tino Asprilla, Nolberto Solano and Shay Given – super players and to many, heroic figures, one and all. And none of them in this book. Sorry lads.

There may be names above who have contributed more to Newcastle United than some of my chosen 20 – and many of those names were on an original lengthy list, scribbled in pencil, crossed out, rewritten, crossed out again ...

My final pick includes a man who played 444 games across 19 years of service – and another who completed not one full season before injury wrecked his career.

Eleven of these men have won major silverware at United, leaving nine who won nought but adulation.

And that is the very heart of the matter, reminding me to stress what this book is not.

It is not a book about the greatest *players* in Newcastle's history, nor even the most influential men – chapters on 'secretary' Frank Watt, who won four league titles and two FA Cups and Stan Seymour, who served the club with distinction as a player, manager, director and chairman – would certainly be included if it were.

No, this is a book about heroes – and a look at why certain icons, across the ages, have been able to quicken the pulse.

To draw up the final list, I have had to address the thorny issue of comparing dusty figures such as Veitch and McCracken – whose epic achievements were sketched in the vaguest detail in the days when Press sports coverage was but a tiny fraction of its 21st century equivalent – with modern day icons.

The Shearer riddle is at the heart of this dilemma. We remain, just a few months after his retirement, in the eye of the Shearer storm with magazine, newspaper and TV specials, books and commemorative DVDs reminding us of his impact.

Yet is he a bigger icon now than his predecessor Colin Veitch was then – a Geordie who captained England and won four major honours with his hometown club?

Shearer is – like Veitch, McCracken, and Bobby Mitchell – one of the long-stayers, yet the relative cameos of Shackleton, Green and Cole also deserve their place.

Many of the figures herein are natural entertainers.

Yet fervent devotion to the likes of McCracken – a cynical defender who manipulated the offside law to disruptive effect – and the destructive ability of Frank Brennan, show that Geordie fans could appreciate the dark arts too.

There is of course, no correct answer to the charge I was given. Indeed, there may not be another supporter out there who would pick the exact same 20, and there is no official 'devotion-meter' on the market to aid the task.

The sheer resonance of names is often a clue, though – and the majority of my chosen names still stir the consciousness of football fans young and old on Tyneside.

Here, then, is my final. There is no definitive attempt to rank them in exact order, and yet the pull of that overriding question is irresistible – just who is the biggest hero of them all?

Read on then, and find out how my answer compares with yours. Forget that talk of a trophy curse, kick back, and revel in all those days when black and white were the only colours that mattered ...

Dylan Younger

*To my father Francis, who gave me my love
of football and of life.*

Colin Veitch

1895-1926: 322 games, 49 goals

IN THE BEGINNING was Colin Veitch.

Before Hughie, Jackie, Wyn, Malcolm, Kevin, Peter, Paul and Alan, Colin was arguably the first genuine football icon on Tyneside. And in these days when Newcastle's reputation as the most feared team in the land is nothing but a dusty memory, Veitch's story is a tale worth celebrating.

Yes, there was a time when United were known for more than raucous support and perennial, agonising underachievement. Under the guidance of secretary Frank Watt, the Magpies won four league titles, in 1905, 1907, 1909 and 1927, two FA Cups (1910 and 1924) and reached another four FA Cup finals (1905, 1906, 1908, 1911). No manager in United's history would again come close to the Scotsman's exceptional record.

In fact Watt's managerial reputation remains criminally under-celebrated to this day, and partly because he ruled before the time when the likes of Bill Nicholson Matt Busby and Bill Shankly worked happily under the title 'manager'. Yet Watt's influence at a club he took from Division Two (Newcastle were promoted in 1898) to becoming established at the very pinnacle of the English game was massive, and to this day he creates a strong case as the most influential figure in United's long history. Indeed, Watt's record means he can stand shoulder-to-shoulder with the very finest managers ever to grace the British game.

But this Edinburgh-born club secretary did not have a feverish media in place to celebrate his legend, and his naturally quiet demeanour did not lend itself to public recognition and acclaim. In short, it remains a stretch to describe Watt, despite his 34-year reign at St James's, as a cult hero in his own right, although he brought many to Tyneside – such as Glaswegian Jock Peddie, whose off-field misdemeanours and 78 goals in 136 games for United marked him out as arguably the first terrace hero in club history.

So many of United's most influential players – like Peddie, Peter 'The Great' McWilliam and Andy 'Daddler' Aitken – hailed from north of the border, products of Watt's comprehensive scouting network in his homeland. But the man who presents a strong case as Watt's most important-ever signing was born in the very heart of the city – although a typical Geordie footballer he most certainly was not.

COLIN VEITCH'S ASSOCIATION with the club – as player and then coach – lasted 31 years after signing for the Magpies in 1895. And, together with central midfielder Andy Aitken, left-half Peter McWilliam, right-winger Jack Rutherford and goalkeeper Jimmy Lawrence – who made a staggering 507 appearances for the club – Veitch was one of the driving forces behind the most successful spell in Newcastle United's history. Standing just 5ft 6in tall, Veitch was a colossus on the pitch – an all-round maestro who so completely mastered all the various arts of the game that he appeared in every outfield position for the club, apart from left-back and left-wing.

However, Veitch, although a capable striker and defender, preferred to direct operations from the half-back line, and central midfield in particular. One of the first football figures to preach the importance of tactics, Veitch's impact on the great Edwardian United side was vast – helping to shape the quick-passing team approach which allowed the Magpies to reach the very pinnacle of the British game and begin the legend that today regularly has the media hailing Geordie football as a 'hotbed' or a 'sleeping giant'.

Veitch's style was the cornerstone of what former Manchester City, Manchester United and Wales star Billy Meredith called "the greatest side that was ever possessed by any club". His pin-point passing was legendary, his control masterful, and one supporter, E.B. Boyd, hailed him as "the best trapper of a ball I have ever seen", in a letter to the

Newcastle Journal after Veitch's playing days had ended. But despite his undoubted ability, Veitch was not the type to dwell on the ball or engage in fancy dribbling skills. He preferred to pass quickly, letting the ball do the work to stretch defences and open up gaps for his forwards to exploit. It is ironic that this approach from Veitch, the earliest of all 20 cult heroes in this book, should even now, 107 years after his debut, be regarded as 'modern'.

Veitch's deep thinking, analytical approach to football made him a versatile player on the pitch, and a trusted lieutenant for club secretary Frank Watt off it. His influence at the club was such that Veitch was the man credited with recommending a new striker in 1908 – and he duly delivered, coming up with an inspired choice in Albert Shepherd, whose record of 92 goals in 123 games brought him into consideration for inclusion in this book.

Respected within the club and increasingly admired on the terraces, Veitch was an easy figure to look up to – despite his lack of stature. With aristocratic good looks, this educated Geordie – he was plucked from well-to-do Rutherford College to begin his United career – quickly emerged as the Renaissance Man of St James'.

At a time when football's followers were making the transition from simply paying spectators to dedicated, passionate supporters, Veitch's extraordinary range of abilities, and his bona fide Geordie roots, made him an instant crowd favourite, even among the greatest collection of footballers in United's history.

Many are the icons within these pages whose off-field antics have added to their cult status, and this is true with Veitch, but perhaps not in the same way as a Gazza or Hughie Gallacher. Articulate and dedicated to the arts, Veitch was a talented musician, conductor, scholar, journalist, actor, producer and playwright and once stood as a socialist Parliamentary candidate after hanging up his boots. Along with team-mate Aitken, he was an active campaigner for footballers' rights, co-founding the Players' Union and then chairing the organisation between 1911 and 1918. And his fame in his home city was further enhanced by his marriage to talented actress Greta Burke, his friendship with the great playwright George Bernard Shaw his work in co-founding the People's Theatre in his native Heaton, and his involvement in the Newcastle Playhouse, the Newcastle Operatic Society and Clarion Choir. Not for Veitch a mate with five bellies.

Shaw was an occasional guest at the Gosforth home of Veitch and his wife – the Round House on Grove Avenue was a special building with circular rooms designed for the Veitchs and befitting the status of a couple who remained glamorous figures in the life of the city long after his playing days.

VEITCH'S CONTRIBUTION TO Newcastle and its football club was so vast that many students of the Edwardian era lay his claim to be considered the most important Magpie ever. Tyneside historian and author Chris Goulding is one such devotee, and he has pushed for a statue of Veitch to be installed in the city centre. Along with Jackie Milburn, Veitch is one of a selected few names from North East sport to be celebrated in the *Oxford Dictionary of National Biography*. The player's fame was further celebrated in modern times in the late 90s play *The Beautiful Game* which recaptured some of the glorious figures from the club's long history. Playwright Mike Chaplin was left in no doubt that Veitch was one of the all-time greats – not least because of his legacy in introducing tactics to the club. "There didn't used to be much movement off the ball," said Chaplin. "What you got was a posse of men chasing it round a pitch. Veitch got the classic passing game going."

Veitch was also credited with a considerable input into Newcastle United's revolutionary offside tactics – a new defensive approach personified by the great Bill McCracken, which would later force a rule change by the FA. Legend has it that the idea, which saw United boast the meanest defence in the land, was first hatched by McCracken, Veitch and Peter McWilliam in a railway carriage following the post-mortem of an away defeat.

Historian Dr Bill Lancaster, of the University of Northumbria, believed Veitch's involvement in such avant-garde thinking helped to shape a legend as large as any in the club's history. "Not only was he the boss of a great team," said Dr Lancaster, "he was the guy who invented the blackboard pre-match tactics talk, and was one of the men who invented the offside trap."

IMPORTANT THEN, WITHOUT question. But a cult hero?

Veitch's popularity in his heyday is so much more difficult to gauge than that of modern-day heroes such as Kevin Keegan, Peter Beardsley and Alan Shearer – due to the passage of time, lack of first hand accounts and the relative scarcity of press coverage in Edwardian times. These were, after all, the days when an FA Cup final win would merit a single medium-length article in the next day's paper. But North East football fans were given a taste of Veitch's popularity with the masses when, in 1998, a special watch given to the player by supporters of the time came up for auction at Sotheby's.

A former family friend of the player had come forward with Veitch's 1905 Championship medal and the watch, which had been bought through public subscription in gratitude for Veitch's crucial role in that title win. Sotheby's football expert Graham Budd pointed out: "The people must have held Colin Veitch in great esteem. It is quite astonishing."

England fans, too, would have cause to celebrate Veitch – he played in four different positions for the national side between 1906 and 1909 and became the first Newcastle player to captain England. Only seven more Magpies have matched that feat since: Jack Hill, Kevin Keegan, Mick Channon, Kenny Sansom, Peter Beardsley, Stuart Pearce, and Alan Shearer with only the latter joining Veitch in skippering England while still a Newcastle player.

But many contemporaries felt that Veitch's versatility counted against him in the battle to hold down a regular specialist starting role for his country, and he won only six caps, facing Northern Ireland, Wales (twice) and Scotland three times, including a 1-1 draw played at St James' Park in April 1907.

The *Journal*'s report on that game claimed that "England were well served by Warren, Wedlock and Veitch. They were a virile and polished half-back trio…if slow in his paces, Veitch placed the ball cleverly and had a hand in the goal that Bloomer netted." Veitch came mighty close to scoring a winner for his country on his home ground that day, striking the foot of the upright.

1906 AND 1907 provided the zenith of the player's international career, as Veitch won five caps in those years – but his match-winning qualities at club level were already beyond dispute. Twelve months before that England game at St James', Veitch had further endeared himself to United fans with a man-of-the-match performance on the same turf in the 2-0 FA Cup semi-final win over Woolwich Arsenal.

The Geordie – proving his versatility by turning out as centre-forward in the absence through injury of Bill Appleyard – scored the first and created the second to book a second successive date at Crystal Palace, describing the first as "one of the best goals of my career". The *Journal*'s report of this match highlights the pass-and-move game in which Veitch and his team-mates excelled.

"VEITCH AND AITKEN were so conspicuously successful in their understanding…Orr, Veitch and Howie were irresistible when they moved off together in possession. The outcome of a series of brilliantly executed manoeuvres, which has amassed the enthusiasm of the spectators, terminated after 20 minutes' play in Veitch sounding the death-knell of the Gunners with a grand goal. Howie passed the ball to Orr, who tipped it forward to Veitch, and the latter caught a bouncing ball with a terrific hook, the unexpected sphere passing far out of the reach of Ashcroft."

A counter-attacking passing move with inside-right Jimmy Howie 11 minutes later showed Veitch's creative abilities once more – but United failed to hit such heights in the final, losing 1-0 to Everton. That was the second of four losing FA Cup final appearances between 1905 and 1911 when Newcastle frustrated their supporters by frequently failing to show their true class on the big day.

BUT 1910, AND a 2-0 FA Cup final replay win over Barnsley, courtesy of two Albert Shepherd goals, buried the notion that United were destined to be perennial underachievers in the famous knockout competition. Having now taken over as team skipper from Andy Aitken, Veitch put in a captain's performance in that victorious replay at Goodison Park.

"Appropriately enough," read the *Journal* report, "Colin Veitch ably fulfilled the responsibilities of his onerous office – the captaincy of the team. His generalship proved a valuable asset in Newcastle's victory, and his directing force had an inspiring effect on his colleagues. Cool and watchful, he collected and placed the ball to the bewilderment of his antagonists, who marvelled at his steadiness and accuracy in feeding his forwards."

Veitch would go on to show his loyalty to his players in a controversial victory speech at a civic reception in Newcastle – criticising the Press for spreading rumours that star striker Albert Shepherd had been in cahoots with bookmakers to discuss throwing a game during the last few weeks of the season.

Throughout a campaign which sealed United's reputation as the most feared club side in the land, Veitch had been at the forefront of the innovative playing style which was regularly referred to as "scientific" in newspaper reports of the day. An epic 4-0 league win at Tottenham had one scribe hailing "the mastery of Veitch, Low and McWilliam", while it was claimed that "Colin Veitch and his colleagues had excited the admiration of all Londoners" with their display.

Veitch was again to the fore in the 2-0 FA Cup semi-final win over Swindon, a match described as "a desperate duel between scientific movement and dash. The real cardinal principle of the game – combination – was the basis of their mark from the outset," read the *Journal*. "Colin Veitch, Low and McWilliam were an irresistible and masterly trio who monopolised the honours for their wonderful success as magicians of the fascinating ball."

Veitch's precision with the ball and his nerves of steel earned him the job as Newcastle's penalty-taker on many occasions – and he frequently saved his side with crucial spot-kicks.

One such occasion was the 2-2 FA Cup fourth round draw at Birmingham in 1906 – a match which proved something of a one-man rescue act. United were 2-0 down at the break, but Veitch, who earned praise from the *Saturday Football Edition* for "keeping the crowd on the tip-toes of expectancy", pulled a goal back midway through the second half, then stayed calm to drive home an equaliser from the spot in the dying seconds.

In all, Veitch would score six times in 45 FA Cup appearances – and was one of only three men, along with Lawrence and Rutherford, who played in every one of their astonishing five final appearances in seven seasons.

BUT IF THE FA Cup too often proved a tale of what might have been, it was in the league where Frank Watt's Newcastle and his trusty lieutenant really cut the mustard. The then 24-year-old Veitch showed his bravery by playing on with a knee injury in the home match with Middlesbrough, which United needed to win to clinch their first ever Championship on 29 April 1905.

Along with Aitken, Veitch was praised in the Press for giving "a masterly display in the middle line" in a 3-0 victory which prompted scenes of mass jubilation and "such a remarkable demonstration of enthusiasm on the occasion of a victory of a football team that was unprecedented in the city".

Even if he was not officially captain then, Veitch was still a natural leader on the pitch, and his all-action style, moving gracefully from attack to defence in seconds, thrilled the crowd. An epic 4-2 home win over Sunderland – Newcastle's first ever derby win in the league, on a baking hot September day – kicked off United's second title-winning season, 1906/07 – and Veitch's defensive capabilities were in evidence in a remarkable game. *The Football Edition* told readers that, "When Bridgett transferred to Hall, a Sunderland goal appeared a certainty. Colin Veitch, however, dropped from the clouds on to the ball before Hall, and enabled Gosnell to break away on the left wing."

A week later, Veitch was on the scoresheet in another 4-2 win, this time away at Birmingham, and the Magpies continued their relentless charge towards glory until the title was clinched by a goalless draw at home to Sheffield United in mid-April. United played the entire season unbeaten at St James' Park, collecting 51 points – three more than their 1905 total – and the *Journal* declared: "They claim the classic hour by outstanding merit both in regard to their aggregate number of points and goal average."

But Veitch and Co surpassed themselves two years later, establishing a new First Division record of 53 points in winning their third League Championship. Veitch scored nine league goals that season, to go with his seven in 1907 and 10 in 1905 – crucial and impressive contributions from midfield as the Magpies lifted the title three times in five seasons. To put that last statistic in perspective, United have managed just one further title – aided and abetted by the great Hughie Gallacher in 1927 – in their other 109 seasons!

As he was in 1905 and 1907, Veitch proved instrumental, earning rave reviews in the 4-2 home win over Blackburn Rovers which clinched the trophy. "Colin Veitch played up to his reputation," read the *Journal*'s match report. "He was a fine support to both the forwards and the backs. The game was not five minutes old before there was evidence of this for, after clearing a fine centre by Anthony, he followed the ball up the field, and soon had a sky at Ashcroft."

That same report wondered aloud why Veitch's England call-ups were drying up, pointing out that "several well-known critics declare that England would do better with Colin Veitch to give the ball to more advantage".

'GIVING THE BALL' was always central to the Veitch credo, and it is perhaps no coincidence that this cult hero's reign should coincide with by far and away the most stunning era of team success in Newcastle history. This book is jammed full of individualist players and characters, some creators with outrageous God-given talent (Len Shackleton and Paul Gascoigne) and finishers with a single-minded thirst for goals and glory (Malcolm Macdonald, Andy Cole, Alan Shearer) who nevertheless failed to shape United into trophy winners. Part of the reason for their lack of silver and Veitch's success is of course down to luck – whether a great players is fortunate enough to have graced St James' Park alongside other talented player and under the stewardship of an accomplished manager, but Veitch's unsurpassed trophy haul as a player – three titles and one FA Cup – is at least partly down to his almost unique strengths as a *team* man.

It is difficult to find match report excerpts which single him out for individual skill, because Veitch's genius was to bring team-mates into the game wherever and whenever possible. Not for Veitch the showmanship of a Shackleton or a Gascoigne – he played the game as the embodiment of his dressing-room tactics talks, believing that teamwork was the key to success. It was an unselfish ethic subscribed to by the likes of Tony Green in his glorious snapshot of a Newcastle career 70 years later, and, in Peter Beardsley in the 80s and 90s.

This newspaper passage from the third round FA Cup win over Blackpool in 1906 demonstrates the player's selfless approach perfectly ...

> "Colin Veitch illustrated to his forwards how to score goals by the dashing run he made through all opposition before tipping the ball to Orr for the latter to score at four yards' range."

An 8-0 home win over Wolves in November 1905 lived long in the memory of all there to witness it, and again Veitch was the conductor, prompting a team of all talents in all the right places. "Of a good lot, Veitch was the best – and that was saying much," read the Saturday evening *Football Edition*. "His tackling and sprints were continually the means of the home forwards being placed in positions of advantage." And five years later, the sophisticated midfield general was still passing teams to death, notably in the famous 6-1 home win over Liverpool in which Albert Shepherd scored four. "Veitch was in rare form once again," read the report that day, "and his manoeuvring of the ball enabled the forwards to get away nicely."

Veitch strolled his St James' Park beat for four more years after that victory over Liverpool, bowing out with a final league appearance at home to Everton in September 1914. But he remained part of the Newcastle backroom team as a coach after World War One, in which, drawing on his leadership experience at United, he rose to the rank of 2nd Lieutenant.

IN COMMON WITH a whole host of Magpie greats too numerous to reflect well on the club, Veitch's long and extremely distinguished career with the Magpies came to an acrimonious end in 1926 when he was sacked as manager of the club's youth team, the Swifts. A career in journalism with the *Newcastle Evening Chronicle* kept him close to the game he loved, although his outspoken views did not always go down well at St James' Park as the club lost momentum following the Edwardian era.

Away from football, Veitch remained active in drama on Tyneside until his death in Switzerland in 1938, where he was convalescing from pneumonia which he had contracted during World War One. George Bernard Shaw once wrote to his widow Greta, who continued to teach drama in Newcastle long after Veitch's death: "The success which you and the circle that gathered round your late husband made of the Newcastle People's Theatre has given you just the experience required for the teaching of dramatic art to novices."

Colin Campbell McKechnie Veitch was clearly not your average footballer, then – mentioned in despatches by one of the country's leading playwrights for his services to the arts. Perhaps the most unusual character in this book, Veitch's reputation as a sophisticated man-for-all-seasons sets him so far apart from the stereotypical image of a working-class footballer. Indeed, with his fine features and natural air of authority, it was easy to mistake this Geordie lad for a natural aristocrat. But for tens of thousands of turn of the 20th century Tynesiders, Veitch – despite his peculiar abilities – was always "one of us", bringing style and success to a working class city in which 30 per cent of the populace lived below the poverty line.

Historian Dr Bill Lancaster has studied the Edwardian era in this region in some detail. "Tyneside was the first working-class area in Britain and formed the first industrial society," he said. "Sport had an immense popular appeal and was the most widespread leisure activity for this new class.

"The sportsmen were seen as being at one with the working man, with their success built on athleticism, masculinity and the will-to-win, attributes they needed in their day-to-day work. In many ways the spectators could feel it was one of them out there winning championships."

In Veitch's case, it was; and the importance of the player's roots in Heaton should not be underestimated when analysing his heroic status on Tyneside. Like Albert Stubbins, Jackie Milburn, Peter Beardsley, Paul Gascoigne and Alan Shearer, Veitch is one of the very few homegrown United stars who can lay claim to greatness in a black and white shirt, and the pride of a Geordie hero at the club has perhaps always been felt a little more keenly. It did after all lure Shearer away from the clutches of Sir Alex Ferguson, tempted Bobby Robson back to this country from his successful sojourn abroad and ensured Peter Beardsley returned to the north east, all in an attempt to return the club to its former glories – namely those heaped upon it in Veitch's time. They all want to emulate Veitch. No finer compliment can be paid.

Where, then does this natural leader of men – with his tactical nous and effortless playing style – sit in the all-time Newcastle Hall of Fame? Club historian Paul Joannou claims he is "perhaps the leading spirit behind the club's Edwardian success", and since that was inarguably United's most golden era, does Veitch not present a case as the biggest hero the club has ever seen?

The argument is certainly there, and we have already seen that Veitch would have his supporters, but if the debate is about iconic, passion-stirring status – and it is – then he has two obstacles to supremacy. The first is the difficulty in comparing status across vastly different eras. Alan Shearer, with no trophies won, had a 48-page supplement dedicated to him when he broke Jackie Milburn's club first class goalscoring record. Veitch, who shares the record with four major playing honours won in black and white, was, relatively speaking, covered by only a tiny fraction of newsprint with no *Sky Sports* specials to remind us of his greatness. We can drag the likes of Veitch out into the light, but the increasing media glare of the last 40 years has not just reflected heroic status – it has helped to create it.

To hail Veitch as a player above the likes of Jackie Milburn may be an argument worth pursuing, but as a cult hero, an iconic figure, there is no contest – even if that has as much to do with the passing of time and an ever-changing media as anything else. Perhaps the other obstacle to Veitch being hailed the biggest hero of all is that, despite his many talents, he perhaps cannot quite match the passion and natural charisma of a Jackie Milburn or Kevin Keegan, nor the bad-boy glamour of a Hughie Gallacher or Malcolm Macdonald. He remains, though, arguably the most influential player in the club's history, as the brains and the heart behind a breathtaking era – a golden age when Newcastle United really did rule the football world.

Bill McCracken

1904-1923: 444 games, 8 goals

MCCRACKEN WAS ARGUABLY the biggest hate figure in Newcastle's history; but he was adored by United fans and is still revered as a legend in the north east.

Laying claim to the title of the Magpies' greatest ever full-back is a handsome, witty, clever, charismatic and colourful Ulsterman, whose tactical genius drove opponents to distraction, opposition fans to fury and forced the FA into a seismic rule change in the mid 1920s. In collusion with left-backs Tom Whitson then Frank Hudspeth, McCracken perfected the first offside trap in the early years of football's development – and kept a vice-like grip on the United defence in the days when they ruled the British footballing empire.

For consistency, longevity (only three players have made more than his 444 club appearances) and silverware, McCracken is up there with the elite. Playing a pivotal role in three title wins for secretary Frank Watt's all-conquering Edwardian side, and the 1910 FA Cup triumph, McCracken's accomplished – if controversial – work helped to shape Newcastle United's very fabric as one of the biggest clubs in the land.

STANDING 5FT 11IN tall, with dark hair, strong features and a brooding on-pitch presence, as befits his image as an imposing figure, Bill McCracken was already big news when he made his debut in

September 1904. An Irish international at the age of 19, both Rangers and Arsenal were hot on the heels of a player who strongly insisted he had no wish to leave his club, Belfast Distillery.

But a hopeful ferry journey across the Irish Sea from the West coast of Scotland, where Newcastle were on a summer tour in 2004, proved unexpectedly fruitful for United director James Telford, and the Magpies shocked the football world by landing one of the hottest properties in the game.

Even before he kicked a ball, the McCracken era – which always smacked of high drama – had brought intrigue and controversy, with the suggestions that he had received an illegal payment to join the Magpies. But Newcastle fans cared not a jot and the air of expectancy was palpable as McCracken lined up for the first time against newly-promoted Woolwich Arsenal for his debut. The Journal match report set the scene for a clash which United won 3-0, launching the career of one of the greatest players ever to wear the black and white shirt:

> "The Tynesiders, whilst they readily acknowledged all enthusiasm to the visitors in recognition of their promotion, were chiefly concerned in another debut of much greater import to them. I refer to the first appearance of McCracken, the Irish international back, in English football. A numerous party of Irishmen, including the father of the stalwart and brilliant son of the Emerald Isle, was present on the stand and, together with the Tynesiders, eagerly awaited the performance of the famous back."

McCracken did not disappoint, "playing superbly" according to a report which also claimed he "saved a certain goal when he cleverly took the ball from the feet of Gooing (Arsenal's centre-forward) in the goalmouth".

Without question United had clinched one of the most important ever signings and, with great names in front of McCracken such as Colin Veitch, Andy Aitken, Peter McWilliam and Jack Rutherford, would go on to win three titles in the next five seasons – reaching the FA Cup final five times in seven attempts. A feat never repeated since.

MCCRACKEN HIMSELF WOULD outlast all those fellow Edwardian greats – playing his last game for the club a full 19 years later, against Cardiff City in February 1923, at the age of 40. Throughout that long and distinguished career, one aspect of McCracken's game stood out – his controversial offside trap. Although a brilliant tackler, a useful passer and dead-ball expert, who was entrusted to take important penalties for the club once Veitch had handed over that onerous duty, the Irishman's lasting legacy to the game is undoubtedly the 1925 rule change which brought attacking football back to British football once again.

But McCracken's rationale was not to help score goals, but to stop them. In his playing day, a striker was deemed offside if there were less than three opponents (usually the two full-backs and goalkeeper) between himself and the goal-line at the moment the ball was played forward. After discussions with fellow tacticians Colin Veitch and Peter McWilliam following one away defeat early in McCracken's United career, he decided this rule should be exploited to United's advantage. The idea was that only one full-back needed to step forward the moment before a through-ball was played, to leave an expectant striker offside.

By playing well up the field, contrary to the prevailing wisdom of the day, McCracken would lie in wait to catch forwards like flies in a spider's web. It was a tactic frequently copied, but the Irishman's anticipation, and his reading of the game made him the undisputed master of the black art. Welsh international Don Davies was a contemporary, and grudging admirer of McCracken's tactics. In a revealing testimony unearthed in Roger Hutchinson's book *The Toon: A Complete History of Newcastle United*, he said: "Where McCracken outtripped all his rivals was in his ability to judge his opponent's intentions correctly, and to time his counter-strokes effectively. Until he retired, no one arose who could match his superiority in that." Davies added that McCracken would "force them to realise that the only antidote to subtlety and deceit was more subtlety and deceit... in short, he made them think, and that has never been a popular mission."

It was, though, an immensely successful strategy – United conceded just 41 goals, a new record low, in their 1909 Championship-winning season, then broke the record again despite finishing eighth in 1920, letting in just 39 goals – eight less than champions West Brom, and bettered it again in 1923, conceding just 37. But the offside trap remained highly controversial – deemed ungentlemanly and against the Corinthian spirit of the game by officaldom and much of the press. It was loathed by opposition supporters for the way it broke up the flowing nature of play, much like the more recent Arsenal back four were derided for making the Gunners 'boring'.

Colin Veitch later admitted he questioned the change in spirit which adopting this approach marked, "We had many misgivings in putting the offside trap into operation, but were astounded how easily the forwards fell into it", while England international striker Charles Buchan declared: "McCracken took the system almost to perfection".

Eventually copied across the land, the FA knew they had to act when a match between Everton and West Ham in December 1924 had to be stopped 41 times for offside decisions! Six months later, on 15 June 1925, the FA made one of the most important rule changes in the history of the game, determining that a forward would henceforth be offside if there were less than two opponents (ie just the keeper) between himself and the goal when he received the ball.

In effect, this meant a full-back could no longer step forward, irrespective of his team-mate, to put a striker offside. The result was a flood of goals, with the average per-game in the top flight rising from 2.44 to 3.45 in one season.

Only one team seemed to buck the trend – Hull City, whose manager, one Bill McCracken, had quickly created a new defensive strategy, ensuring that his team kept five successive clean sheets at the start of the season! Former FIFA president and FA secretary Stanley Rous admitted in 1979 what the rest of the football already knew – that McCracken, more than anyone, had forced the FA's hand 64 years previously. "He became so adept at playing forwards offside that the law had eventually to be changed," said Rous.

MCCRACKEN'S CUNNING HELPED make him a feted anti-hero on Tyneside, where fans, being fans, delighted in the frustration of opposing forwards and spectators. But everywhere else, he ran a gauntlet of hate, pelted with missiles by opposing fans and once mobbed by raging pitch invaders at Manchester City. *Evening Chronicle* reporter Stan Bell, looking back at the player's career in 1962, declared: "Bill was booed off every ground in the country apart from St James' Park.

At Villa Park, a supporter threw his pipe at him and hit him on the head. At Stamford Bridge a spectator spat at him and I recall a match at Roker Park when Bill was pelted with oranges and bananas. This amazing character thrived on it all."

Indeed, bearing in mind McCracken's refusal to buckle or alter his ways under arguably the fiercest abuse ever afforded to a United player, it is tempting to regard him as the strongest character ever to wear the black and white. Long-term sports correspondent Bell certainly thought so, describing him as "The daddy of them all... the greatest full-back to turn out at Gallowgate and the most colourful personality ever to wear the black and white strip."

McCracken always insisted he never gave a second's thought to the abuse he received – nor the regular missiles of fruit which he insisted was "more than you could get in one greengrocer's shop", adding "they booed me off every ground – not that it worried me. The more they shouted, the harder I played".

And when the offside tactics did not do the requisite of winding up the crowd, there was always McCracken's cantankerous nature to do the job instead! He recalled in interview with the *Guardian* in 1967 provoking a mass brawl on the pitch during one game for Belfast Distillery, when he had to escape the punches and make a dash for the dressing room after having his shirt and shorts ripped off by angry supporters.

Not that McCracken had much modesty to preserve.

Then aged just 16, he had sparked the fracas with an over-zealous tackle in a match against Wesley – only for the victim's brother, also playing that day, to seek revenge.

"I dodged, and the chap hit his brother right in the eye," he recalled. "There was a hullabaloo. Spectators came on to the field, fighting all around me. I wasn't hit, though. I just made the dressing room with only my socks and boots left on!"

Yet McCracken's legendary cheek made him all the more loved on Tyneside – where he and his disciples revelled in the irritation of countless failed attacks. During an epic 8-0 home win over Wolves in November 1904 – then United's biggest ever league win – the cocky Irishman, only two months into his English League career, hung back to amuse the fans with fake gestures of surprise and panic whenever the opposition crossed the halfway line, shouting sarcastically to the crowd:

"Look here! Look here!" McCracken was also fond of telling strikers caught in his offside trap to "use your brains!" while long after his playing days, he would reveal that he chanced upon the technique as a direct result of his teenage cheek in one game for Distillery – insisting, aged just 16, that he should play in the same position as established star Jimmy Welford. "When I got on the field, Jimmy, who had been with Celtic and Aston Villa and was at end of his career, said to me: 'Where do you want to play, kid?' I said, a bit cheeky, like, 'Any full-back position'. Anyway, Welford said: 'You play up in front of me'. So I did the grafting, and he just stayed there. I could see that all sorts of decisions could be given if that system was used. So I did it…"

MCCRACKEN'S STRENGTH OF character and legendary chutzpah may have helped afford him iconic status on Tyneside – but it also landed him in hot water with the authorities. He received a one-month ban when, having been sent off for questioning a referee's decision against his team-mate Frank Hudspeth, he then wrote to the FA telling them exactly what he thought of the official concerned. The player's front also brought untold damage upon his international career. Ireland's No. 1 defender went 13 long years without representing his country, after a row with Irish FA officials over appearance money.

McCracken, a regular international since his debut in 1902, had become increasingly embittered about the £2 appearance money on offer to him and his team-mates, in comparison with the £10 paid to English internationals. On his way to Belfast for a Home Championship clash with England in February 1906, and backed up by Everton's Billy Scott, McCracken, who had already written to the Irish FA to make his point without reply, decided to force home the issue.

Taking up the tale years later, he told the *Guardian*: "I went to Johnny Ferguson, the secretary, and told him that Scott and I would play if we had the money. Ferguson said it would cost £40 to call a meeting to get that passed, so I said he could save himself £30 by giving me the £10. He got at me, he was sarcastic, then he said he would finish me in football.

"I used to carry a bit of cash around, and took £100 from my pocket and said: 'Hell, Johnny! You cover that, and I'll bet you won't finish me in football. You can stop me playing for Ireland, but that's all.' He wouldn't bite, but I didn't play in that match. Scott did, though, and they didn't ask me to play again for Ireland until 1923."

In fact, McCracken's sharp mind was for once playing tricks on him – the record books show that, following that 5-0 home defeat in his absence, he was picked once more for the national side in 1907, until that 13-year exile in which he refused to apologise for his monetary stance. Bridges were belatedly built again in 1920, and he would play three more times before a farewell appearance against Scotland in 1923, at the grand old age of 40.

No longer playing league football at the time, his performance that day against the great Scottish winger Alan Morton was a poignant reminder of what Ireland had been missing for more than a decade. Chelsea's Sam Irvine joked with McCracken afterwards: "You had a bloody cheek doing what you did to Morton; you played him out of the game", and McCracken, regarding the performance as "a great finish to my career as an international", added: "I never allowed him a touch of the ball".

McCracken was Hull City manager at the time, and clearly still had plenty to offer as a league player – but was not allowed to show it, with Newcastle steadfastly refusing to release his registration. "I was too loyal," he would later reflect, referring to his 19 years with United. "They kept me on the transfer list for 10 years until I was managing Hull City, in case I should play for another club."

But that fall-out – yet another in a long line of bust-ups between the club and some of its most distinguished servants – did not prevent McCracken, after spells bossing Hull, Gateshead, Millwall and Aldershot, working again for the Magpies as a Southern scout until 1958, when newly-arrived manager Charlie Mitten, himself a maverick who had eschewed the serfdom of playing for Manchester United to risk everything in moving to Colombia, outside FIFA's auspices, for a king's ransom and earn himself a ban from playing in Britain, showed him the door.

Supporter R Greenfield wrote to the *Evening Chronicle* to complain, criticising the "arbitrary and shoddy" treatment of "Newcastle's oldest servant".

AS A SCOUT, McCracken had been instrumental in bringing 1955 FA Cup-winning hero Vic Keeble, and highly-rated inside-forward George Eastham to Tyneside in more than a decade of talent-spotting, and would go on to work in a similar role for Watford into his 90s, recommending a young Pat Jennings to the club. His eventual retirement from scouting, at the grand old age of 94, came about when a fall left him walking with a stick in January 1978, and he was honoured with a special presentation of a Long Service medal from the FA for services to the game the following week. Almost exactly a year later, and just nine days short of his 96th birthday, Bill McCracken passed away in a Hull hospital, leaving the *Evening Chronicle* to wax lyrical about "an astonishing soccer personality and Newcastle United's greatest and oldest exile".

McCracken had been the last survivor of the Magpies' first ever FA Cup win in 1910 – a game which showed the big-hearted side of the provocative Irishman. Indeed, the man in the next chapter would surely not have been become quite as big a hero on Tyneside to this day, were it not for the intervention of McCracken at a crucial stage of the 1910 Cup final replay against Barnsley.

Centre-forward Albert Shepherd had gone into the game under a cloud of suspicion about underhand involvement with bookmakers – but he would re-emerge as a fans' favourite after scoring both goals in the replay, with McCracken handing over his penalty-taking job to his team-mate at the last minute. But if Shepherd took the glory in that replay, the tie was only taking place thanks to McCracken's efforts in the first game. The Irishman had put in a superb performance in the original 0-0 clash at Crystal Palace, leaving the *Football Edition* to purr: "Will McCracken has never been seen to greater advantage than he was at the 'glass house'". It had been, according to contemporary reports, a match that the Magpies could and possibly should have lost.

A repeat performance of that one-man rescue act came in the 0-0 final draw with Bradford in 1911, after Newcastle had travelled to Crystal Palace as holders and favourites. But, after weathering the storm, the Magpies – shorn of the injured Shepherd up front – could not repeat their replay heroics at Old Trafford this time, going down 1-0 to the Yorkshiremen. In truth, the Magpies had reason to thank the ever-reliable Irishman on countless occasions during his 19 years' service, and match reports of the time are chockfull of references to the timely interventions of a man who ruled the United defence with consummate ease.

A 3-1 home win over FA Cup holders Aston Villa in 1906 left the *Newcastle Journal* declaring that "their forwards were so cleverly tackled by McCracken and McCombie that they rarely threatened", while a year later the same newspaper was hailing "the powerful kicking of McCracken" in the 5-2 victory over amateur side Corinthians which allowed United to lift the 1907 Sheriff of London Charity Shield.

The report on the 1910 FA Cup semi-final win over Swindon records one of McCracken's trademark goal-saving tackles.

> "Wheatcroft received a pass in front of goal, and took aim," read the *Football Edition*, "but his judgement was upset by a charge from McCracken, who was just in time to avert danger, for the effect of his charge was to send the ball wide."

Fast forward nine years to 1919, and, in his first appearance after the Great War, the *Sunday Sun* gleefully reported that the now veteran Irishman had hit the ground running at home to Arsenal, "McCracken was loudly cheered for effectively stopping Blyth at point-blank range at the last moment. He and Hudspeth did all that was necessary with a ball that was very tricky on a bad pitch – as one onlooker put it, it was like a billiard ball with side on it."

YET, DEVOTED AS he was to the defensive arts, United's legendary full-back also boasted the passing skills to make some telling contributions in attacking manoeuvres. He created, for example, a fine Cup semi-final goal for Albert Shepherd in their 1911 win over Chelsea with a typically clever early through-ball – while the assured full-back was also regularly relied upon to dispatch important penalties. He scored one such spot-kick in the 3-0 home win over Everton which clinched the 1909 title – a game played in a carnival-like atmosphere which had everything, including a dog on the pitch! "The crowd prolonged their cheering when the black and white Dane in the possession of the club appeared from the paddock and careered joyously across the field," read the *Journal* match report.

It's a wonder McCracken didn't play it offside!

The player's bravery – he frequently played on after painful collisions – was another factor which endeared him to the black and white faithful and this came to the fore in helping the Magpies clinch their second league title in 1907, when he took the field carrying a leg injury to help clinch a 3-0 home win over Bristol City in the title run-in. "He played against Bristol City when unfit, and received further damage," read the *Football Edition*. "We wonder how many players are endowed with the Irishman's pluck?"

McCracken's influence in these title wins can also be shown in a defensive record which was the envy of the land. The Irish schemer did more than anyone to create a solid platform for the forward-thinking aristocrats in front of him to build on and wreak havoc. The *Journal* delivered news of the 1907 Championship arriving on Tyneside with this testimony: "The solidity and efficiency of the defence is emphasised by the fact that not a single goal was scored against Lawrence, McCracken, Low and McCombie in 12 matches."

Meanwhile, the *Evening Chronicle* greeted the 1909 title triumph by declaring: "The Tynesiders could boast a faultless defence, and so excellent was the foundation laid in this department that the Newcastle attack were afforded a veritable glut of goal-scoring opportunities." The McCracken effect is self-evident in the league table of that year – the Magpies' 41 goals conceded was a massive 16 less than runners-up Everton.

But, crucial though he was to Newcastle's era of domination, the silver which McCracken lifted in black and white – his haul of four major honours is the equal highest in the club's history – is only part of the legend he left behind on Tyneside. In truth, the years he played on after winning that last trophy, the 1910 FA Cup, did as much if not more to increase his status among supporters.

FANS LOVE PLAYERS who show a bit of loyalty to the club they adore, and while most understand footballers leaving to increase their chances of glory – like Albert Stubbins, Peter Beardsley, Paul Gascoigne and Malcolm Macdonald – a man who sticks by through thick and thin is even more greatly revered. Bill McCracken was one such and, having tasted life at the top of the league, he could have been forgiven for jumping ship earlier. As it was, following a third-place finish in 1912, United would never again break into the top four until after McCracken had left in 1923. Indeed, three times he would endure the ignominy of finishing in the wrong half of the table, in the days leading up to the Great War when, in a complete reversal of style in comparison to the modern United, Newcastle's attack failed to match the mastery of their backs.

Tynesiders' love of their former stalwart was rekindled when McCracken made a brief return to the region to manage Gateshead in 1932, prompting his former team-mate Colin Veitch, who had moved on to a career in sports journalism, to capture the mutual feeling of respect between the Irishman and the people of his adopted homeland. "I know that Bill spent the happiest years of his life on Tyneside," wrote Veitch, "and I know that he will not regret returning to a district where he has so many friends. He was a popular figure with the Magpies from the moment he landed at St James' Park in 1904 until the time that his playing days finished and he departed for Hull in 1923."

Unfortunately for Gateshead, McCracken, who had already impressed as a manager at Second Division Hull, leading them to the 1930 FA Cup semi-final, was soon tempted back down south by Millwall, to leave Veitch declaring: "All his old love for the North has been increased by the treatment he received at Redheugh Park. Hence he has taken some time to make up his mind – but the offer was too good to turn down." He left behind a reputation arguably larger than any Newcastle player that had gone before, and one which still bears comparison now with the greatest heroes the club has ever produced. And, as a clinical, indeed cynical, defender, McCracken stands shoulder-to-shoulder with Frank Brennan as perhaps the two biggest defensive giants in Newcastle's history. Both special players, they have achieved the not inconsiderable task of earning enduring devotion for their defensive achievements at a club long obsessed with attacking football.

In McCracken's case, his undoubted skill as a tackler and man-marker has undoubtedly been overshadowed by his tactical genius. A feature by the *Newcastle Journal* upon McCracken's final departure from the North East when he resigned as Gateshead manager in April 1933 made this very point. "McCracken's first-rate full-back play and the way in which he could make an opponent 'perform to his tune' was sometimes overlooked by many people who remembered only his penchant for throwing forwards offside. He could do all that was required of any defender in the way of tackling and kicking; and was particularly skilful in outwitting the tricky winger who held the ball."

A further taste of the defender's status came when the North East press once reported that a letter from a Belfast fan addressed simply to "The Best Full-Back in Britain" duly arrived on McCracken's doorstep during his playing days. Indeed, for his quality as a player, the success he brought to the club, his loyalty, passion, bravery, off-field controversy, charisma, strength of character and, perhaps above, all, his uncanny ability to wind up the opposition, McCracken ticks all the right boxes as a bona fide cult hero.

That last point cannot be overemphasised for a Tyneside public who revelled in the angry reaction the Irishman provoked among opposition players and supporters – at times McCracken must have seemed like one of their own on the pitch to stir things up a bit. "How's that, man?" he would gleefully shout at a forlorn-looking striker after catching his latest victim offside. Perhaps only the passage of time and a relative lack of media coverage in McCracken's heyday prevent this supremely confident loveable rogue mixing it with the biggest guns of all in Newcastle United idolatry.

There is another thought – the men whose names are maybe bigger in the consciousness of the club's modern history, Jackie Milburn, Hughie Gallacher, Kevin Keegan and the like, are goalscorers; William R McCracken, meanwhile, was a stopper in every sense of the word. He certainly did not play what Ruud Gullit would one day call 'sexy football' – and we have to accept that watching stop-start United games regularly punctuated by McCracken's offside appeals must have been a peculiar – and not a universal – joy. But if the player's very position on the field is counting against him in the final reckoning, it shouldn't, because McCracken was a true master of his chosen art. As a player who brought a new and devastating tactical dimension to the game, he is also indisputably an all-time great.

For his single-handed destruction of some of the finest attacks in the land over a massive 19-year period with United, and for the impish joy he took in it, McCracken's name would surely live on even without his involvement in that epic offside rule change of 1925. McCracken was Newcastle's very own smiling assassin even before the term had been coined, and the club have never quite seen his like since. Welsh international Don Davies, in his description of the player's armoury, once asked: "Who but a snake charmer would fall in love with a serpent?"

Thousands upon thousands of Newcastle fans – that's who.

Albert Shepherd

1908-1914: 123 games, 92 goals

HIS INITIALS ARE AS. He was an England international and became a No. 9 icon on Tyneside after leaving his Lancashire club for Newcastle United...

He created a goalscoring legend which puts him up there with the very greatest strikers ever to don a black and white shirt...

But, unlike Alan Shearer, this Newcastle legend won the League title with Newcastle, then rose to the occasion when needed most in the FA Cup final the following year, scoring both goals to bring the trophy to Tyneside for the first time. Step forward, Mr Albert Shepherd – the first true striking great that Tyneside ever did see.

Yes, there was Jock Peddie, who scored 78 goals in 136 games to become a huge favourite on the terraces – and we must also consider that Glaswegian's No. 9 successor Bill Appleyard (88 goals in 146 games). They were two superb frontmen and colourful characters in their own right at a time when football was beginning to take a firm grip on the passions of the Geordie public.

Peddie, who played for the club between 1897 and 1902, paved the way for a succession of centre-forward heroes, earning adulation in his goalscoring feats and creating fascination through constant run-ins with the United hierarchy. Appleyard, too, is knocking on the door of our final list of 20 cult heroes, and, unlike Peddie, his claims are strengthened by major silverware. Nicknamed 'Cockles', this 14-stone former North Sea fisherman helped United to two league title wins and two FA Cup finals, and roused United fans for five years with his bustling, barnstorming style through the middle. The burly Appleyard was also a skilled billiards player, the footballers' champion no less, and managed to keep Tyneside's public entertained with regular exhibition matches around the region.

Heroes both, for sure, but Albert Shepherd's record, and the gripping yarn behind his finest hour in a United shirt, suggest that he was a cut above, and earned a place in the hearts of Tynesiders reserved in the following century for only a treasured few. Indeed, in the 92 years since he played his last game for the Magpies, only two men have ever bettered Shepherd's strike-rate at United. Shepherd also holds the distinction of becoming the club's first-ever Cup final winning hero, setting the tone for a club which would, in later years, become synonymous with the glamour of that competition.

EVEN IN THE 21st century, there are those Newcastle fans who would rather their team won the FA Cup than the Premiership title, despite the latter being indisputably more prestigious in the modern game. But back in Edwardian days, there is little doubt that the Cup was the big one, the trophy which every player and fan in England dreamed of. Shepherd, operating under a cloud of suspicion created by his own directors, and ending an agonising run of three successive Cup final defeats, made those dreams come true in 1910. And his two-goal man-of-the-match display in that 2-0 replay win over Barnsley is in itself almost enough to guarantee Albert Shepherd's place in the pantheon.

But before that epic tale of derring-do is thoroughly dusted down, consider also the following...

- Shepherd scored 92 goals in 123 games for United
- He became the first Newcastle player to break the 30-goal-a-season mark in 1909/1910
- His strike-rate of 75 per cent is surpassed only by Hughie Gallacher and Andy Cole
- His 16 FA Cup goals in 19 games gives him the best FA Cup ratio in United history
- He twice finished as the First Division's top goalscorer

– He once scored four goals for the Football League XI against Scotland

– And grabbed four goals on FIVE other occasions for the Magpies

Little wonder that the legendary Charlie Buchan described Shepherd as the greatest striker ever to play the game until Gallacher burst onto the scene in the mid-20s. But, while Gallacher had to wait 18 months to touch silver on Tyneside, Shepherd needed just six, netting 11 times in 14 league appearances to help bring the 1909 Championship to Gallowgate.

Shepherd, having signed in late November, had missed half a season, yet still finished as the club's top goalscorer that year. He started as he meant to go on, scoring a goal and making one on his debut in a 4-0 away win over Nottingham Forest on 28 November and the £850 transfer fee paid to Bolton Wanderers was soon beginning to look like a bargain.

The *Journal* hailed "a successful debut in a Newcastle jersey hallmarked by a clever goal" in which the new signing had "hooked the ball over Maltby's head and scored at his leisure after 28 minutes' play".

But this was no great find that had been unearthed by United – Shepherd arrived at St James' Park as an established star name, an England international, and with 90 goals in 123 games (a record almost identical to his Newcastle figures) under his belt at Bolton. He also had a hat-trick against the Magpies to his name in a 4-0 home win for Wanderers in April 1908 – and his form in previous clashes with United had brought him an influential fan in the Gallowgate ranks. Skipper Colin Veitch was much celebrated within the club at the time – even having a hand in team selection – and when chairman Joe Bell asked his captain's opinion about who could fill the departed Bill Appleyard's boots in November 1908, Veitch pointed him in Shepherd's direction. Having had a helping hand from one fellow United cult hero to start his black and white adventure, Shepherd would get more valuable assistance from another to add to his legend in the FA Cup final 17 months later.

But first there was a League Championship to win, and Shepherd managed to find the net on his home debut against Sunderland, his second game for United. However, it counted for little, coming in a humiliating 9-1 defeat at home to Newcastle's derby rivals, and setting a record which still stands to this day as the worst home defeat in the English top flight. Incredibly, it did little to break United's stride as they continued on towards their third championship win in five years – a triumph completed with a record 53 points, seven ahead of nearest rivals Everton.

Established stars such as Bill McCracken, Peter McWilliam, Jackie Rutherford and Jimmy Howie had been left out of the side in that home defeat to Sunderland. Secretary Frank Watt would not make the same mistake again, and his record buy scored 10 goals in his first 10 games to become the new darling of the Gallowgate terraces.

Spectators had long since developed into fans on Tyneside and Shepherd was one of the first players to attract heroic status among supporters who were fast falling in love with the finest footballing side in the land. Four of Shepherd's first 10 United goals came in a stunning 4-0 away win at Notts County in January 1909 – just two months after his signing, and one of the most colourful tales of his six-year reign as King of Tyneside would emanate from his performance that day. It later emerged that Shepherd had special reason to be motivated – he wanted to catch a train just after the match to visit family and friends in Bolton, and had negotiated a bizarre deal with club directors that, if he managed to score four goals, he could walk off the field early – leaving Newcastle with just 10 men!

But the eager Shepherd did not get too much of an early finish – having to wait until the 75th minute before bagging his fourth, then, with the match won, feigning a limp to hobble into a waiting taxi and head for nearby Nottingham railway station.

United's directors certainly got their end of the bargain, though – with a stunning performance which left the *Newcastle Journal* correspondent, writing under the heading 'Shepherd's Great Achivement', in raptures,

"Albert Shepherd, who made his debut for Newcastle at Nottingham two months ago, marked his second visit to Lacetown with an admirable example of the goal-getting powers which won him fame as a Bolton Wanderer. Shepherd's goals were, of course, the feature of the match and the brilliant Wanderer certainly seems to be developing his 'tween backs dash' to wonderful effect. His runs were electrifying and the pace with which the sturdy Newcastle centre covered the ground astounded everyone."

The report went on to hail Shepherd's fourth strike that day as 'a masterpiece'. "The Newcastle centre outwitted Montgomery and left him easily in the run, sailing away with tremendous pace towards goal. Shepherd volleyed with cannon-like velocity from fully 20 yards' range just inside the corner of post and upright... The beauty of the point lay in the fashion in which, after beating Montgomery, Shepherd gave Morley no opening for a spoiling charge, drove a second sooner than Iremonger had anticipated and in such an unlikely direction. It was a masterpiece."

STANDING JUST 5ft 8in, Shepherd was by no means tall for a centre-forward, but with a purposeful gaze and square-jawed demeanour, he was a stocky man who looked as if he meant business. Compared since to Malcolm Macdonald for his speed, strength, power and direct, surging runs on goal, he certainly shared Supermac's penchant for the spectacular, although unlike SuperMac, Shepherd was also hailed as a master of the dribble, and, unlike his 1970s successor, did not seem to attract published doubts over any perceived lack of technical ability.

That is, perhaps, at least partly due to a vast difference in the type and amount of media coverage afforded to the game in different eras, although The *Journal* certainly went into detail to give their readers a first description of new boy Shepherd on his debut in 1908. The report, hailing the player's ground-breaking running style, in contrast to the target-man approach so prevalent at the time, also paints a vivid picture of Shepherd's on-pitch persona.

> "Albert Shepherd is a type of forward who is absolutely new to the many types who have figured in the history of Newcastle United. Of medium height, his big assets are his build and weight – he is broadish and solidity itself – and his fearlessness and dash were admirably exemplified on more than one occasion on Saturday. When Shepherd is placed well forward, and gets a prospect of a run between backs, goals are always in prospect, and, when in possession of the ball, he never avoids the backs to any extent."

His perfectly-timed, rip-roaring 'tween backs dash' proved to be a favoured tactic which thrilled Tyneside crowds, but Shepherd also seemed to possess subtler skills as a player – highlighted in another four-goal display against Preston in January 1910, a landmark performance which saw the United forward break the 20-goal-a-season mark set by Jock Peddie. Indeed, the full range of Shepherd's attributes seemed to have been in evidence during a match which, according to the *Journal*: "marked a new epoch in the Tyneside career of the prince of marksmen". He had, said the newspaper, "blazed with a vigour that was characteristically Shepherdian".

Those tactics ranged from intimidation – forcing the defender's error which led to an own-goal for United's second of a 5-2 win – to delicate dribbling skills. "It was amazing," read the report, "because the methods adapted by Shepherd varied from his usual sweeping runs 'tween backs on two occasions to artifice dribbling round a disorganised pack in front of goal".

A special player, then. But Shepherd also had that ability – shared in future years by the likes of Gallacher, Jackie Milburn, Kevin Keegan and Peter Beardsley, to rouse his team almost single-handedly. His influence on team-mates was immense, and is documented in another press report of the time which gives us a colourful snapshot of Shepherd the player.

> "The mood of the powerful Lancastrian seems to exert an extraordinary influence on Newcastle United," it read. When Shepherd was reticent, Newcastle moved slackly… when Shepherd thundered at the fortress, his colleagues thundered in powerful unison."

This was, remember, already a side feared the length and breadth of the land when Shepherd, aged just 23, had arrived from Bolton Wanderers to spearhead a team full of celebrated internationals. Yet, almost immediately, he had become its heartbeat, its talisman. Shepherd's uncanny ability to rise to the big occasion, coupled with a regular output of extravagant goals to light up Saturday afternoons at St James', made him arguably the biggest terrace hero Newcastle had ever seen. A particular knack of scoring against derby rivals Sunderland did his cause no harm, either – by the time he left Newcastle in 1914 he had scored eight times in 10 games against the Wearsiders.

UNITED LOST AN FA Cup semi-final to Manchester United in Shepherd's first seasons on Tyneside, but he at least had memories of an inspirational two-goal display in a 3-0 fourth round replay win over the old enemy at Roker Park in March 1909. The result, avenging that infamous 9-1 home defeat, was hailed by the local press as the greatest win in Newcastle's history, announcing United's coming-of-age as a top-flight side, of superior class to a club they had once looked to for inspiration.

As for Shepherd, he was, said the *Journal* "unquestionably the star artist, and deserves unstinting praise for the two dazzling sprint dribbles that enabled him twice to defeat {Sunderland goalkeeper} Roose".

There was more to come. In the 1909/10 season, Shepherd's best for United in which he scored 31 goals, he marked his third appearance of the season with a hat-trick on his old Bolton stamping ground, reversing his feat of the year before in a Bolton shirt. The Saturday tea-time *Football Edition*, noting amusedly that several misses by Newcastle's centre-forward were enjoyed by the home crowd, agreed, tongue-in-cheek that "apart from his three goals, the ex-Trotter did very little".

Three months later, Shepherd would go one better in an extraordinary 6-5 Newcastle defeat at Liverpool, a marvellous spectacle of a match which would be echoed in that infamous 4-3 reverse at Anfield for a Championship-chasing United under Kevin Keegan some 87 years later. This time, though, the Magpies threw away a 5-2 first-half lead, four of them scored by Shepherd with the pick of the bunch being his second. "Then came the grandest goal of the match," read one report, "Shepherd outwitting a couple of opponents and shooting from fully 30 yards' range. The ball travelled with such speed that it rebounded from inside the net and came 20 yards out."

Newcastle's front line earned high praise for having "absolutely bewildered the home defence" in the first half. But in true Newcastle United style, the away side imploded after the break, with the unlikely Liverpool revival spearheaded by two goals from ex-Magpie Ronald Orr.

One year later, another four-goal effort would not prove to be in vain at home to Liverpool, inspiring United to a 6-1 win in October 1910, with Shepherd matching that feat with another four six weeks later in a 4-1 victory over Nottingham Forest.

BUT SHEPHERD'S BIGGEST contribution to the club folklore undoubtedly came in the 1910 FA Cup final replay – and the background to his man-of-the-match display is worth recalling to capture the drama and significance of the day.

Like so many United idols since – and a couple before – Shepherd's status among supporters had been enhanced by a colourful, vibrant personality. United's most successful centre-forward to date was a born joker who liked a drink or three – a passion he indulged by running a pub in Bolton after hanging up his boots. He was also a strong-minded, occasionally moody individual to boot, who attracted his fair share of trouble.

Put this rebellious, jack-the-lad image together with his fondness for a wager and it is not too difficult, even 96 years later, to understand how scurrilous rumours could begin to surface in a one-club town about United's golden boy. Even so, there was no evidence provided or suggested at the time to back up the suspicion of some club directors that Shepherd had planned to take a bribe from bookmakers to undo his team in the FA Cup semi-final with Swindon.

Even his team-mates were stunned when the star striker was instead fielded in a side full of reserves for a 1-1 draw with Arsenal the day before – and left out of the semi-final starting XI. The Magpies cruised to a 2-0 victory to book their place in the FA Cup final at Crystal Palace against Barnsley, but when news leaked out about the reasons behind Shepherd's startling omission, Tyneside was in uproar. To put it into modern context, imagine the fallout if Freddie Shepherd accused Alan Shearer of fixing a game and insisted he did not play in a semi-final!

Exactly.

The rest of the squad were also incensed and backed Shepherd to a man, and when press reports highlighted the damaging rumours, there was even talk of a players' strike. Skipper Colin Veitch noted: "We insisted on Shepherd's reinstatement for the final against Barnsley".

The players got their way, but, after a dull 1-1 draw in the final at Crystal Palace in which Shepherd was largely kept quiet by some concerted rough treatment from his markers, rumours again resurfaced that he had been "nobbled".

With virtually no supporter interaction in press reports of the day, it is nigh on impossible now to accurately gauge the fans' feelings about the gossip; yet supporters could be forgiven for feeling a trifle bewildered by the whole situation.

But it was serious enough, certainly, for every one of the United side to believe they had a point to prove in the replay – which they duly did, thanks to Shepherd. At this stage, the Magpies were in danger of becoming the nearly men of the FA Cup. The 1910 replay was, after all, their fifth final tie, having lost in 1905, 1906, 1908 and drawn with Barnsley the week before.

United had been favourites for each game, and the pressure on Frank Watt's accomplished, all-star line-up to finally rise to the occasion and prove their class was immense. Throw in the added weight of Shepherd's individual circumstance and it seems that the Lancastrian entered that replay under more pressure than any United player in the club's long history.

Yet he rose to the occasion. United's black sheep had the ball in the net during an all-action first half, but his strike was ruled out for offside. He then made sure by finishing off a classic team passing move with characteristic aplomb – pouncing like a tiger on a 'tween the backs' pass from Sandy Higgins – then stepping up to score the first penalty in a Cup final to finish off the Tykes.

In a team performance hailed as the best ever seen in a Cup final, Shepherd took centre-stage and his dramatic transformation from villain to hero was greeted with ecstasy by the travelling black and white hordes in a 76,980 crowd.

"The enthusiasm was tremendous," read the *Journal* report. "One thought the heavens had fallen from the volume of the roar…Shepherd certainly deserves a special world of praise for the brilliant marksmanship by which he scored a couple of goals. The first was the result of a daring dribble and shot in the face of a stout challenge by the goalkeeper and the second was the due reward of a thrilling, subtle manoeuvre, for a penalty which he himself scored, and was only conceded when his legs were swept from under him after he had tricked three opponents."

Such was the strength of feeling over Shepherd's treatment by the club that regular penalty-taker Bill McCracken happily handed the chance over to his team-mate for United's second, and the Lancastrian's day in the sun was complete. "He was a bit of a lad and used to play billiards," recalled McCracken years later. "The rumour got around that he had been talking to bookies, but Albert wasn't like that. Anyway, I said that if Albert didn't play in the final, I wouldn't. He played. In the replay Albert scored once in the first half then near the end of the game we were awarded a penalty. I was the penalty-taker. I walked up as if to take the kick and on the way said to Albert: 'Fancy it? Go on, take it', and walked away.

"I wanted to get him re-established, and by the roar of the crowd, I knew he had scored."

Shepherd's efforts – and the previous rumours which had dogged him – were not forgotten in the jubilation of a first-ever FA Cup win for the club.

FOOTBALL MAY BE big business in the 21st century, but it is sobering to note that the 1910 cup-winning heroes produced a crowd of 6000 to acclaim their feats – and that was just the figure of a warm-up greeting party at Carlisle – where the United side stopped off before continuing their train journey back to Tyneside.

Back in Newcastle, team skipper Colin Veitch, in his victory speech at the Pavilion Theatre, broke off from the congratulations to remind the listening public that "rumours regarding the players should not be taken as being correct without hearing the players' side of the question". He added that "one of our colleagues has suffered in this respect, but has undoubtedly vindicated himself since". Nobody needed Albert Shepherd's name spelling out, nor could anyone in the North East of England be left under any doubt as to what the team's victory had meant.

The *Journal* report of the homecoming train journey paints a vibrant picture of a jubilant public enthralled by their heroes' achievements – starting United's long love affair with the oldest cup competition in the world.

> "At Brampton, Gilsland, Haltwhisle and Hexham, crowds swarmed round the saloon and even the officials were infected by the germ of excitement. From Blaydon and Elswick, fog signals demonstrated the joy of the railwaymen and at every little point into the city, cheering crowds roared their delight at the sight of the Cup. They look in at the window and shouted 'Well done boys – at last!' Everyone seemed to say 'At last'. It was the chief

remark of all the informal gatherings from Southport to Preston. The newspapers said so, and every addition to the party from Carlisle to Newcastle said it."

Hopes were high that the wait would not be long for the Magpies' second Cup win – and they were further fuelled the following season by the irrepressible Shepherd, who scored 33 times in 38 games, including an incredible spell of 18 strikes in 13 matches which earned him his second, and final, England cap – in a 2-1 home win over Ireland in which he scored his only international goal.

Like many Newcastle stars before and since, Shepherd felt hard done to by the England selectors, his only other cap coming in his Bolton days, but he took out his frustration on the opposition, particularly in the FA Cup. Shepherd proved to be the driving force behind United's run to the 1911 final against Bradford, netting in every round up until that point. But, after scoring a hat-trick in the 6-1 first round win over Bury, then making his mark against Northampton, Hull (two), Derby and in the 3-0 semi-final win over Chelsea, the black and white rollercoaster shuddered to a halt.

Shepherd had been carried off the pitch during a 2-2 draw with Blackburn in the penultimate league game of the season, and a serious knee ligament injury – sustained in a collision with Rovers keeper Jimmy Ashcroft – would agonisingly rule him out of the final. Without their talisman, Newcastle lost 1-0 to Bradford in the replay – having failed to score in 180 minutes of football; how they missed their prolific forward, and they would not win another major trophy for 13 years.

As for Shepherd, the seriousness of his injury meant his best days at Newcastle were unquestionably behind him. Like Len White nearly half a century later, Shepherd would re-emerge afterwards, but as a shadow of his former self. The *Evening Chronicle Football Edition* marked the incident on 15 April 1911, when one of their finest ever players lost his sparkle for good. "In a rush for goal, Shepherd and Ashcroft collided, and Shepherd fell," read the report. "He was immediately attended to by the trainer and directors and as he was carried from the field on a stretcher, his moans could be heard all over the ground."

It was a sad and ignominious exit for a 25-year-old in his prime, but the fans' favourite, after missing the entire 1911/12 season, made a comeback at the start of the following campaign, scoring in a 1-1 home draw with Sunderland in his second game back. The *Football Edition* remarked that Shepherd looked "just like his old self", but the sharpness did not last. He would play just 28 times in three seasons after his injury, and while he scored 13 goals – a respectable enough return for many strikers – Shepherd was struggling to regain his old form and sharpness, eventually retiring from the game in 1916, two years after moving to Bradford City.

BY THE TIME he left St James', as a 28-year-old, Shepherd's status as the greatest striker the club had ever seen was not in dispute. But the task, some 92 years later, of ranking his status against the biggest heroes in United history is infinitely trickier. Media exposure for footballers was a tiny fraction of the relatively obsessive, modern-day equivalent, and so, as with his fellow early cult heroes, Shepherd stands at a disadvantage to so many of his rivals elsewhere in this book. Managers will cue up for a soundbite to tell the world how brilliant Alan Shearer is – but in Shepherd's day, there was no such thing as a manager, let alone one who would talk to a press, which was by necessity parochial, rather than national, in nature. A relative paucity of information, and the long passage of time, mean that names such as Albert Shepherd, Bill McCracken and Colin Veitch will obviously not resonate as strongly with supporters today as the likes of Peter Beardsley, Kevin Keegan and Alan Shearer.

Yet that does not mean they were any less celebrated in their day – and the accounts of general FA Cup fervour in 1910 show admirably that Edwardian Tynesiders were arguably even more fanatical about their football as their modern-day, arguably sanitised equivalents. Reaching back through the fogs of time, there remains plenty of evidence that Shepherd was a true Newcastle United icon, and in the cult hero stakes, this stocky Lancastrian remains an all-rounder who deserves to cast a long shadow over the club's history, out of all proportion to his 5ft 8in frame.

Shepherd had a touch of Paul Gascoigne's bad-boy reputation, Len White's pace, Hughie Gallacher's genius, Supermac's eye for the spectacular, Albert Stubbins' goal-poaching instinct and, perhaps most importantly, a bit of Jackie Milburn's big-match temperament. He boasts, at 75 per cent, a stunning goals-per-game ratio, which, if we use that evidence alone, marks him out as one of the best three strikers

Newcastle has ever seen, behind Gallacher (82 per cent) and Andy Cole (81). It is worth pointing out, too that Cole, did not match Shepherd for longevity, playing less than two full years on Tyneside to the latter's five-and-a-half, and half of that in the second tier of English football.

But it is perhaps the driving force Shepherd provided to the 1909 title and, even more significantly, the 1910 FA Cup, that cements his place in the pantheon. They are, after all, two more major trophies than were ever won by Kevin Keegan, Peter Beardsley, Tony Green, Malcolm Macdonald, Paul Gascoigne and Alan Shearer in a black and white shirt – and contemporary reports noted the extraordinary influence Shepherd had in those successes.

Shepherd has, in common with the likes of Green and White, a nagging feeling that he could have achieved so much more had injury not harmed his career while still in his prime. Yet for all his considerable, ability, fame and striking prowess, it remains difficult to put him on a level pedestal with the likes of Gallacher and Milburn – possibly with a few more years, fully fit, at the top level with United, all the rest may well have been playing catch-up.

As it is, United fans owe so much to a player who, as a chainsmoking, hard-drinking publican, died 77 years ago in his native Bolton, aged just 44. Shepherd, after all, was the man who finally brought the FA Cup home. He was perhaps the first to bring undisputed striking class to St James' Park, and, by feeding Tyneside's thirst for colourful characters and rousing football, he embedded a tradition of the cult of the centre-forward which continues unabated to this day, shaping how Geordies feel about their club and their heroes.

Hughie Gallacher

1925-1930: 174 games, 143 goals

AT 5FT 5IN, Hughie Gallacher might just stand above them all. Whichever way you look at it, the wee Scot is the epitome of a cult hero, and his legend lays claim to being the finest player ever to wear the black and white shirt.

You can keep your Alan Shearers, Peter Beardsleys and Kevin Keegans – surely only Jackie Milburn can seriously stand up to that challenge – and what a debate that would be between the pair in football heaven. Milburn, of course, would be too modest to push his own virtues – thankfully, since Hughie might just lose his temper! The Scot, you see, was a character brimful of colour – a man whose God-given genius and arch, tempestuous nature made him a true icon of the terraces. Passion for football, for hell-raising and for life ebbed out of every pore of Gallacher's tiny frame – and the folk of Tyneside loved him for it. If Alan Shearer is the consummate model professional, Hughie was a wee Scots scallywag – yet he still managed to bring the league title back to St James', a feat he accomplished with some style.

Gallacher's life was a rollercoaster adventure, and its tragic early end threw his achievements into even greater focus – and they were many. Those who champion Milburn or Shearer as the club's No. 1 cult hero should consider the following…

- Gallacher was the last Newcastle captain to win the league title, in 1927, scoring 36 goals in the process
- At 82 per cent, he has the best strike rate of any United player, past or present, scoring 143 in 174 appearances
- He was hailed by Frank Watt, the most successful manager in United's history as "the greatest player the game has ever known"
- 68,836 fans came to St James' Park in 1930 to watch his return for Chelsea on a Wednesday afternoon, with many more thousands locked outside

That figure still stands to this day as a club record, and is now surely an irrefutable and permanent testament to an adoring Newcastle public.

Twenty-seven years on, those fans were to have their world rocked even more deeply than when their hero had been sold against his wishes to the London club when, on 11 June 1957, they learned of a shocking incident at 'Dean Man's Crossing', which has gone down in Tyneside folklore. The following morning's *Newcastle Journal* summed up the tragedy as well as any, under the headline: "HUGHIE OF THE MAGIC FEET IS DEAD" . . .

> *"On the charge list which will be placed before Gateshead magistrates this morning will appear the name of Hughie Gallacher.*
>
> *But his name will not be called. Instead, a police officer will announce that Gallacher is dead. Gallacher, whose magic feet fascinated English and Scottish football followers more than 20 years ago, was found decapitated yesterday near the main railway line at Low Fell. Two trainspotters, a boy and his sister, saw a man fall in front of the 10.50am York to Edinburgh train, just about a hundred yards from the crossing known locally as 'Dean Man's Crossing'.*
>
> *Gallacher, who was 54, had been summoned to appear at Gateshead Court today accused of assault, ill-treatment and neglect of his 14-year-old son, Matthew. Matthew was taken from Gallacher's care on May 28, pending the result of the court hearing."*

At a heart-wrenching inquest, the coroner Mr W Carr recorded a verdict of suicide on the death of a legendary footballer, who was wracked by shame, guilt and depression. Before jumping in front of the train, Gallacher had written to relatives – and to Carr himself – to apologise for the trouble he had caused, and to declare that, even he had lived to reach 100, he would never forgive himself for striking Matthew. The former goalscoring wizard had been accused of throwing an ashtray at his teenage son during a family row. Gallacher's eldest son, Hughie Jr, told the TV documentary *Looking for a Legend*: "I knew there was upset and trouble, but I didn't think anything like that was going to happen, over nothing at all, really. It was just a mad moment, the police got involved, and it snowballed."

Two days before his death, a contrite Gallacher visited Matthew, staying at the home of his sister-in-law Dorothy Armstrong, to tell him: "Look after your Auntie Dolly, she has been a good pal to you". The following day, he told Mrs Armstrong he was not going to work, but going "for a slow walk". The last person to see Gallacher alive, was the 13-year-old boy, Gordon William Glaholm, who watched him die. Glaholm was the grandson of Gateshead FC chairman William Tulip – one of Gallacher's old clubs. And he told the inquest that the last word spoken by the Scot was "Sorry", for knocking down the boy's umbrella as he climbed over the fence on to the tracks.

Before Gallacher jumped on to the line, the unfortunate eye-witness recalled: "He seemed to hesitate, and swayed backwards and forwards." It was a pitiful end to a life which brought so much joy to the Geordie corner of the world, but like everything in Gallacher's realm, it smacked of high drama. And the temper and emotion which ultimately helped led to his downfall, not to mention the pathos of his passing, have all helped to turn this little Scotsman into a huge icon on Tyneside.

One measure of the man, is the sheer number of colourful stories still told about his life and times in a Newcastle shirt, starting with his dramatic club record capture on a wild Lanarkshire night 32 years before his untimely end. The legend began, for Newcastle fans at least, in the Airdrie boardroom, with discussions of a transfer, which would rock United to its foundations ...

Manager Frank Watt – although referred to as secretary, as was the fashion of the time – was on the lookout to bring fresh attacking impetus to help bring the glory days of Cup finals and league titles back to the club. Newcastle had been rebuffed FOUR times in their attempts to sign 22-year-old Gallacher – who had scored 100 goals in 129 games north of the Border, and had scored twice for Scotland against England earlier that year.

The final throw of the dice was Watt's idea – to turn up at an Airdrie boardroom meeting uninvited, to push home their case. The date was 8 December 1925, and Watt, accompanied by directors Robert McKenzie and John Graham, was about to deliver an early, very expensive Christmas present to the St James' Park faithful. Arsenal, Chelsea, Sunderland and Everton all coveted Gallacher's talents – but Airdrie, then a major force in the game and Scottish Cup holders, had given no encouragement to any of his suitors. Watt recalls a similarly frosty reception when he bumped into his opposite number Willie Orr outside the ground . . .

"My people will never transfer Gallacher," Orr had said. "You fellows haven't an earthly chance. I am surprised to see you here – really I am. You're just wasting your time." But a determined approach – and a readiness to flash the cash – was to win the day. The Newcastle delegation begged their way into the boardroom at the end of the meeting, and refused to buckle at talk of a near-British record £6,000 for the player. To spend that kind of sum was important to Newcastle. Sunderland had set a new record the week earlier in paying £6,550 for Bob Kelly. At one point the player himself was whisked back to the club – having to change out of his pyjamas – to ratify the move, and he later recalled:

> *"I was sitting in front of the fire in my pyjamas and dressing-gown when there was a knock at the door. When I opened it, there was the Airdrie manager, Mr Willie Orr, soaking wet, for it was a wild night. He had come to tell me that Newcastle United had made a firm offer for me."*

Gallacher agreed to the deal – but there was still some late night bargaining to be done, with Airdrie's directors sceptical about how Newcastle had planned to pay such a huge sum. Watt, describing his favourite moment of the deal, takes up the tale…

"'Like this,' I answered quietly. All eyes were upon me as I pulled from my pocket a cheque-book, walked to the table and, amid profound silence, wrote out a cheque for the full amount, asked Mr Graham and Mr McKenzie to sign on the dotted line, and then handed the cheque to the astonished Airdrie directors."

The transfer which was to concrete the cult of the centre-forward at Newcastle United was complete. But before Gallacher was to even set foot on the St James' Park turf, he had already suffered from the emotional turmoil which was to boil beneath the surface of the likeable Scot all his life – and which only served to endear him to his public all the more

Married at 17, Gallacher had separated from his first wife and endured the death of his baby son – facts little reported at the time, which all helped to convince the player that a new start was in order. Ready for a fresh environment, it is perhaps not surprising that Gallacher took to his new home immediately, declaring in a matter-of-fact way even before his debut: "I soon felt I should be happy at Newcastle United." But if this was to prove a marriage made in heaven, the bride seemed to have a few last-minute jitters at the altar. The Scot long remembered the surprised reaction of the home crowd – who, in the days before television, were seeing the player in the flesh for the first time – when he ran out of the tunnel for his first appearance at home to Everton.

"It was a bit of a shock to hear the roar of welcome I got from the Newcastle crowd," he said. "Half-hidden by the roar was a gasping noise that I heard clearly enough. Obviously a lot of people had not been prepared for seeing such a wee fellow coming out among the giants." The fans were not alone, with Newcastle centre-half Charlie Spencer admitting: "We were staggered by his size. Then, soon after the match began, I turned and gave my fellow defenders the thumbs-up. We knew a real star had joined us."

How right he was.

Twenty minutes into the game, Gallacher scored the first of his many goals for the club, then set up Stan Seymour for a simple finish before adding his second to make it 3-1 – only for another world-class centre-forward, Dixie Dean, to prevent a winning debut for Hughie by completing his hat-trick in a 3-3 win. The *Newcastle Football Chronicle* purred: "No sooner did he touch the ball than one sensed the artistic player. There were times he beat three or four men by clever dribbling. Newcastle have at last found a leader of real quality."

After just six games, Gallacher had scored 11 times, and a four-goal showing in a 5-1 home win over Bolton in the fog had left the crowd delirious. Gallacher went on to score 25 goals in 22 games in his first season in a black and white shirt, and had begun to establish a goals-per-game rate which, unless FIFA follow through with president Sepp Blatter's idea of making the goalposts bigger, will surely never be beaten.

Newcastle fans had loved Veitch, made a legend of McCracken and idolised Shepherd, but Hughie was different. Hughie took heroic status to new levels. United had found the first true superstar of their 32-year history, a player who would leave a legacy and tradition which few centre-forwards have been able to live up to. Jock Peddie had scored 78 times in 135 games for the club, Bill Appleyard 87 in 145 and Gallacher's immediate predecessor Neil Harris 101 in 194. Albert Shepherd of the 1909 Championship winning side, with 92 strikes in 123 games, had set the benchmark – but Gallacher was to obliterate it. And, as much as he was stirring souls on the pitch, he was raising heart-beats off it as well.

'DAPPER' IS THE word used most often to describe the player's appearance at this time. Though on a tiny fraction of today's wages, Gallacher still managed to live a playboy lifestyle in the 1920s, a slave to fashion and revelling in the razzmattazz of his newfound superstar status in the city. Resplendent in his smart double-breasted suits, fedoras and white spats, Gallacher dressed like a gangster (he idolised screen icon Jimmy Cagney), was courted like royalty, and was a regular sight in the pubs and dance-halls of Newcastle, drink in one hand and rolled-up umbrella in the other. The ladies in particular loved him for it – and he took full advantage of the opportunities which came his way – but his passion for the high life did nothing to dampen the ardour of true football fans across the region, as, in the early days at least, he always produced the goods in training and on match days.

Local legend has it that a favoured trick would be to neatly cut piles of plain paper, stick a couple of real notes on top, and draw audible gasps from fellow drinkers by waving his wad around in the city's bars.

It is not, you might imagine, the sort of trick to endear yourself to a predominantly working-class public. But Gallacher had the impish charm to pull it off – and Tyneside was in thrall to his celebrity. A working-class boy, whose footballing genius and hard-living lifestyle seemed to cock a snook at the authorities and employers everywhere, in fans' eyes Gallacher could do no wrong.

In fact instead of feeling envious, Tynesiders seemed to celebrate the success of a natural rebel who had effortlessly escaped from the hard work and drudgery of blue-collar life in 1920s Northern Britain. Perhaps because of a shared sense of hardship, Geordies have always welcomed a Scot – and vice versa. Gallacher was not the first to discover this, and he felt so at home that he would settle in the region long after his playing days were over, just a few miles from St James' Park. He responded to this adulation in kind – always ready to sign autographs, stop for a chat or, more significantly, accept a pint. That habit in particular would cause problems further down the line. But for now, there was the small matter of bringing the league title back to his adopted home – a feat for which he will forever be remembered on Tyneside.

IN THE SUMMER of 1926, nobody's star shone brighter in Newcastle – maybe even in Britain as far as footballers were concerned – than Hughie Gallacher. Yet still it was a huge shock when the club's directors handed him the captaincy. This was a hot-headed player whose skills often attracted rough treatment on the pitch – and who was not slow to retaliate, or give the referee a piece of his mind. It was like making Wayne Rooney captain of England today.

Gallacher was later to admit he felt he was not captaincy material – yet still he remains the most successful skipper the club has had in the last 80 years, the only one in that time to bring the coveted Championship trophy back to Newcastle. While the three title wins in the first decade of the century were a triumph of professionalism and teamwork, the 1927 success owed much to the magic – and strong-willed personality – of one man. Gallacher hit all four in a 4-0 win over Aston Villa in the first game of the season, then, since he lost the toss before the game, sent a typically cheeky message to the Newcastle fans declaring that he "intends not only to take classes in that art, but to put in intensive practice in all his spare time".

Two consecutive home defeats to Burnley and Bolton were no laughing matter, but a Gallacher-inspired 4-2 home win over Manchester United got the ball rolling again. The Mighty Atom – one of his many nicknames – scored the only goal of the game to beat Liverpool, then hit the target again in a 3-1 away win at Everton. The word was spreading across clubs throughout the land that Newcastle – and Gallacher in particular – were a force to be reckoned with. The Scot's goalscoring display in a 5-1 win over Birmingham left the *Sunday Sun* newspaper searching for new superlatives to describe "a mercurial Gallacher, shooting from what appeared to be impossible positions with stinging force and accuracy, and always weaving insidious passages goalwards, such as to reduce his opponents to the very brink of despair."

A stunning hat-trick secured a 3-1 win at Tottenham in November and United fans started daring to dream about a fourth league title. But if the best of Gallacher was there for all to see at White Hart Lane, his dark side was also in evidence. The cheeky Scot was far from a saint on the pitch, and his penchant for goading opponents seemed to provoke rough treatment as much as did his undoubted genius. Such was the case in North London, as tempers flared following a succession of fouls from the home defenders, and the referee had to stop the game and ask both teams to calm down following a free-for-all.

Verbal abuse, taunting defenders about their lack of ability and constant kicks and elbows when the referee looked away, were all part and parcel of the Gallacher package, and if the Scot did not quite give as good as he got in the days when many fouls were overlooked, he gave it a darned good try. "He had a vicious tongue," said fellow Scotland international Bob McPhail. "I learned swear words from Hughie I had never heard before." It is a rare thing for a player to be appointed as minder to his own captain, but Gallacher's incendiary tendencies were such that manager Frank Watt appointed Bob McKay to keep a close eye on the skipper at all times. Watt, though, was more than happy to take the rough with the smooth – and if anything, Gallacher's spiky nature merely endeared him to the United fans even more. If they weren't applauding his goals, they were wincing at the abuse he took or encouraging his spirited retaliation – they simply could not take their eyes off Newcastle's stick of dynamite.

His popularity was growing week-by-week, and when Newcastle beat West Ham 2-0 on 4 December, they went top of the table – albeit on goal difference – for the first time since their 1909 title win. It was almost exactly a year to the day since Gallacher arrived, and his first 12 months on English soil had proved beyond the United directors' wildest dreams. That West Ham win was significant since it showed a much under-rated aspect of Gallacher's game, and one which, his champions argue, helps to put him ahead of the likes of Jackie Milburn and Alan Shearer in the pantheon of United greats. Having put his side ahead, Gallacher created a goal out of nothing with a mazy dribble and cut back for Stan Seymour to drill home – a perfect example of the Scot's creative play. Seymour was to score 19 goals that season, and McDonald 23 – many of them created out of nothing by a killer pass or clever dribble from Gallacher. In the early season 4-2 win over Manchester United, the club's record buy may have scored just once, but he laid the other three on a plate for McDonald (two) and Seymour, showing a touch uncommon among centre-forwards of the day, and marking him out as a player equipped to excel in any attacking position on the pitch.

That creative ability sets Gallacher apart from some of his celebrated successors in the No. 9 shirt. Milburn and Shearer fans might argue, with some justification, that scoring goals was easier in the 1920s, but, according to contemporary reports, the Scot created many more chances, for himself and his team-mates, than those men who followed him. A blistering shot, and a natural goal-poacher's instinct completed the package – and the second half of the 1926/27 season rammed home the message emphatically. Santa was a Scotsman as Hughie dropped in on St James' Park to deliver two goals in a 5-0 win over Cardiff on Christmas Day, while a first-half hat-trick in an 8-1 FA Cup win over Notts County was doubly significant.

The Scot had seemed unlikely to take part minutes before kick-off, suffering from a fever and a temperature of 100 degrees, while one of his goals that day, balancing the ball on his head for a few moments before volleying it home, was regarded as one of his most audacious. Back on league duty, a home match against Derby in February had to be stopped twice for the much-abused Gallacher to receive treatment. But typically, he battled on showing the toughness and raw-hearted courage, which so endeared him to the working man of the North East, and scoring in a 3-0 win to keep the title momentum going.

A superb hat-trick in a 7-3 victory over Everton put the Magpies back on top of the tree, and a crowd of 45,000 – notably 9,000 up on the attendance for Gallacher's debut – watched a game which inexorably turned the title tide United's way. Watt's side would not relinquish top spot again, with Gallacher keeping the pressure on by scoring both in a 2-1 victory at Blackburn– the first strike being hailed later by Stan Seymour as the finest ever scored in a black and white shirt.

"I remember I passed the ball to Hughie and sent him off on a 30-yard dribble down the wing," recalled Seymour. "I tore down the middle. The goalkeeper came out to narrow the angle, expecting like me, that Hughie would send ball over as I had a clear shot at goal. That was too simple. Hughie pushed the ball gently through the goalkeeper's legs."

Seymour watched Gallacher's talents at close hand week-in, week-out, and was left in no doubt about the man's standing as a player. He would later claim: "He was a nonpareil. Stanley Matthews has only a fraction of his casual genius. No one made soccer seem so easy." But if that goal at Blackburn was one of his best, the matchwinners against title rivals Sunderland and Huddersfield – both securing priceless 1-0 wins – were to prove his most important in a black and white shirt. The latter left St James' Park marvelling at how he had outjumped 6ft England defender Tom Wilson to head home a goal which gave United's skipper one hand on the League Championship trophy.

United needed just a point at home to Sheffield Wednesday in their penultimate match – but Gallacher was determined to sign off in style, scoring both goals in a 2-1 win that brought the title back to Tyneside for the first time in 18 years. Gallacher's mark of 39 strikes that season (36 in the league in just 38 games) would stand for 67 years, until Andy Cole sensationally went two better in the 1993/94 season. But it would truly have horrified everyone connected with the club to know that they had just won their last English title for at least the next 80 years.

One man of course, does not a title-winning team make – but Hughie Gallacher seems to have gone mighty close with his contribution to Newcastle United in 1927. As the *Northern Echo* reported: "In Hughie Gallacher, their centre-forward and captain, they possess a footballer and leader who stands alone in the matter of skill. It was largely due to his brilliancy and the support he received from his colleagues that Newcastle United gained League honours."

Little did Gallacher know that he had lifted his first and last trophy with the club – but if silverware was to elude him in the next three seasons, personal glory and adulation did not. Season 1927/28 brought 21 league goals in 32 games, as an ageing Newcastle side slipped to ninth in the table. United dropped a place further the following year, but Gallacher's star still shone brightly, with 24 goals in 33 games.

TO ADD TO his popularity on the terraces, the people's hero was forever in trouble with the authorities. Decades later, a *Sunday Sun* correspondent would claim the Scot "made George Best look like Mary Whitehouse," and while that was a blatant exaggeration, there was a kernel of truth therein.

Gallacher certainly attracted the wrong sort of headlines and, despite his huge influence on the pitch, doubts seemed to surface in the boardroom. A late night fight with team-mate and future brother-in-law George Mathison on the Redheugh Bridge resulted in an arrest, and shocked the St James' hierarchy. It was a pattern that would be repeated throughout the young star's life – drink bringing out the devil in a soul always battling to keep a lid on the fire within. Four years later, as a Chelsea player, he would miss a return visit to St James' having been arrested and fined for being drunk and disorderly – fighting with Fulham supporters at midnight on the Thursday before the match outside Walham Green Underground station.

But Gallacher always had an excuse – telling the court, according to a *Journal* report of the time that he had been "goaded with an accusation which had always been foreign to his principles"! But if being drunk 36 hours before a match was deemed unprofessional, Gallacher would think nothing of enjoying a couple of pints in the Strawberry pub with supporters right before kick-off – and local legend has it that a team-mate was sent to haul him away from the bar double-quick on one occasion, for fear he should miss the match.

If getting Gallacher to kick-off on time was one thing, persuading him to stay on the pitch was another – a 7-2 defeat at home to Burnley, in which Newcastle's star man was engaged in a particularly bruising battle with his nemesis, centre-half Jack Hill, almost resulted in the Scot walking off the pitch in disgust. "I got so fed up with the bustling I was getting that I tried to walk off the field," he later recalled. "Fortunately, I was persuaded by some of my team-mates to play the game out, but it was a near thing." Yet Gallacher would never bear a grudge, and later recommended Hill to the St James' Park board, precipitating the big defender's switch to United only months later.

Gallacher's constant rows with officials helped to make him a marked man wherever he went, and he brought another league match – at Everton – to a standstill when he refused to take a free-kick, having been offended by the referee's numerous requests to reposition the ball. Again, Newcastle team-mates persuaded him to play on, but United's centre-forward was booed off the pitch at half-time.

Loved as he was by the United followers for the passion which he displayed, it is perhaps easy to see why his popularity was not always as high with the opposition. Indeed, Sunderland wing-half Alex Hastings – a Scotland team-mate, no less – once declared: "I never hated anyone so much on the field." Referees no doubt agreed – and one official in particular, Bert Fogg, could be forgiven his anger at wee Hughie on New Year's Eve, 1927, when he had to endure a running battle with the player during Newcastle's 3-2 home defeat to Huddersfield. Gallacher was furious at having two penalty appeals turned down and Fogg decided enough was enough after one verbal tirade.

"He asked me my name and I replied that if he didn't know my name he had no business being on the field," said Gallacher.

"So I asked: 'What's your name?'

"'I'm Mr Fogg,' he said.

"'Aye, and you've been in a fog all match,' said I."

But Gallacher did not stop there – asked to go into the referee's room after the match to apologise, he lost his temper again, with some reports claiming that, upon finding the unfortunate, naked Mr Fogg bending over to go into the bath, Hughie gave him a helping hand with his right boot!

Considering Gallacher's one-man war upon match officials, it is ironic that his last involvement in the game was to referee a host of charity matches across northern England and Scotland in his late forties – a habit which again brought sanction from the FA, who warned him he would be banned from all involvement in football if he continued to officiate matches involving "unaffiliated teams"! But Gallacher's quick tongue was not exclusively reserved for officialdom. Former team-mate Albert Chandler had cause to regret taunting the striker towards the end of his Newcastle career, after telling him in a match against Sheffield United: "I don't know how some people get their caps."

"I told him," said Gallacher, "that we only got our caps because we were always playing against mugs like him."

BUT GALLACHER'S LEGENDARY cheek was to bring a heavy price. That run-in with Bert Fogg resulted in a two-month suspension, and commentators at the time started to predict a premature end for his tumultuous love affair with United. Arsenal came calling as early as the summer of 1928, and while their overtures were rejected, there seemed support in the boardroom to cash in on the club's superstar. Gallacher lost the captaincy that summer – despite having led the club to League title success. He admitted, looking back, that it was the right decision: "I was not sorry; my impetuous nature was unsuited to the responsibility."

Scotland – then the strongest of all the home nation sides – gave Gallacher an outlet from these worries. Although their centre-forward was still serving that two-match domestic ban, the Scottish FA kept faith in him for an upcoming date with England at Wembley – and it was to prove one of the most memorable of all time between the old enemies. Gallacher, although for once not on the scoresheet, inspired his side to an epic 5-1 win and became immortalised as one of the Blue Devils, or Wembley Wizards, for their sensational display.

The Belshill battler was a true national hero in this era, scoring all the goals in a 4-0 win over Northern Ireland in 1926, a hat-trick in a 4-2 home win over Wales in 1928 and surpassing himself by scoring five in a 7-3 win over Northern Ireland the following year. In all, he scored 24 goals in just 20 appearances for his country, a mark only bettered by Denis Law and Kenny Dalglish, who needed 55 and 102 caps respectively to reach their joint top total of 30 goals.

Despite his immense achievements on Tyneside, Gallacher would late pick a remarkable reception from French fans as one of his biggest thrills in football, having excelled while playing for his country at the Colombes Stadium, Paris. "When the game finished, the whole of Paris seemed to be shouting 'Vive le Gallacher!'" he said.

It wasn't always plaudits from opposition fans, though. A devastating performance for the Scottish League against the Irish League in 1925 offered Gallacher the opportunity to take his capacity for troublemaking to new heights. Gallacher had enraged the home crowd by scoring five goals in succession in a 7-0 win. Turning on all the tricks, his exhibition football had brought a scribbled death threat from Irish supporters to his dressing-room at half-time. "By the time the final whistle blew I was about the most unpopular man in Belfast, and Belfast in those days was not the sort of place where one wanted to have a lot of enemies," he said. But Gallacher was not be deterred from visiting friends in the city that night – and if he had not taken the threats seriously beforehand, that would soon change.

"I had another player with me and we were on our way back to the hotel, walking along a dark street, when a shot rang out," he said. "The bullet pinged against the wall not far from my head. Believe me, I covered the 200 yards back to the hotel in better than even time." He would later enliven an already sensational tale with the witty aside: "I should have extended my stay in Belfast – it seems I still hadn't managed to teach the Irish how to shoot straight!"

It was not the last time Gallacher would be forced to run a gauntlet of hate, showing a capacity for trouble which would amuse and fascinate his followers, but cause consternation in the boardroom. An ill-fated club tour to Italy, Czechoslovakia, Hungary and Austria in the summer of 1929 would bring trouble by the bucketload, with Continental fans incensed by what they saw as British unfairness – downright indifference. The Newcastle bus was stoned in Milan, then United were accused of not trying after an 8-0 defeat to Bratislava, but the match against a Hungarian Select XI in Budapest would be the stormiest of the lot.

The Magpies went down 4-1, full-back Alf Maitland was sent off, and the Hungarian players and officials became convinced, having smelt alcohol on their underperforming opposition, that United's players had taken to the field drunk. Spat upon during their retreat from the field, the team – with Gallacher and Maitland identified as ringleaders – were hauled up before the English FA over the incident. And while the players were forced to admit that a bottle of whisky had been passed round before kick-off and at half-time, the authorities somehow accepted their version that the refreshment was purely medicinal!

Gallacher appeared in person to answer the charge, and Maitland backed up his successful defence that "it was a boiling hot day so we rinsed our mouth out with a little scotch and water". As you do.

More fireworks were to come from Newcastle's star man before even the close season was out. Perhaps feeling jaded at all the scandal, perhaps disillusioned at the departure of an influential team-mate in Stan Seymour or perhaps worried at the impending arrival of a new centre-forward from Dundee United in Duncan Hutchison, Gallacher shocked Tyneside with a transfer request.

It was hastily withdrawn, but those close to the club were well aware that Gallacher's opponents were gaining sway in the boardroom. An FA fine for penning a series of newspaper articles entitled "Inside the Football Game" had brought more controversy upon the Scot's head, and the player's capacity for courting trouble showed no signs of abating.

Years later, Gallacher's forthright views as a sports journalist for the local Newcastle press would even bring a ban from the St James' Park shrine he once called home. But, in the early part of the 1929/30 season, the supporters were delighted to see their hero put all his troubles behind him by starting like an express train, with 11 goals in his first 10 games. That their hero could still perform for them despite all his troubles, all his travails, told them all they needed to know. He was a supremely gifted god of the game.

Superhuman Gallacher would hit 34 in what was nearly a disastrous season for United; and he crowned an astonishing personal season with a sterling display to inspire his side to a 1-0 win over West Ham in the final game to ensure the Magpies beat the drop. Hughie had saved United almost single-handedly. The stuff legends are made of.

Little did anyone know, Gallacher had just played his last game in a black and white shirt. Making his dazzling display to keep Newcastle in the top flight all the more amazing, a huge controversy had broken out on the morning of the game, with newspaper reports claming the Geordie icon had been offered by the board to bitter rivals Sunderland. Newcastle feverishly denied it. Gallacher believed it, but still he signed a new contract for the following season – in those days players had little choice - and that, his legions of fans thought, was that.

And it was…until Chelsea chairman Claude Kirby knocked on the player's door in Belshill on 24 May 1930 to tell him that the two clubs had agreed terms. It was a *fait accompli* and Gallacher, while saddened to leave his beloved Tyneside, was too proud to hang around once he knew Newcastle's board wanted him out. He admitted he agreed to the near British record £10,000 move "with the greatest regret", and added:

> "The whole business was a complete shock to United supporters. Believe me, it was just as much a shock to me. The reason for this I don't know to this day; perhaps they were just short of money."

The promotion at Newcastle of first-teamer Andy Cunningham – he had never seen eye-to-eye with Gallacher – to become the first player-manager in British football was hailed as one reason for the sale. But there was no possible justification in the eyes tens of thousands of distraught United followers. The sale came when Gallacher's popularity was at an all-time high – only weeks earlier he had given up a precious Scotland cap against England in order to play for his beloved relegation-threatened side against Arsenal.

That decision infuriated the Scottish FA, who became reluctant to pick English-based players, or 'Anglos', for years afterwards, but in Newcastle, the *Evening Chronicle* had summed up the city's feelings: "Our hopes are renewed, our prospects are brightened! All together now, hats off to Hugh Gallacher!" Those hats were now off to wave Hughie a tearful farewell, but the great man later revealed that he told 'a certain member of the Newcastle board':

> "I shall be back on Tyneside when you've said goodbye to Tyneside. It may not be as a player, but I know I shall get back somehow; and I'll be amongst my friends in the North East."

AFTER PLYING HIS goalscoring trade at Chelsea, Derby, Notts County and Grimsby, Gallacher would get his wish in 1938 when he returned to the North East to play for Gateshead, for the princely sum of £500. "I have been north, south, east and in the Midlands, but no place can compare with Tyneside and its people," he said. "My transfer to Gateshead is one of the greatest things that ever happened to me." There came, in between his travels, divorce from his first wife, Annie McIlvaney, a subsequent bankruptcy at least partly caused by the resultant court costs, and a 12-month ban for drink-driving after a collision with a cyclist.

Rows and misdemeanours and tall tales followed Gallacher around the country. But his return to Tyneside – home of his second wife Hannah – precipitated one of the happiest spells in his life. Together they would raise three sons in the town and enjoy a period of stability long after Gallacher played his last game for Gateshead in September 1939, when the Second World War brought his League career to an end. Denied a job in football – he asked Newcastle and Gateshead if there were any vacancies but was "told all the jobs had already been promised" - he took work at Huwood's mining machinery factory on the Team Valley Trading Estate.

Even in the days of the maximum wage, this was something of a comedown for such a footballing superstar, but Gallacher, who had long railed against a system which he felt denied him and his ilk their due riches as players, insisted he was not bitter. He was transferred, in his time, for a total of £23,000 – a huge sum in between-the-wars Britain. "Not much of that money has found its way into my pocket," he said. "and I'm still having to work for a living. Not that there's anything wrong with that - I'm still a fit man. Where I work on the Team Valley Trading Estate, I have found friends and security. Not every footballer is in the same happy position." Rumours of illegal payments followed Gallacher around the country, and after hanging up his boots, he told an FA inquiry that he once received a £300 under-the-counter payment as part of one transfer.

THROUGHOUT HIS CAREER Gallacher further furnished his rebellioius reputation by revelling in his unofficial role as a footballing shop steward and once negotiated, for himself and his Newcastle team-mates, a hefty bonus for one crucial FA Cup replay. This illicit deal was set up during the train journey on the way to the match, responding to the chairman's initial refusal and threat to drop the rebels by pointing out: "It's too late now as the kick-off is in two hours."

The money was duly paid, and maybe even Gallacher was forgiven the late uprising when he scored twice in the first 11 minutes to put United on the road to victory. This was one player who could talk the talk and walk the walk. But despite his best efforts, football, while bringing Gallacher fame, failed to deliver fortune. It is a sobering thought for today's multi-millionaire players that a true genius like Gallacher had to return to his working-class lifestyle to survive.

Nevertheless, Gallacher the ex-player still enjoyed the fame and affection of a living legend on Tyneside. That sense of security would continue until his wife's death from a heart complaint in 1950 left her husband distraught and alone, taking refuge in drink, and heading for his own tragic end seven years later. An overall goalscoring record of 463 goals in 624 games was impressive enough as an epitaph – but more importantly, Gallacher left as his legacy a legion of epic stories on Tyneside which have been eagerly passed on from generation to generation. No player before or since has sparked so many tales and downright gossip as Hughie Gallacher – down to the downright comical yet pervading rumour that he put a curse on United before throwing himself on the railway tracks in 1957.

There are more believable reasons why the Magpies have failed to win a domestic trophy since, but try telling that to ex-manager Ruud Gullit, who was so perplexed at the club's long search for silverware that he recruited a local priest, Canon Robert Spence, to sprinkle holy water and exorcise any demons from within St James'! But no story is told more often – and few can whet the appetite for the game of football more – than the tale of Gallacher's first return to St James' Park as a Chelsea player on 3 September 1930.

Some reports – such as that of then United manager Frank Watt – claimed there were as many as 40,000 locked out of the ground, on top of the 63,386 (at the time of going to print, a record for a midweek league match in England) that were packed inside. The fans, many of them perched precariously on the roof of the stands, had come to say goodbye to their idol following his heart-breaking close-season move, and the memory of that Wednesday afternoon, Gallacher would later recall "put the auld lump in the throat".

It was a remarkable outpouring of affection for a player who tapped into the Geordie bloodstream like no other before or since. He would later tell North East football journalist Arthur Appleton that it was "the most touching and memorable occasion of my football life". There will never be another tribute quite like it. But Gallacher deserved it; for his legendary cheek and bravado, his aggression and courage, his undoubted genius with a football and the way he poured his heart and soul into the black and white shirt.

Gallacher's legend is a very different one to that of the other truly huge names in Newcastle's history. Try to imagine the likes of Milburn,

Keegan, Beardsley and Shearer repeatedly arrested for fighting, kicking a referee into the bath, and being accused of being drunk during a game. The wee Scot was at best a scamp and at worst a rogue – yet the people of Tyneside warmed to him all the more because of his faults. Today's modern pros – helped by agents and PR consultants – would blanch at the very thought of some of Gallacher's escapades. But in an era when players still socialised with their fans, Gallacher's fondness for a drink, his quick temper, downright cheek and canny eye for making a few quid simply marked him down as 'one of us'. Gallacher was a god amongst men. Shearer was a god apart.

Only a select few manage to pull off the dual role of off-pitch rebel and playing genius. Decades later, Paul Gascoigne threatened to become the closest thing to a modern-day Hughie, but without matching his predecessor's achievements or sticking around long enough to build up a similar legend. And if striking successors Milburn, Macdonald and Shearer were so often hailed as "the complete centre-forward", Gallacher's glittering array of skills marked him out, in many eyes, as the complete player. He did so much more than score goals, although he did plenty of that. His vision, passing and dribbling ability were up there with the likes of Stanley Matthews, Tom Finney and the man he loved to watch after his own career ended, Len Shackleton. In terms of strike-rate, and thanks at least partly to a game which has become ever more defensive since his 1920s heyday, Gallacher will probably always remain No. 1. But, to those in the know, the sheer magic he created in a black and white shirt has never been bettered either.

No-one has researched the complete days of Newcastle United more than official club historian Paul Joannou. So perhaps we should listen when he claims: "*Gallacher is, in my opinion, the greatest Newcastle United player in the whole of their history.*" But for a epitaph which fittingly captures the emotion and hero worship Gallacher generated in this part of the world, the *Journal*'s Ken McKenzie did a mighty fine job the day after the great Scot took his own life on 12 July 1957:

"There is no one fit to tie the laces of the Gallacher-that-was," he wrote. "May the earth rest lightly on Hughie Gallacher, I am sure that many will join me in that wish, remembering the days of his greatness when he gave pleasure to thousands – it would not be far from the truth to say millions – and roused the Gallowgate roar to thunder."

Albert Stubbins

1936-1947: 218 games, 237 goals

WHO HAS SCORED more goals for Newcastle than any other player? Most Newcastle fans would say Alan Shearer – with the author of the quote above a close second. But, according to some sources, the real top man is a pug-nosed, ginger-haired Geordie who spent his childhood in the US of A, and is captured for posterity on the world-famous album cover of the Beatles' Sgt Pepper's Lonely Hearts Club band. (If you've got it, that's him peeking over Marlene Dietrich's shoulder, just along from Lewis Carroll.)

Step forward away from such lesser lights, Mr Albert Stubbins. Rumour once had it – before Sir Paul McCartney solved the mystery many years later – that Stubbins was picked for that Beatles cover alongside other great names such as Fred Astaire and Marlon Brando because John Lennon liked the name, and it certainly has a solid 'working-class hero' ring to it. But Stubbins – in the black and white of Newcastle United and the red of Liverpool – also produced the achievements to match the image – and it's not nonsense to suggest he is one of the most legendary players in the club's history.

THE TRAGEDY OF Stubbins' football career – though he never once publicly bemoaned it – was that he hit his peak during World War Two, when there no full-time football was played in England, and so his heroic goalscoring exploits are not recognised in official records.

Hence Shearer, at 202 first class goals is now acknowledged as the United record-holder, ahead of Milburn on 200. Throw in the latter's wartime tally and Wor Jackie stands on 239 – and there the debate starts… because different sources put Stubbins' final record at either 245 or 237. Whichever source is used, Stubbins, sadly, can never be compared on a level playing field to those other two greats, having prospered in the regionalised war-time leagues, where many teams had to rely on guest players and defences were generally acknowledged to be less disciplined and organised than in the full-time game.

That said, there are plenty of admirers who would hail Albert Stubbins – the man with the rocket shot which, it was rumoured, once broke a keeper's arm in his Liverpool days – as the top man in the Magpie annals. Jackie Milburn and Sir Bobby Robson were two famous North Easterners who cherished Stubbins as a childhood hero – and he remained a celebrated figure in his native North East, forever stopped on the street for a chat, right up until his death in 2000. Robson described the red-haired 6ft speed machine as "my boyhood hero – the centre-forward I hero-worshipped as a young lad, a marvellous goalscoring centre-forward".

Indeed in the shadow of the country's struggle with Nazi Germany, and when the folk of Newcastle most needed a hero, flame-haired Stubbins stepped forward, delivered and shone like a beacon. He played the game with style, panache and a smile as wide as the Tyne.

Stubbins' spectacular development in the early 40s made him THE find of war-time British football, and, even six decades later, the statistics go a long way to explaining his place in the pantheon. In a black and white shirt, Stubbins plundered:

- 29 hat-tricks (more than double Hughie Gallacher's 14)
- Four successive hat-tricks
- Five goals in a match five times
- Four in a match six times
- 40 goals-a-season or more on four separate occasions
- and 39 goals in 24 games against Middlesbrough!

Stubbins would go on to prove his undoubted credentials in the post-war First Division, grabbing 83 goals in 180 games for Liverpool and blasting five when called up for the Football League XI in 1950.

Like Peter Beardsley 40 years later, Stubbins found hero-worship on Merseyside as well as Tyneside, scoring the goal which won them the title in 1947, when he outpaced Wolves' centre-back Stan Cullis to slide the ball home. There were, in common with many a Magpies idol, no trophies for him at United, but the skills he flaunted on the St James' Park pitch, and the excitement he brought during arguably the most difficult decade of the last century, made him a true war hero as he lit up a depressing and difficult decade.

Off the pitch, this natural gentleman proved a marvellous sporting ambassador, and a powerful role model to the younger players at St James' – one in particular. "I idolised the man and learned from him the dignity and humility needed to help carry the burden of being a star," said Milburn. With his famous good humour and grace, his artistry and pace, Stubbins seemed to provide the perfect antidote to the grief, fear and strife of living in a country at war.

Since he was such a true gent on and off the pitch, the one blot on Stubbins' disciplinary copybook came as a real shock, when he was sent off after responding to constant rough treatment from Sunderland's Jimmy Gordon at Roker Park by flattening the full-back. "The ground was silenced. It was unbelievable," Milburn remembered, recounting a tale which nevertheless did his hero's street cred no harm, while Stubbins, who insisted he was taking retaliation for an assault on little Ernie Taylor, declared afterwards: "I grabbed him by the throat, pushed him down and knelt on top of him!"

But, Sunderland defenders apart, Stubbins' style was not a physical one – indeed he was a far cry from the traditional battering-ram centre-forward, personified by the man who, combined with the war, ruined the Geordie's England career, Tommy Lawton. Instead, Stubbins had to make do with one Victory international appearance – scant reward for a player who terrorised defenders with his pace, guile and shooting ability across the country for 16 years. His knack of being able to shoot from almost anywhere kept United fans on the edge of their seats, while they delighted in his deft body swerve and confident ability to take on any number of defenders during his countless sorties on goal. "He could shoot from anywhere once he was on the run," said Milburn. "I've seen him go through and hit them from 50 yards."

Never mind the quality of the defences – a point much debated by supporters and pundits alike in retrospect – Saturday afternoon escapism at Gallowgate had never been so thrilling, nor as welcome. The passionate fervour which Stubbins' exploits created was enhanced by a new piece of FA legislation in 1939 – compulsory playing numbers, allowing fans for the first time to easily identify, and identify with, their heroes.

With Stubbins – who had originally started out as a wing-half – used as an inside-right for his first season and a half as a Newcastle player, Billy Cairns was the first to wear a No. 9 shirt which would become increasingly prized over the decades. But Stubbins' spectacular success when eventually converted to the centre-forward's role would mark him out as the first to bring heroic status to one of the most famous numbered shirts in football. At just under 6ft and in his size 11 boots, Stubbins certainly had the stature for the job. "I don't know whose inspiration it was, but one particular day I was selected to play centre-forward, and I felt completely at home," the player remembered years later. A legend was born.

YET HIS RISE to stardom on Tyneside so nearly got off to a false start when the teenage Stubbins signed for derby rivals Sunderland as an amateur. He had also played for amateur side Whitley & Monkseaton, but the youngster's presence of mind paid dividends when he insisted on an unusual agreement with Sunderland which allowed the 16-year-old to leave if boyhood team Newcastle came in for him – as they did in March 1936.

Stubbins had only been back in the North East a few years, having spent much of his childhood in New York and Detroit – but he knew where his heart lay. His subsequent rise through the ranks of the 'A' Team and reserves to the United first team was meteoric, up until the point when he poked home his first-ever senior goal in front of the Gallowgate crowd, in a 3-2 home win over Burnley, on 10 September 1938.

It was Stubbins' fourth appearance for the Magpies and although he scored many more spectacular efforts over the years, he would always remember that first strike at St James' as his proudest moment in the game. "I was so excited, I could hardly breathe," he said. "There is nothing that has ever equalled the thrill."

Ten days later, and after only a handful of games in a black and white shirt, Stubbins' emergence warranted a page lead feature in the

Newcastle Journal. "Meet Albert Stubbins, 19-years-old football expert, whose performances in Newcastle United's forward line have been sending the crowds at St James' Park into raptures," read the review. "He came into prominence only this season after one previous game with the first team and now, after only four matches, the Wallsend boy's ability has become the topic of the hour with United supporters."

The same report also highlighted Stubbins' canny attitude in preparing for the future – stressing that the youngster was already proficient in book-keeping and shorthand since "Football, says Albert, will not keep him for all his life". The shorthand in particular would come in handy almost throughout Stubbins' days in his role as a part-time – and latterly full-time – sports reporter. But before he took up the pen, he would keep the headline writers busy with his own prowess on the football pitch.

The press and fans alike were entranced by the skills and power of the new boy, with early comparisons being made to greats such as Charles Buchan and Tommy Lawton, though Stubbins insisted: "I never copied anyone's style, I just did what came naturally". Yet the Wallsend lad had certainly added hard work to his God-given gifts. His bemused mother once told reporters that, as a young boy, her Albert would be up doing sprint training in the fields before school every day. That dedication, coupled with the natural ability of a sportsman who also won medals at baseball, athletics, boxing and swimming, turned Stubbins into a formidable competitor.

For one full season before the outbreak of war, and the 1939/40 campaign in the new wartime Northern Regional League, he would work the inside-right channel until an injury to Billy Cairns gave him his big chance against York City in November 1940. Stubbins found the net in a 3-0 win, but was still sharing the No. 9 shirt with Cairns until the start of the 1941/42 season. His amazing season-by-season tally from that point is worth recounting in full – even if, due to the lack of official records in wartime football, there is still debate over some of the fine details.

The North East press archives claim that Stubbins' wartime tally was 245 goals in 199 games and overall 250 in 228. However, Newcastle United's official club historian Paul Joannou puts those figures at 231 in 188 in wartime and 237 in 228 overall. What is not in doubt is that Stubbins scored 40 goals or more in his last four seasons at Newcastle and his average goals-per-season tally is over 30. Joannou puts his five full seasons as United's No. 9 at this, with the *Journal/Evening Chronicle* figures in brackets:

1941/42: 33 (38) goals
1942/43: 42 (40) goals
1943/44: 43 (44) goals
1944/45: 43 (42) goals
1945/46: 40 (43) goals

As the figures suggest, the fact that Albert Stubbins was THE sensation of British war-time football is beyond dispute, and his red-hot form produced some astonishing scoring sequences, including scoring 16 goals over in nine successive games, and that amazing total of 39 goals in 24 games against Middlesbrough (little wonder the Teessiders tried to buy him from Liverpool for £18,000 in 1951). Boro bore the brunt during Stubbins' most eye-catching run in January and February of 1941, when the flame-haired assassin scored 15 goals (a respectable season's total for many strikers) in just five games! That run included four successive hat-tricks as Stubbins hit 4, 3, 3, 3, and two – with his 'failure' in the last game costing club director Stan Seymour a fat cigar, since he had bet his star striker he could make it five in a row.

Stubbins later well remembered that game against York City, in which he hit the underside of the crossbar with two minutes left. "The boys kept on feeding me the ball and, although I hit the woodwork several times, I just couldn't get the ball in the net a third time," he said.

Press reports of the time during this five-game scoring run capture the excitement which the barnstorming Geordie brought to the Magpies line-up. After four goals in a 7-1 home win over Sheffield Wednesday, the *Sunday Sun* declared that Stubbins "at centre-forward, in the absence of Hugh Billington [a wartime guest player], put up his best game of the season for United" and hailed his "amazing pace off the mark" and "splendid finishing". Three more goals came in a 6-2 home win over Boro, with the same newspaper praising his "fast, thrustful football, full of skill and powerful finishing" in an overall "dashing display".

Stubbins then managed to score three against the Teessiders away the following week – albeit in a 4-3 defeat – to leave the *Sunday Sun* marking his exploits with understated praise. "Ten goals in three matches in a row," read the report, "– not a bad record"!

A War Cup hat-trick against Rochdale was next up, with the *Journal* reporting that a 3-1 away win owed everything to "the amazing ball control of Stubbins."

Among many memorable performances, two more stand out, one in Stubbins' final season on Tyneside when gates, just after the war, although with the league still in wartime format, were back up to around the 50,000 mark on Tyneside. A five-goal display in an epic 9-1 home win over Stoke on 22 September 1945 had the Newcastle crowd delirious – a game also notable for the superb marking job done by young full-back Bobby Corbett on the great Stanley Matthews. Stoke's goalkeeper that day was Denis Herod who later recalled, "before the game somebody told me that Stubbins couldn't head the ball. By half-time he'd scored three with his head and left me out cold following an aerial challenge!"

But the game Stubbins would later pick out as his personal finest in a black and white shirt came on 28 April 1945 – a 4-2 War Cup win at home to Bolton. Stubbins remembered: "I got three goals in the first half, all with my right foot", and the *Sunday Sun* noted that "the leadership of Stubbins was a marked feature of the early play". Still, it is telling that Stubbins' favourite display should come in a match which saw United crash out of the Cup at the quarter-final stage – they had gone down 3-0 at Bolton in the first leg, losing 5-4 on aggregate – and he was destined, like many United idols before and since, not to win silverware on Tyneside. Indeed, the closest he came was as a guest for derby rivals Sunderland in 1942, when he wore the red and white stripes in a losing War Cup final against Wolves. It is, perhaps, just as well for his fame and popularity on Tyneside that Stubbins did not manage to end up on the winning side that day! Sixteen years later, he recalled the bizarre situation which led to him wearing the colours of his club's bitter rivals in a cup final. "In wartime football there was a rule that if a team was knocked out in the early stage of the cup competition, then you could be approached by another club to play for them in the later stages," he explained. "Raich Carter was the Sunderland captain and I played in their two-legged cup final against Wolves. We lost – but not a lot of people know that I played in a cup final for Sunderland."

STUBBINS' LACK OF honours – and a long-held thirst to test himself against the best which had never been properly quenched during wartime football – led to a transfer request which hit club and fans like a bombshell in the late summer of 1946. Now a regular part-time scribe in the *Evening Chronicle* and *Sunday Sun*, Stubbins penned his usual column on the eve of the new season, under the headline "United Fit and Ready for the First Hurdle".

He would play just three more games that season, scoring once, before Newcastle – finally accepting they could not, as a Second Division club again, match his ambitions – decided to grant his transfer request. No fewer than 18 clubs immediately registered an interest in Tyneside's prolific goal machine, but when United set the price at above £10,000, all but three withdrew, leaving Liverpool, Everton and Notts County left in the race.

On Thursday September 12, the *Evening Chronicle* reporter Stan Bell reported that, "The biggest auction in football took place at St James' Park today, when Liverpool and Everton offered £13,000 for Albert Stubbins". The fee was actually second to Arsenal's record-breaking £14,000 paid to Wolves for Bryn Jones just weeks before, and Liverpool finally won the day when manager George Kay and chairman Bill McConnell offered to set Stubbins up with part-time journalism work at the *Liverpool Echo*.

Tyneside's favourite striker, having worked as a shipyard draughtsman on the Wear throughout his United career, was already determined to spend his years in journalism after hanging up his boots. Stubbins later recalled how he was relaxing at the flicks when news got through to him in spectacular fashion about Liverpool's bid. He told Liverpool journalist John Keith: "I was sitting in the Newcastle News Theatre when a notice suddenly came up on the screen saying 'Would Albert Stubbins please report to St James' Park'." Liverpool had also helped carry the day by acting faster – and with a degree of guile. Knowing Everton would be in the hunt, the Liverpool delegation attempted to throw their derby rivals off the scent by attending an afternoon reserve game at Goodison Park, then stealing away at half-time for a quick drive up to the North East to do a deal.

Heart-broken Newcastle fans were handed a consolation when the club went out and spent every penny of the £13,000 fee on a man who would soon become known as the Clown Prince of Soccer, Len Shackleton. But salt was rubbed into still sore wounds when they had to sit by and watch their exiled favourite son win the title with Liverpool – just as Peter Beardsley would after leaving North East shores in the 80s. And Stubbins' contribution could not have been more dramatic. In the climactic title-deciding final game of the season at Molineux, where Wolves needed only to draw and the visitors to win, he used his famous pace to outsprint centre-back Stan Cullis to score the decisive goal in a 2-1 win and take the Championship trophy to Merseyside.

Worse would come five years later for the United faithful, when a double strike in a 3-0 home win for Liverpool over Newcastle would effectively end the Magpies' 1952 title challenge – after competing in the top four until the turn of the year, United would win just three more times in their last eight games following that result, but at least picked up a glamorous consolation in the form of the FA Cup.

Stubbins, meanwhile, would score 83 goals in 180 games for Liverpool – despite suffering from a muscle complaint which hampered his fitness for two years – to prove conclusively he was a great performer in league football, and is remembered today on Merseyside with perhaps as much fervour as on Tyneside. However, he was never in any doubt, when questioned in his later years, about where to find the best supporters in football, and this empathy for United fans is at the core of Stubbins' legend in the North East. "You know, I've played before quite a few crowds in my career, but there is no crowd like that at St James'," he told the *Sunday Sun*. And a guest appearance on the pitch aged 73 before a home match with Southend in 1992 brought the old memories flooding back. "When I went out of the pitch I knew I was in front of a largely young crowd who would never have seen me play," he said. "But the welcome, the ovation I got, was wonderful, from wonderful supporters. It proved that if you make a name at Newcastle United, your name will always be known. Yes, going out on that pitch again after all those years, and getting such a reception… that was special, very special."

Stubbins was overcome with emotion – and concussion – when he renewed his love affair with the Gallowgate crowd as a returning Liverpool player in a 3-0 friendly win for the Merseysiders on

Valentine's Day, 1948. The *Journal* reported that he had to ask United defender Frank Brennan what the score was after suffering a 20-minute memory blank after a heavy contact with the ball on the crown of the head. "Indeed, he contributed to securing his side's third goal without having any clear recollection of how it transpired," read the report, while a fully recovered Stubbins told the United fans afterwards: "I should like to thank everyone for the reception. There's nothing quite like the Gallowgate crowd."

Stubbins missed a penalty that day, but he did not miss much else in a red shirt, scoring the fastest 50 goals in Liverpool's history and going on to produce his finest representative performance, a five-goal display for the Football League XI in a 6-3 win over the Irish League on 18 October 1950. The Geordie centre-forward had broken his nose a few days before against Bolton, but was determined to play, insisting: "The injury is uncomfortable and breathing not too easy, but of course I still have my good looks." He lined up for the game alongside luminaries such as Tom Finney and Stan Mortensen, but stole all the headlines the next day.

The *Journal* report drooled: "Stubbins must receive full marks for the excellent manner in which he took his chances. The centre-forward's positional play and accurate shooting were first class, and he looks like starting favourite for the centre-forward position in the England team which meets Wales at Roker Park on 15 November."

That predicted call-up never came, with Stubbins' only England appearance coming in a 'Victory International' during his Newcastle days which sadly was not given official recognition – a 1-0 defeat to Wales at West Bromwich Albion's ground, The Hawthorns, on 20 October 1945. Three years later, a chance to step into Tommy Lawton's boots for a first official cap went begging again after one of three transfer demands at Liverpool had produced a lengthy stand-off between club and player.

In October 1948, the *Journal* noted: "Had Stubbins not put himself out of football from the start of the season by refusing to re-sign for Liverpool, and requesting a transfer, he would probably have succeeded Lawton as England centre-forward; instead Jackie Milburn has taken over …"

The comparisons between those two Geordie icons was often made in the late 40s and early 50s, and while there is no doubt that Milburn, overall, must be hailed as the bigger hero in the region, many fans from the era regarded Stubbins as the finer player. The *Guardian*'s obituary upon Stubbins death in December 2002 made that point, declaring that Milburn is "a greater icon on Tyneside than Stubbins, but many fans and journalists believe that Stubbins was a still better centre-forward".

Whoever had the edge, Sir Bobby Robson was left to rue, after Stubbins' death, the fact that Newcastle could not keep the older player in harness a while longer alongside his young pretender. "Albert was a fabulous player, both for Newcastle and for Liverpool," he said. "I only wish he could have played more games with Jackie Milburn – imagine that partnership."

For his part, Milburn was always quick to acknowledge the impact Stubbins made on his own game – and the good nature of a man who remained, with his flat nose and red hair, instantly recognisable and immensely popular on Tyneside right up until his death. "He gave me all the encouragement in the world when I first came to Newcastle," said Milburn. "If I had a bad game, he was the first to put his arms around me with a few words of advice. And he was so polite that he would step aside to give you the chance of a goal."

Yet if Stubbins exuded an air of humility, he was also a fierce competitor with a confident belief in his own abilities, and with the will to push himself to the limits of his potential – attributes which brought a wartime Newcastle side some epic victories over the years. Milburn remembers that before one game, Stubbins winked at him and whispered: "I'll score three today", before going out and doing just that, all in the first half. Yet that confidence never emerged as cockiness or arrogance. After making a short playing comeback for Northern League side Ashington (Milburn was involved again in setting up the coup for his hometown team) Stubbins, having left Liverpool the season before, made a massive impression on supporters, despite leaving the club after just a handful of games in the autumn of 1953.

When his newfound role as a centre-back had, after a promising start, earned mixed reviews, he decided to cut short the arrangement, yet the Supporters Club still arranged a presentation of a clock to the 34-year-old, and secretary George Tait declared: "It will be a token of our appreciation of a grand sportsman and a gentleman who would be a credit to any club". Stubbins even went back on a vow not to play up front again when Ashington, staring relegation in the face, begged him to return as a striker the following March. "We got to the stage where Ashington needed eight points out of 10 to avoid the bottom of the Northern League," recalled Stubbins. "So I went to centre-forward, and we got nine points out of the 10. It was a nice way to finish."

With that Superman rescue act in the bag, Stubbins concentrated on journalism – writing for the *Shields Weekly News* as a court and council reporter before specialising once more on football with *Shoot Magazine* and the *Sunday People*. But he still found time to earn rave reviews for a coaching stint in America in 1960, when he was christened "the Babe Ruth of British soccer" after guiding a makeshift New York Americans side to a win over Bayern Munich and draws against Burnley and Nice in a summer international tournament.

The *Evening Chronicle* reported at the time that Stubbins had proven to be an innovator as a tactician and coach: "Fielding three full-backs and three half-backs, the team completely curbed the more stylish continental sides". More praise came his way when he won a Lifetime Achievement award from the Football Writers' Association in 1984, and he declared: "I hope I'm not sounding egotistical, but it's lovely to think that what you achieve on a football field as a young man can still bring you recognition 40 years later". Those long memories of supporters would lead to another cherished memory for Stubbins in 1987, when a House of Commons celebration dinner in honour of the player was held – and a telegram from Sir Paul McCartney would shed some light on who was behind his inclusion on that world-famous Sgt Pepper album cover. Stubbins told the *Journal*: "For some years I had speculated about why the Beatles had chosen me for their record cover. For a long time, I thought it was because of John Lennon. Apparently he was no football fan, and the only two names he's heard of, being a Liverpool lad, were Albert Stubbins and Dixie Dean. He rather liked the sound of them . ."

But Stubbins would believe that theory disproved when McCartney's telegram arrived at the House of Commons, to solve a 20-year mystery. It read: "Well done, Albert. For all those glorious years of football. Long may you bob and weave. Paul McCartney."

Stubbins' celebrity status – frequently stopped when out shopping or playing his regular Thursday afternoon snooker session at the Chalk 'n' Cheese club in Newcastle's High Bridge Street – was a source of constant surprise and delight to the man in his later years. "I find it fascinating that I walk down Northumberland Street in Newcastle or Lime Street in Liverpool and strangers stop to talk about football," he told the *Journal* in 1987. "Young boys ask me for my autograph and, whenever I visit Liverpool, taxi drivers sound their horns and give me a wave as they go past." Stubbins' refusal to be bitter about how Adolf Hitler's untimely intervention in Poland harmed his football career is another facet of the player's character which endeared him to supporters.

As part of that same *Journal* interview he declared: "There are no regrets. I played for two great clubs and when I hung up my boots I felt satisfied with what I had achieved. Who can say that it would have been the outcome in another era?" Yet that is the tricky question we have to ask if we are to give this natural gentleman his due reckoning in the Newcastle United Hall of Fame. And to do it, to compare Stubbins with his own boyhood hero, Hughie Gallacher, and his striking successors such as Milburn, Len White, Malcolm Macdonald, Alan Shearer et al, we must confront the thorny issue of rating wartime football. Great players such as Stanley Matthews, Frank Swift and Stan Cullis all played the wartime game – as did Milburn as a winger, and the latter always defended the standard, declaring: "A goal is a goal and it's hard enough to score them at any time". Stubbins' United team-mate Jack Clark once pushed the Wallsend lad's claims as Newcastle's all-time great in a letter to a local newspaper, insisting: "I know people will say it was wartime football, but they have no idea how good it was".

Stubbins himself reckoned Newcastle had a strong side in the early 40s, with Scottish international defender Bobby Ancell, centre-back Jimmy Denmark and England star Dougie Wright in harness. He also had great regard for fellow striker Ray Bowden, saying: "Ray was a really excellent player and it was so sad that the war interrupted his career". The guest system in operation at the time ensured that even the smaller clubs could boast a few star names, and Stubbins himself later insisted: "I can't say I found a lot of difference between war-time and peacetime football. Everyone still picked up the points".

And yet, and yet…

The constant change in line-ups, the smaller crowds and a relative lack of emphasis on training and coaching surely means that defences were less organised and that the results cannot have been contested quite as fiercely as in the real thing of the Football League. Stubbins' tragedy – if you can call it that – is that he can never be truly regarded as the greatest player in Newcastle's history after playing seven out of his nine seasons at St James' in the wartime game. His spectacular scoring ratio of 109 per cent – dwarfing his nearest challenger Hughie Gallacher's 82 per cent – would surely never have been repeated in the Football League, even if Stubbins' First Division record at Liverpool in his late 20s and 30s showed he was still dangerous at the highest level. Yet there have been and there remain plenty ready to push Stubbins' considerable claims, irrespective of the quality of the Northern Regional League.

The *Sunday Sun* claimed in 1960 that "Albert ranks with the all-time greats who have won the No. 9 jersey in English League soccer," while the *Evening Chronicle*'s John Gibson, who covered United for decades, insisted that "few centre-forwards have captured the imagination like this Wallsend-born son of Geordieland, whose dashing style captivated countless thousands of fans". Former United skipper Joe Harvey – on the opposing side to Stubbins many times before the Yorkshireman signed for Newcastle – acknowledged that "his goal tally was breathtaking". And even allowing for a touch of bias, we should heed the words of Stan Seymour, who, when a director at Newcastle in Stubbins' pomp, rated the No. 9 higher than England icon Tommy Lawton. "The only advantage Lawton might have over Stubbins is with his heading," declared Seymour, "Stubbins is cleverer on the ball". Praise indeed. But, up against a host of names elsewhere in this book, lack of silverware is another cross Stubbins has to bear in posterity, and even though the game's big prizes were not there to be won during his days on Tyneside, he is bound to suffer in comparison to the likes of Gallacher, Milburn and Wyn Davies on this score.

But as the magnanimous Stubbins was always quick to point out, his is not a tale of what might have been. After all, who could have done more in wartime for the Magpies than score 231 games in 188 wartime games? Could Gallacher or Milburn have proven any more dangerous?·And who, in that bleakest of eras, could have done more to light up Tyneside and bring much-needed glamour and excitement to the life of the region? Circumstances beyond his control may prevent Stubbins challenging for the title of Newcastle's greatest ever player. But when it comes to United heroes, surely only a select few stand above him.

Len Shackleton

1946-1948: 64 games, 29 goals

HAS THERE EVER been another quite like Shack? Will there ever be?

Not according to those privileged enough to watch him – or honoured enough to play alongside one of the very few English footballers who can indisputably lay claim to the title 'genius'.

That he is not among the very biggest legends in Newcastle United's history is surely only due to the brevity of his black and white adventure – he played just 17 months on Tyneside. Yet he was a hero from that famous day one against Newport County – and his vast array of on-pitch trickery ensures that, even in the next millennium, this brash Yorkshireman remains the yardstick by which every other ball-playing Magpie has ever been judged.

In short, if you stick to the notion that Shackleton was the most gifted ever to grace the Gallowgate turf, you cannot go far wrong. Look to no higher authority than Jackie Milburn on this one. "Shack was the greatest ball-player of all time," said the United's legendary No. 9. "He could balance the ball on a snowflake. He was a born entertainer, and always original and inventive."

Yet, even his biggest fans had to admit that Shackleton's unpredictability could cause a team problems. Milburn added: "Shack didn't know what he was going to do next, so what chance had us mere mortals playing with him?"

His refusal – or innate inability – to curb those individualistic tendencies would ensure a premature end to his Newcastle career, and there is no disputing that, much to the chagrin of United fans, Shackleton went on to give greater service down the road at derby rivals Sunderland, scoring 100 goals in 348 games. But the anguish which that seismic £20,050 transfer brought to Tyneside is a measure of the ardent following which he had already built up in a thrilling, yet all-too-brief rollercoaster ride at St James'. Newspapers were inundated with letters from angry supporters, while workers staged a protest demonstration at the Armstrong Vickers factory on the banks of the Tyne as news unfolded of the record-breaking deal.

Shack left no legacy of silverware behind – indeed, he stands alongside Kevin Keegan in this book as one of only two players never to have played a game for Newcastle in English football's top flight. At just 64 and 85 appearances respectively, Shackleton and Keegan also have two of the shortest careers among the 20 chosen cult heroes in this book. But while Keegan has a sensational managerial career to strengthen his credentials, there was no such second coming for his predecessor.

So why, ball skills apart, put an arrogant Yorkshireman, who completed not one full season for United, up there on a pedestal with the likes of Gallacher, Milburn, Beardsley et al?

There are several reasons – but the clue to the biggest is in the title of the man's own autobiography: *Clown Prince of Soccer*. Quite simply, Len Shackleton was a born entertainer, and the Gallowgate crowd adored him for it. A natural rebel, he brought character, humour and magic to United's game; when Shack's one-man show rolled into town, the St James' Park crowd were treated to Saturday afternoon escapism at its best. Okay, Leonard Francis Shackleton was not the only attraction in an attacking line-up that also boasted the gifted Tommy Pearson, strikers Charlie Wayman and Roy Bentley and a pacey young winger called Milburn – but he was undoubtedly the ringmaster. Standing just 5ft 8in tall, Shack did not need to rely on physical strength to beat opponents – instead his wonderful close control and vast array of tricks would allow him to glide past opponents, while his visionary passing could also leave defences stranded.

A master of the unexpected, Shackleton would push the ball along, drag or pass it with any part of his boot – while his party piece of rebounding the ball off the corner flag would bring the black and white house down. His pinpoint ability to place the ball meant his scoring record, as an inside-left or inside-right, was impressive enough with Newcastle, at almost a goal every two games. But even his own team-mates acknowledged that scoring goals was nowhere near the top of Shackleton's priorities – he would rather entertain the crowd and embarrass the opposition.

A 4-1 home win over Cardiff in November 1947 was a case in point, when, with the pressure off following an early Jackie Milburn strike, Shackleton played to his adoring gallery almost throughout. Milburn later recalled: "He and Tommy Pearson gave an exhibition – they kept the ball between them with six or seven defenders around them, frightened to death to tackle – and this happened for 90 minutes."

Shackleton did deign to venture forward enough to get on the scoresheet on this occasion – but his impish delight in tormenting the opposition in other areas of the pitch was the priority.

But if the fans adored him for his gleeful one-upmanship, it did not meet to universal acclaim within the club. Indeed, a split within the United camp was evident as early as this, just a year into his Newcastle career. On the one hand were admirers such as centre-half Frank Brennan , who, in an interview with the *Journal* back in 1972, waxed lyrical about how Shackleton was many years ahead of his time. "He was doing things with the ball that they are only giving names to now," he declared. "Fair enough, you had players who gave their all. But Shack was the complete showman. Entertainment-wise, 10 minutes of Shack was worth 15 or 20 minutes of the greatest comedian on the stage – what he could do with the ball!"

In the other camp were men such as skipper Joe Harvey, who worried that Shackleton's unpredictability and refusal to work to a team pattern would scupper the side's chances of success in the long-term. Harvey told then manager George Martin: "We'll never win anything with Shackleton in the team – we've got to get rid of him."

Slap bang in the middle stood Jackie Milburn, an acknowledged fan of the inside-forward's genius who nevertheless acknowledged that "he had no interest other than entertaining the crowd – he'd rather beat three men than lay on a winning goal". Nevertheless, Jackie remained grateful for Shackleton's influence in helping the Geordie adapt to an unaccustomed centre-forward role only weeks before that win over

Cardiff – when Milburn emerged as the hat-trick hero in a 5-3 win at Bury in the game which sparked the career of United's most celebrated No. 9. Shackleton also got on the scoresheet that day and Milburn's son Jack, in his biography of his famous father, recalled the influence Shack brought to bear on a nervous Milburn Snr. "Don't worry Jackie, I'll look after you," said the ever-confident Shackleton, before feeding Milburn a stream of passes to help him became an instant centre-forward hit.

"Len Shackleton was a master craftsman, and thanks to him I got among the goals," said Milburn, who added: "I clicked with him because I expected the unorthodox. If he ran one way, I ran the other and sure enough the ball always found me. On the other hand, Len's quick-witted humour often caused me to laugh outright and lose control of the ball!" The issue of how to slot such a precocious individualist into a team game is one which has tormented many managers over the decades – but Milburn's declaration here perhaps suggests that the very best players have no problems adapting to such an 'unpredictable' ball-player.

Sadly, Newcastle did not have men of Milburn's calibre in every position and, while Shackleton's off-field personality was also a big factor, his perceived lack of cohesion with the rest of the United side certainly added to his early departure from St James' Park. Shackleton would later admit that his lack of silverware – he won not one major trophy throughout his career – would be his biggest regret in football, followed by the fact he won so few (five) England caps. His frequent international snubs have been put down to a clash between Shackleton's rebellious nature and the old-fashioned conservatism of the post-war English FA. But the grey men of Lancaster Gate cannot be blamed for his lack of club honours. Indeed, although Shackleton's genius is never questioned, the debate about his true effectiveness as a player was debated long after his retirement through injury in 1957. The *Daily Telegraph*, in a feature on his career in December 1970, came to a sobering conclusion. "In an era when to be a star is to be a stereotype, one wonders what would be the effect if a new Len Shackleton were to emerge," the *Telegraph* pondered. "I have the feeling that he would find it just as difficult to achieve recognition."

Yet lack of recognition among football lovers was never a problem – rather a lack of international caps and silverware. Shackleton's Division Two promotion with Newcastle – although he was sold to Sunderland three months before it was completed in the May 1948 – remains his most notable honour as a club player. And there are those Newcastle supporters who maintain that his 17-month Tyneside sojourn, barren of silverware, does not make him a United great. But in terms of cult heroes, there is surely no debate.

SHACK'S MAVERICK, CHEEKY persona coupled with the magic of his footballing arts, always made him deeply popular on the terraces – even if club directors and even team-mates were not unanimous in their praise. And never mind 17 months – five minutes was enough for the black and white faithful to take the new boy to their hearts. No discussion about Shackleton's contribution to Magpies folklore can be complete without reference to one of the most exciting days in club history – that six-goal debut in a record-breaking 13-0 win over Newport County. It is worth recalling that Newcastle fans were at the time still smarting from the sale of crowd favourite Albert Stubbins to Liverpool for a massive £13,000 (the second highest British transfer fee of the time), when United director Stan Seymour shocked Tyneside by persuading the board to spend every penny on the relatively unknown Shackleton.

Seymour was captivated by the skills of a player who had scored 171 goals in 217 games for Bradford Park Avenue, and who had guested for Huddersfield and Bradford City during the war. Indeed, Shack himself was shocked at the size of the fee – prompting row No. 1 with the United hierarchy, when he accepted a £500 signing-on fee, believing that would be around the expected standard 10 per cent of his fee, which he guessed to be less than £6,000!

If the player himself was surprised at the size of the deal, so were the rest of United's squad. Frank Brennan later recalled that he and his team-mates were a tad bemused at the deal.

They need not have worried. Three days after signing on 5 October 1946, Shackleton laid the opener on a plate for centre-forward Charlie Wayman at home to Newport County. The new boy managed to miss a penalty before making up for that with an astonishing double hat-trick – the most successful debut in club history– including a three-goal burst in just 155 seconds. Pity the poor fellows who nipped out to the gents at that point! By half-time, Wayman had three goals and Shack four.

Frank Brennan, who watched Shackleton's rapid transformation into a terrace hero, declared years later than he had never seen anything quite like it. "Who was this player Len Shackleton? The players and supporters alike were soon to know," said Brennan. "The display of football from the new boy was unbelievable...I am sure that all these spectators, the players and myself had never seen before or since an exhibition in one game by any player. This was Len Shackleton. Shack exhibited the almost impertinent skill which delighted his colleagues and supporters and infuriated his opponents. He was taken to the hearts of all the fans in this one game. Has this happened at Newcastle since? I doubt it. I say there hasn't been a player with Shack's appeal before or since."

Despite playing in front of the biggest crowd of his life – 52,137 were packed in at Gallowgate – and lining up alongside star names such as Pearson, Milburn, Wayman, Bentley and Brennan, the cocky 24-year-old Tyke had stolen the show. Quite apart from the six goals, the crowd loved Shack for his on-pitch swagger, including, at one point, putting his foot on the ball and taunting his marker by beckoning him closer. Little wonder that, as Brennan said, "the opposition were frightened to go anywhere near him by the end".

Never had a new hero been so quickly established, and Shackleton followed up by scoring in a 1-1 draw away to Southampton, finishing the season as the club's joint second highest scorer with 22 strikes in 38 games. Yet Shackleton would later claim that he regretted his astonishing introduction to Tyneside, since it created so much expectation and put him on a pedestal. "And the only place to go from a pedestal is off it," he added. "After that even if I scored three goals in a match, it was regarded as a flop. I couldn't win, even though that sort of memory lives with you forever."

Yet those who followed Shackleton's career closely would find difficulty accepting that he was never happy on a pedestal! This was a player with the on-pitch swagger of a man who knows he has God-given gifts way above the players around him. Not surprisingly, this did not go down too well with everyone.

Even before he had arrived on Tyneside, his penchant for tormenting opponents had brought criticism at Bradford. The *Telegraph* noted that "the locals had tired of the impish pranks of this precocious youngster, who seemed to like nothing better than grafting on to his magical skills a merciless goading of the opposition which had players itching for revenge". And Shackleton himself acknowledged that the approach from Newcastle had come at the right time, admitting: "I was losing some popularity with the Bradford crowd, so I was glad to listen to the pleadings of Newcastle United director, Mr Stan Seymour."

Yet Shack – perhaps because he did not stay long enough for his star to fade, or perhaps because he found the perfect audience for his showboating football in the North East – never lost any popularity with the Magpies faithful, nor did he on Wearside despite playing for seven seasons in red and white.

Joe Harvey could perhaps have been forgiven for his stance on Shackleton's lack of team ethics since he had been the intended victim of his fellow Yorkshireman's showmanship. The incident occurred when the two faced up to each other in a Bradford derby before either made the move north – although Shackleton, playing for Park Avenue against Harvey's City, paid a high price for his intended cheek. "Joe was a tough nut and always tried to kick hell's bells out of me, so in one game I got the ball and decided to get my own back," remembered Shackleton. "I manoeuvred so the referee was between me and Joe, and made sure Joe couldn't get the tackle in. Then, like a clever so-and-so, I decided to stand on the ball, slipped over and did my ligaments in, and was out of the game for 17 weeks. So much for trying to make a mug out of Joe Harvey!"

Harvey would later recall with a wry grin another occasion when the pair were on opposing sides – when Shack and Sunderland came calling at St James' Park. The United skipper said: "Nodding towards the press box, Shack told me: 'That's where I'm going to end up – criticising you!'"

He was as good as his word.

But if Shack certainly brought more than his fair share of hilarious diversions to Gallowgate when he signed for Newcastle, his influence in that first season was also undoubtedly shown on the pitch, with United finishing as the division's top scorers on 95 goals – albeit 10 points off the promotion pace in fifth spot. A measure of the side's frustrating inconsistency is that they wrapped up their season by losing 4-2 at – wait for it – Newport County, who had been so humiliated on Tyneside just seven months earlier.

THAT FIRST SEASON in black and white also proved to be as near Shack would come to silverware, when the side reached the FA Cup semi-final (he would match that feat twice at Roker Park) only to be thrashed 4-0 at Elland Road by a Charlton side who had endured a sleepless night thanks to food poisoning.

United would go on, of course, to greater heights in that competition after losing Shack, along with fellow crowd favourites, Wayman, Pearson and Bentley. But tellingly, centre-back Brennan – who lifted the Cup with United in 1951 and 52 – would pick the Second Division side Shack dominated as the greatest Newcastle team he had ever played in.

It is tempting to dream about what else the club could have achieved if they had managed to keep Shack and Milburn in harness – as it is, Shackleton's exit from the club, like so many of United's star names before and since, was precipitated by a series of fall-outs with the club's hierarchy. And, although a clearly bitter Shackleton would later claim it was a relief to escape what he termed "a chocolate club" because "they melt under pressure", it certainly came as a blow to the Yorkshireman at the time.

He had declared when joining Newcastle that he was joining "the best sporting folk in the world," and, when he looked back on United's decision to accept Sunderland's bid in February 1948, he recalled: "I had no real desire to leave the Magpies and the Tyneside crowd, but behind the scenes things happen in the life of a professional footballer that cannot be publicised and I thought it was best for both United and myself to seek a new club."

Decades later his feelings about the way Newcastle United had been run and their perceived lack of ambition came to the fore in an interview with the *Evening Chronicle* in November 1990, in which he declared: "Sunderland supporters are a little more demanding. They wouldn't put up with the Christmas Club attitude that has been running Newcastle all these years…but if you go another 30 miles down the road to Middlesbrough the supporters are much harder to please – they want a free Bovril and a bullfight at half-time!"

It is tempting to trace Shackleton's famous disdain for club directors back to his treatment and departure from St James' Park, where nobody, he claimed, would take credit for the decision at the time. "There was Alderman McKeag and Stan Seymour senior, and there was manager

George Martin. They all said they didn't want me to go – but they were all keen to blame each other for my departure."

In his own words, Shackleton joined "a much more professionally-run club" when he went to Sunderland and he got his revenge on the grey suits of the boardroom in that now-infamous blank page of his life story *Clown Prince of Soccer* under the Chapter Six heading 'What the Average Club Director knows about Football'.

Shackleton was still a Sunderland player at the time and, a quarter of a century later, when asked how he managed to escape censure from the club for his literary cheek, he said: "Easy. Every director came up individually, nudged me, winked and thought I was talking about the other fella, not them."

However, if the criticism was directed anywhere it was surely at St James', rather than Roker Park. Shackleton had been embroiled in a series of rows from day one of his Newcastle career – and if this made it easy for the board to cast him in the role of troublemaker, it did his popularity on the terraces no harm at all.

Indeed, his role as a determined rebel, standing up to authority, made him all the more adored by supporters, while he earned respect from team-mates as one of the earliest and most outspoken critics of the way clubs used to milk their superstar players.

Shackleton's hackles first rose over the issue of his technically illegal £500 signing-on fee – which he deemed derisory and which the club refused to pay up front. Shackleton later claimed he had to fight to get all of his promised cash, while he also took United to task – along with skipper Joe Harvey – over the issue of club houses, which were promised to both when they signed and which were still to be provided at the end of the 1946/47 season, nearly 19 months after Harvey's arrival and seven months after Shack's.

That particular row, although finally settled, rumbled on throughout United's FA Cup semi-final defeat to Charlton – just another example of mis-management behind the scenes which would dog the club at almost every turn, and even in the height of their 1950s Cup-winning heyday.

Another fall-out came at Christmas 1947 when Shackleton – along with goalkeeper Jack Fairbrother – ignored a request from manager George Martin for the whole team to spend Christmas Day watching prospective FA Cup third round opponents Charlton in action at

Middlesbrough. But perhaps the final straw came during that FA Cup tie at Charlton when Shackleton, worried about his 15-month son who had been taken ill before the match, had agreed to play, on condition that manager Martin would book a taxi for him to take him straight to the train station.

The taxi failed to materialise, and the player, having belatedly found one himself, felt even more aggrieved when he had his expenses claim queried by the board! The expenses issue was at least in part down to Shackleton's reputation with directors as having an eye for the fast buck, and he was marked out as a ringleader whenever the players, mindful of the fact that the Magpies were pulling in the best attendances in England, understandably grumbled about their wages.

Indeed, the Magpies pulled in an average of 56,299 in the 1947/48 Second Division promotion season – a British record until Manchester United topped it in 1968 in the top flight – while a massive 64,931 crowd watched Shackleton's last match at St James' Park, a 4-1 win over Luton on January 3, when Jackie Milburn scored a hat-trick.

Shackleton's subsequent £20,050 move to Sunderland at least allowed him to continue playing professional cricket for Benwell on the banks of the Tyne, while this all-round sportsman managed to lift silverware as a golfer when he pipped Jackie Milburn to the 1971 North East Press golf tournament!

Shackleton's skill with a ball would belatedly transfer itself to the tennis court when, in middle age, he claimed to have wiped the floor with the opposition in a summer tournament while on holiday in Morecambe, after picking up a racket for the first time. "I'd entered it just for a lark," he told the *Journal*. "I'd never stepped on to a tennis court before – but blow me if I didn't go and win the tournament. My opponents thought I was kidding when I kept asking which court I had to serve to and where I had to stand."

TALENT, IT'S TRUE, goes a long way to explaining why Shackleton was so loved by Tynesiders – but attitude had an awful lot to do with it too. This was the same player who, on being offered schoolboy terms as a 15-year-old at Arsenal (he was devastated when the Gunners released him a year later) told manager George Allison: "Another thing – If I decide to sign for Arsenal, you'll have to buy me some boots. These aren't mine, and I can't afford to get any."

Decades after Shackleton worked his sorcery in a black and white shirt, it is easier to recapture the hilarity of this naturally mischievous character than it is to fully convey his mastery of the ball. Numerous anecdotes remain about a player who once admitted he was constantly plagued by "that imp inside me which makes me fool around". If the imp stopped him achieving the honours he deserved, it at least brought him more than his fair share of adulation from the terraces.

Skipper Joe Harvey once recalled his bemusement when, with Newcastle leading 1-0 at home to Tottenham (thanks to a Shackleton goal), the Clown Prince spent an age lining up his team-mates in the box for a last-minute corner, gesticulating and shouting out directions – only to tap the ball a few inches over the line and trot back to the halfway line smiling and telling his captain: "By the time they fetch that, the game will be over!"

Big Frank Brennan recalled another occasion when Shackleton's improvised gamesmanship delighted the United crowd – but enraged the home supporters in an epic 2-0 FA Cup quarter-final win at Sheffield United in March 1947. Blades fans had worked to help clear heavy snow from the pitch in order to get the game played – and Shackleton, who would later pick this as one of his most memorable matches for the Magpies, was to take full advantage of the unusual surrounding conditions, with his team 2-0 up and longing for the final whistle.

WITH BRAMALL LANE open on one side to the adjacent cricket pitch, where 5ft snow drifts were piled high, Shackleton had already incurred the wrath of the referee once for timewasting after he had dribbled towards that side of the ground and belted the ball as hard as he could into the snow. Brennan takes up the tale of Shackleton putting his incredible ball-bending skills to unorthodox use. "Instead of using the ball he smacked it into the cricket pitch. Away into the snow went the ball boys. It was a funny sight… with only their heads visible. Eventually the game re-started after the referee had had a few words about wasting time. I am sure this was done by the referee to soothe the seething home crowd. With two minutes to go there was a repeat situation. With baited breath we watched as he turned in an almost identical situation to boot the ball into the cricket field. Then, as if he remembered the ref's warning, he turned towards the opponent's goal. He sailed the ball up in the air towards the goal…slowly it turned in its flight and drifted back into the cricket field. Even the ref had to smile. The crowd went mad…Newcastle won."

Like Paul Gascoigne four decades later, Shackleton's appetite for on-pitch mischief never waned as the years passed and he continued to amuse and enchant Sunderland supporters right up unto his enforced retirement through an ankle injury in 1957. He later recalled one favourite moment which thrilled the Roker Park crowd, when, with his side 2-1 up against Manchester City, he bemused his team-mates and the opposition by dribbling the ball towards the touchline next to the dugout, then stopped dead in his tracks and waited. "The City defenders didn't know what to do. It wasn't conventional enough for them, and so for a minute no one came towards me," he remembered. "I put my foot on the ball and pretended to look at my watch. Then I started brushing my hair back. The fans loved it. "Roy Paul (City captain) was mad, as you would expect. He came tearing in like a mad bull. I dragged the ball back so that he went sliding out on to the cinder track, and I then passed it calmly to a team-mate."

Shackleton certainly played football with a smile on his face, and, in his post-playing days as a sports journalist, was constantly critical of the game's increasingly organised, regimented approach. Perhaps not surprisingly, he picked Gascoigne as his favourite player in the late 80s, while, in an interview with the *Journal* in 1985 he declared: "Football's given me a good living, but it's too organised now. It's like watching a game of chess, and who bothers to do that? That's why gates are down. I don't believe there is any room given to entertainment or improvisation these days – it's all about results."

We have, therefore, a fair idea what he would make of the even more organised, defensive Premiership game in 2006.

But if Shackleton the confirmed entertainer was exactly the type of player for Newcastle fans to take to their hearts, then results are also important when we rate the biggest cult heroes in the club's history. And this is where Shackleton must lose out to the very biggest United legends – trophy winners like Milburn, Colin Veitch, Bill McCracken, Hughie Gallacher, Bobby Mitchell, and Wyn Davies. And perhaps we should not be too harsh on Shackleton's relatively lackadaisical approach when we analyse why he did not win trophies at Newcastle – after all, the more professional, single-minded Alan Shearer won nothing in black and white either, and he did not arrive, as Shackleton did, at a club in the Second Division, only to be shipped out 17 months later.

Instead we should regard it as one of the misfortunes of club history that United seemed at the time ill-equipped to handle, and get the best out of, arguably the finest footballer ever to have graced the Gallowgate turf. Leonard Shackleton's party piece was flicking a coin from the top of his foot into his jacket pocket – but the Clown Prince was so much more than a circus act. Just consider these glowing words from a team-mate who is himself a legend still at St James' Park – big Frank Brennan.

> "It was a pleasure being able to play in the same side as Len.
> Thank you for giving me this great experience. It was only
> for one season, but a book could be written about it."

It takes a special footballer to make such an esteemed fellow pro speak in these terms. But all those supporters who were privileged enough to watch an undoubted master at work between October 1946 and February 1948 will appreciate Brennan's feelings.

It is easy to see Shackleton's deserved place in the Newcastle United pantheon as a testament to Tyneside's obsession with adventurous, magical football. So many supporters may have longed, at various times, for their side to be a touch more pragmatic – and surely never was that feeling so strong as during the 1996 title run-in, when Kevin Keegan's cavaliers threw away English football's greatest prize, the Premiership. But, like it or not, for better or worse, attacking football is now ingrained in the fixtures and fittings of St James' Park, and men like Shackleton – and their special bond with the fans – help us to understand why.

Trophies are all well and good – and would be so, so welcome, but the excitement of a genius at work, the comedy and spectacle of watching your hero stand, foot on ball and hands on hips, goading the opposition, is what makes cold wet Saturday afternoons worthwhile.

In an age of agents, marketing deals, media hype and 90-mile-an-hour football, this is a lesson worth heeding. Would that there were more like him. As Shack told the *Sunday Sun* back in 1991, nine years before his death, "I just wish our game had more of a smile on its face and that occasionally they'd let the dust settle on the pitch, and show the supporters what pure football is really like."

Jackie Milburn

1943-1957: 494 games, 239 goals

JACKIE MILBURN WAS, and perhaps always will be, No. 1.

Midway through Newcastle's history came the man to stop all arguments about the club's greatest ever hero. And in truth, it is difficult to see another player ever overshadowing his legend. There are arguably more gifted players elsewhere in this book, certainly a few more colourful personalities and a perhaps even a couple dusted more liberally with the stardust of charisma than J.E.T. But the man who so aptly lived up to those famous initials generated a love never equalled on North East shores.

Indeed, transcending the boundaries of sport and garnering respect from all walks of life in this region, Milburn is a strong contender for the greatest cult hero – within or without football – that the North East of England has ever seen. There remains one unshakeable truth underpinning Milburn's magnetic and almost universal appeal – and it has little to do with football. But consider first his huge achievements on the pitch...

- Milburn won three FA Cups, scoring in two finals
- He scored 20 goals to help United to promotion in 1948
- He is the club's record league goalscorer with 177
- He holds the club appearance record for a striker with 397

– He scored nine hat-tricks for the club
– He remains, with 23, the club's record FA Cup goalscorer

Milburn's mark of 200 competitive goals was, of course, eclipsed in Alan Shearer's final season as a player at St James' – and the two inevitably invite comparison as Geordie centre-forward heroes who both served the club for a decade or more. Milburn's champions traditionally point to the fact that his 200 were League and FA Cup strikes, while Shearer had 30 European goals, including Intertoto Cup, to boost his tally – competitions which were not open to his predecessor.

Another point often raised in support of Milburn is his wartime tally of 38 goals (plus one Charity Shield strike) which, according to club historian Paul Joannou, makes him the 'unofficial' highest scorer in United history on 239, although other sources insist Albert Stubbins plundered 245 in wartime to claim the top spot. Milburn's goalscoring feats are all the more impressive since, unlike Shearer, Hughie Gallacher and Malcolm Macdonald, he made many of his United appearances stuck out on the right wing before his true ability as a centre-forward was uncovered.

Yet debates about goalscoring statistics – diverting though they may be – do not even begin to capture the essence of Jackie Milburn's enduring fame in his homeland. In fact, to a large extent, they are beside the point.

Milburn's status diminished not a jot when Shearer rammed home his 201st competitive strike against Portsmouth on 4 February 2006 – because the legend goes so much deeper than that. Milburn remains to this day, 18 years after his death from lung cancer, the most deeply loved figure in the club's history, and this has as much to do with the man off the pitch as the player on it. Yet Milburn's personality contained none of the restless energy of a Kevin Keegan, the exciting, rogueish passion of a Hughie Gallacher, nor the outrageous exuberance of a Malcolm Macdonald.

In a way, Milburn's extraordinary appeal was in his ordinariness.

True, he was a warm, charming and quietly charismatic man – but his greatest qualities, and ones which endeared him so much to the people of this region, were a kind heart and the natural modesty of an Ashington pit lad; qualities which never left him, despite his stellar achievements. Indeed, his son Jack, in his biography of Jackie, *A Man of Two Halves*, described that his father only came to realise his true popularity in his last few days, as he fought a losing battle at home with cancer. Jack recounted: "Get-well cards, letters, flowers and fruit flooded into the house and the telephone never stopped ringing, and I reckon it was at that time that Dad actually realised he had so many genuine friends in the world."

His son argues that up to that point, and throughout his career, Milburn – partly influenced by an innate inferiority complex, which he talked privately about in later life – never had any idea of his worth to a society in thrall to his stardom.

HE RECOUNTED HIS father's shock when, upon being made a Freeman of the City in 1980, he was asked for his autograph by Cardinal Basil Hume, while another autograph-signing session, at a 1988 Football Writers' Association event in London, surprised Milburn when the queue for his signature dwarfed that of guest-of-honour Pelé!

In a tale retold by sportswriter Alan Oliver of Newcastle's *Evening Chronicle*, Milburn admitted: "That was one of the most embarrassing moments of my life". Milburn's genuine modesty underpinned his entire career, and it is arguable that he might have been an even more fearsome proposition as a striker if he had the on-pitch conceit of a Macdonald or Shearer. He once admitted "I lacked a bit of devil as a player" and contemporaries attest to feeling bemused by his relative lack of self-belief.

After one away defeat to Stoke City, in which Milburn played as a winger, he confessed to feeling outclassed by Sir Stanley Matthews, adding: "He made the ball do everything but unlace itself and name its maker. After that superb display, I felt I should go home and burn my boots, for as a footballer, I realised that I could never, for all my natural speed and great enthusiasm, hope to be in the same class as this distinguished player."

Yet England colleague Sir Tom Finney may beg to differ. Before an England match away to Wales in October 1949, he recalled Milburn's pre-match jitters, "Jack said: 'That Tommy Jones is playing again. I never do well against him.' I told him not be daft and go out and get a hat-trick. He did." Finney concluded: "He did have an inferiority complex. He never thought he was as good as he was."

Milburn would later admit to as much, insisting that his lack of confidence came from a traumatic incident in childhood when, after winning his fifth event at school sports day, his exhaustion – as he threw himself to the ground – was misinterpreted as posturing by his watching father, resulting in a real hiding later on at home. Jack Milburn recalls that his father admitted: "Maybe my father's intentions were the best in the world and I've certainly never had a big head, but that thrashing laid the foundations for an inferiority complex I have fought all my life to overcome."

It is well-nigh impossible to judge how modesty ends and insecurity begins in analysing Milburn's career, but he doubtless carried himself throughout with an almost complete lack of ego. His request to play in the reserves instead of the first team after recovering from injury at the start of the 1951/52 season is yet another example of his selfless attitude. "After I recovered from my injury, I thought it unfair that the forward line should be changed just to accommodate me, so I asked Mr Seymour if he would play me in the reserves, and he agreed," Milburn later recalled.

It is difficult to imagine the likes of Macdonald, Keegan and Shearer adopting the same approach – and remember that Milburn, at this time, was at the very height of his fame as Newcastle's goalscoring, FA Cup-winning hero.

AWAY FROM THE pitch, Milburn's self-effacing, charming manner marked him out as a natural gentleman and fans lucky enough to meet the great man always left afterwards feeling his reputation had been enhanced. Quite simply, he always had time for people, and cousin Jack Charlton remembered that a walk through Newcastle city centre with his elder relative was always a slow affair, so regularly was he stopped by ardent supporters. Quoted in Mike Kirkup's biography, *Jackie Milburn: In Black and White*, Charlton declared: "He was everybody's friend. If you ever walked through Newcastle with him, you got stopped every two minutes; everybody said 'Hello' to him ... Memories of him playing football were very important to people, but there's got to be more than that for him to make that kind of mark on the area and the society."

Mary O'Dowd, who wrote to the *Evening Chronicle* to express her grief at Milburn's passing in 1988, captured what it was like to meet her idol. "I heard the news while listening to the radio and am not ashamed to say that I shed quite a few tears... I was lucky enough to meet Jackie – he had a modesty and naturalness which made it so easy to be able to talk to him". The deep grief felt by O'Dowd was matched across the North East on 9 October 1988 – and a 'state funeral' a few days later when it seemed the entire region thronged the streets to pay their respects. Milburn's death was felt almost as keenly as that of a family member in thousands of households, and in these parts it is no exaggeration to compare this phenomenal and almost unique display of public mourning, with the funeral of Princess Diana nine years later.

Milburn's daughter Betty, in an interview with the *Newcastle Journal* a year later, captured the scene as countless thousands lined the streets to greet the funeral cortege all the way from Ashington to Newcastle. "We came out of the house in Ashington and there were firemen saluting," she said. "All the way through Ashington to Newcastle, all along the route, there were people standing. Old people, young people, were paying their respects to a man who last played football 30 years ago – thousands sharing our day of mourning. It was a truly beautiful experience. I stood back and saw the love and respect being shown towards Dad. It gave us the strength to get through the day and it is something which we will never forget."

It is also, arguably, an occasion which will never be matched for a footballer in these parts; a day when the cliché came true – the city stood still.

If you need any further proof of Milburn's standing, bear in mind the following...

> - He is the only player in Newcastle's history to have a stand named after him
> - He is the only footballer ever to have a statue erected in his honour in the city centre (and another one in his hometown Ashington)
> - He won – by a landslide – a poll by the North East press in 1987 to find the North East's greatest post-war player
> - He had a musical play – simply entitled *Wor Jackie*, written about him and performed at the Theatre Royal
> - A massive crowd of 45,404 – and legends such as Ferenc Puskas, Sir Bobby Charlton and Sir Tom Finney

– turned up for his belated testimonial in May 1967
- He was the subject of the first ever episode of ITV's
This Is Your Life to be filmed outside London
- He was the first footballer to be made a Freeman of
the City of Newcastle

That latter occasion left Milburn – always acutely aware of his humble roots in a pitman's terraced house in Ashington – typically non-plussed, declaring "What am I doing etched on a wall with all those fine folk?"

But perhaps the most moving occasion of all for Milburn in retirement came back at the Civic Centre in 1987 when the Newcastle Sports Council awarded him a special honour – the Wilkinson Sword of Peace for his services to sport in the region. The event proved emotional for everyone present when the assembled throng burst into a spine-tingling rendition of 'The Blaydon Races' as the Duke of Edinburgh made the presentation. Son Jack recalled that "Dad had to fight back the tears. He really didn't know which way to turn".

Throughout decades of North East life, this sort of adulation for 'Wor Jackie' has been an accepted truth – and attempts to analyse the reasons behind such depth of feeling always go beyond his ability with a ball. Season ticket-holder and lifelong supporter Ian Parker, now in his early 70s, watched Milburn as a teenager and believes that personality weights heavy in any assessment of the Milburn legend. "He was such a nice fella, so well respected," said Ian, of Burnopfield, Newcastle-upon-Tyne. "Nobody ever heard a bad word said about Jackie – and I can't think of another footballer at the club that you can say that about. Every mother wanted their son to grow up like Jackie – he was proud of his Geordie roots but never arrogant and never lost his temper as a player."

Timing, too, played its part. "Everyone needed a hero after the bleakness of the war years, and so everything Jackie did – everything he was – was magnified. He was the perfect guy to hang your hat on."

Ten years after he last kicked a ball for United, a feature by Harry Thompson on Milburn touched upon this universal appeal, and acknowledged: "His popularity transcended social barriers, and also had a passing impact on people to whom sport in general and soccer in particular were mysteries they did not care to penetrate." Thompson earmarked three main factors in the Milburn legend – his dashing style of play, his sportsmanship and an endearing personality. "With all this," he added, "picture the emergence of Milburn upon a Tyneside and North East just releasing itself from war weariness, yearning for a brave, uncomplicated figure to cheer, and before the forced sophistication of TV and the competition of the car. Then, maybe, you can understand the Milburn impact, the like of which is unlikely to be seen again."

Milburn's kind heart off the pitch undoubtedly affected his countenance on it; unlike many of the rebellious firebrands which have brewed passion on the terraces over the years at St James', he was never once cautioned in a black and white shirt, and remained a model of sporting dignity throughout a long career. His erstwhile skipper Joe Harvey once described Milburn as "gentle and generous in victory, always first with the handshake in defeat." While Bobby Charlton was perhaps the most eminent deliverer of a line in praise which peppers the Jackie Milburn pantheon. "No one in football ever had a bad word to say about Jackie," he declared, "and he never had a bad word to say about anybody."

Bearing in mind that Milburn worked as a tabloid sports journalist for many years after playing, that is quite an achievement!

If there remains, in all this hero-worship, too much sentimentality about the life and times of what was, in many ways, an ordinary working-class bloke from Ashington, then that is not Milburn's fault. He was probably, in truth, correct to be embarrassed at times about adulation which has proved to be an unmatched phenomenon in the history of North East sport. But, before we paint a picture of a living saint which certainly would have the great man turning in his grave, it must be noted that much of the strength of the Milburn legend is built on lofty perceptions – and expectations – of a Tyneside footballing public who have always, perhaps more than in other areas of Britain, longed for a hero. And in Milburn, they found a man who never seemed to disappoint their expectations, never shattered their illusions. With no roguery (á la Hughie Gallacher or Gazza) or harshly competitive edge (think Keegan, Shearer) to offend tenderer sensibilities, it was easy to presume, from a distance that Jackie Milburn, with his widespread appeal, really was 'All Things to All Men' – not to mention women and children. He wasn't, of course. But by carrying on in his own courteous, modest way, and always affording time to his disciples, he allowed a movement of adoration to build momentum like no other before or since.

Can there be anyone else in this book for whom the following words – uttered by Cardinal Basil Hume upon Milburn's death – would not seem ridiculous? "There was a quality of goodness about him which inspired others," said Hume.

The record books are full of other glowing testimonies to Milburn as a man – while his presence throughout the other chapters of this book, as critic, point of reference, prized team-mate, friend, supporter, personal champion, advisor or measuring stick, are testament to his vast influence upon the fortunes of Newcastle United and its people. The last point is one worth stressing – Milburn has set the standard against which all cult heroes at the club have been judged since. "More gifted than Jackie Milburn," "As popular as Milburn" are regarded as the highest praise possible to other Magpie favourites of all eras.

Yet very few – even in the height of Keegan-mania or the recent frenzy of celebration over Shearer's achievements – ever dare to claim that their favourite is *bigger* than Wor Jackie. Indeed, although the nickname has been copied at times (Bobby Mitchell was "Wor Bobby" to some, while there has even been an attempt to establish "Wor Al" in recent times) it is telling that Milburn, in his fond term of reference, is the player to be most deeply accepted as 'wor' or 'one of us'.

There are solid historical reasons for this. Having come from bona fide Geordie mining stock and having combined his early playing career with shifts down the pit at Woodhorn and then Hazlerigg Colliery, Milburn had nothing to prove to any of the supporters about hard-work and commitment. He would often take the field at St James' having worked the 'early shift' the night before – starting at midnight on Friday through until 8am Saturday, before joining thousands of United supporters in the long queues for the bus into Newcastle city centre to begin his match preparations. "Often they would yell at me to get to the front of the queue, but I waited my turn like the rest," he recalled. Eventually, when the onerous regime looked like taking its toll on a player rapidly emerging as the biggest star in the Magpies' ranks, fellow workers rallied round to persuade the colliery manager to give 'Wor Jackie' Saturdays off – by threatening all-out strike action.

A year later, Milburn, who had been working as a fitter, belatedly managed to wangle exclusion from below ground duties when, on the advice of a friendly doctor, he employed the tried-and-trusted method of picking at his ears with a matchstick and convincing medical staff at the Royal Victoria Infirmary he was suffering from external otitis, or inflammation of the ear. Few begrudged Milburn the break, as he was finally spared the underground shift a full five years into his playing career at Gallowgate. Indeed, after trawling the record books for any "dirt" on the great man, it seems that this trick with a matchstick, and a couple of ill-advised transfer requests, is as damaging as it gets for Milburn the player.

The first request – quickly turned down by club directors, came in October 1948 after Milburn, returning from an England win over Northern Ireland in Belfast, had had his head turned by talk of earning big money – outside of football but alongside his footballing contract – in the South East.

The second request was apparently engineered by director Stan Seymour who, three years later, was tempted by a tentative approach from Portsmouth into tipping the newspapers off about a £30,000 price tag for the player – and successfully urging Milburn to ask for a move in writing. Fortunately for all parties concerned, there were no takers at what was then a massive price tag – although Milburn was furious when Seymour insisted the whole saga had been sparked by the player's unrest.

Throw in his managerial failure at Ipswich – about which Newcastle fans care not a jot, and which seemed to stem at least in part from his lack of ruthlessness – and a public criticism of Portman Road predecessor Sir Alf Ramsey for his lack of support, and you have as full a picture as you can get of Milburn's 'dark side'. Controversy may have stalked every move of United icons such as Gallacher, Malcolm Macdonald and Paul Gascoigne, but it rarely got close to Milburn.

For all that, this Ashington lad was no media recluse – he had a keen sense of humour, a lively way with words and a natural cheery charisma which, like Macdonald and Keegan, allowed him to light up any room just by walking into it. His son Jack recalls that Milburn Snr, despite his modesty, once admitted he was aware of the effect his personality had on others. "I could never understand that of myself, but felt very blessed for it," he said. It all helped turn Milburn into the biggest star United had ever seen – even if he remained perplexed at being put on a pedestal above so many other great names.

When Kevin Keegan signed for the club in 1982, for example, Milburn agreed to pose for pictures with the new boy – but wondered aloud why Len White, Malcolm Macdonald or Wyn Davies had not been asked as well. "Shouldn't it be Len, Malcolm or Wyn in the photograph with Kevin and not me?" he said. That humility from a fellow hard-working Geordie with a God-given talent, an infectious personality, dashing good looks and a kind heart, turned Jackie Milburn into Tyneside's favourite son.

ACHIEVING EFFORTLESS SUCCESS in a fairytale ascent to soccer stardom yet keeping a level head and a common touch, Milburn was the son/friend/brother/son-in-law that all North Easterners wanted. But of course, there is one other thing that deserves a little emphasis before we close the book on this man's iconic status – and something which, had it not been true, would have rendered all the above redundant outside his own circle of friends and family... he could play a bit too.

Standing 5ft 11in tall and J.E.T-propelled, Milburn's unconventional striking style marks him out as one of the most exciting Magpies ever to don the black and white shirt. Pace was always at the heart of his game – before he had even made his debut, he shocked Albert Stubbins, then the fastest man on Newcastle's books, by outsprinting the United No. 9 in training, while Sir Tom Finney would attest to Milburn winning all the races at England camp, too. Such was Milburn's class he competed as a teenager in the prestigious Powderhall sprint meeting at Edinburgh, while he was reported to have clocked a superb 9.7 second personal best in the 100 yards. Stunning speed and a natural eye for goal were two of Milburn's chief weapons as an outstanding right winger at St James' – and Sir Bobby Robson, who watched the great man as a childhood fan at United, would later insist it was a close call which position he mastered better.

Yet those two attributes also marked him out as a potential through-the-middle striker and, although he was initially reluctant to answer the call in October 1947 from manager George Martin – who was suffering from a shortage of recognised striking talent – on reflection, it seems a surprise that the transformation had taken so long. It was, after all, more than four years into Milburn's Newcastle career, and he had scored 17 times from the wing in season 1946/47 – and 38 times in two war-time seasons before that. History records that Milburn's doubts were shared by skipper Joe Harvey, trainer Norman Smith and director Stan Seymour, who insisted the winger was not good enough in the air to fill the centre-forward's role.

But Martin, as recounted by Roger Hutchinson in his book, *The Toon – a Complete History of Newcastle United Football Club*, stood his ground, insisting: "You're wrong all of you. Not only will Jackie make a centre-forward, he'll get a cap into the bargain."

The prediction looked less ridiculous when Milburn hit a hat-trick in his first game as United's No. 9 – a 5-3 win at Bury – and he was soon leaving defenders trailing in his wake on the way to goal as he plundered 20 goals in 40 games that season to help Newcastle back into the First Division. An epic 4-2 win over Sheffield Wednesday clinched promotion and brought the first honour of Milburn's career – and he would later recall the atmosphere that day as the best he ever experienced, eclipsing even the three subsequent FA Cup final victories.

A FEW MONTHS later, and just a year after his centre-forward conversion, Martin was proved right when Milburn received his first England cap – and scored – in a 6-2 win over Northern Ireland. He would score another eight times in an international career that brought just 13 appearances over seven years – a scoring ratio which suggests that Milburn might just have emerged as one of the all-time England greats, if only he had been given more chances.

In truth, he did not help his cause by pulling out of an England tour in the summer of 1949, to go to America instead with Newcastle. Milburn insisted at the time that his reason was partly "because of the lack of urgency among team and supporters alike" at England level.

In common with United team-mate Bobby Mitchell, who found Scotland a cold environment after the 'band of brothers' mentality of the St James' dressing room and the passion of the crowd, Milburn failed to truly settle in the England camp. He later admitted he felt he never received proper service from international team-mates, felt that some were too intent on furthering their own interests rather than playing like a team and even went so far as to suggest that "one or two of them were outright snobs".

However Milburn's attitude merely endeared him all the more to Newcastle fanatics, who may well have been supportive of director Stan Seymour's failed attempts to get their prized asset released again from England duty before a match against Northern Ireland in 1950. Although not, in this instance, motivated by the player, this was the second time United had requested Milburn's withdrawal and the situation did not help the player's chances of establishing himself. Over ensuing years, Newcastle fans were to become convinced that old-fashioned anti-North East bias was hampering their idol's international career as he was continually dropped then re-selected throughout his six years of England duty – but the emergence of Nat Lofthouse as England's reliable No. 9 was another telling factor. With his prodigious aerial ability, Lofthouse was a more traditional all-round centre-forward, and was doubtless deemed a safer bet than the unconventional Milburn, who preferred the ball to feet and who would roam right across the front line in search of openings.

Heading was never Milburn's strong point – he was once left with a sore head after being told to practise heading a heavy laced leather ball for four days solid by England boss Walter Winterbottom. But Milburn, whose representative career peaked with an England hat-trick over Wales in a 4-1 win at Cardiff in October 1949, and another for the Football League in their 3-1 win over the Irish League the same season, had other attributes. Although he played in the Brazil World Cup of 1950 – having a good headed goal ruled out for offside in the 1-0 defeat to Spain which ended England's chances – those qualities were to be shown to so much more devastating effect at club level.

Having played his part in keeping himself and the England squad alive on their return flight from Rio – Milburn noticed a problem with one of the engines and alerted the pilot, who had to make a quick landing for overnight repairs before crossing the Atlantic – Tyneside's favourite son quickly resumed his favourite pastime, bringing thrills and spills to the St James' Park crowd.

Boasting superb close control at speed, relentless energy, unquenchable spirit and a thrilling knack of heading straight for goal, Milburn played the game like a young man in a hurry. Although a gentleman on and off the pitch, he was a tenacious player, and would frequently launch himself into a trademark hooked sliding tackle to retrieve the ball from defenders who had had the nerve to dispossess him – a challenge which Peter Beardsley would also perfect in later years. Milburn was happy to try his luck at goal from any angle and with either foot, and often took goalkeepers by surprise with the ferocity of his shooting, despite very little backlift. It was a heady concoction which the Newcastle fans, born and bred on a diet of attacking football, could hardly fail to resist. It is perhaps little wonder that former Newcastle team-mate and close friend Bob Stokoe described Milburn as "the most exciting thing I have ever seen on a football pitch".

Milburn's sweet striking of the ball, his deadly accuracy and the sheer grace of his movement left supporters and press alike in raptures. Journalist Harry Thompson spoke of "days in the mud when only Milburn seemed to matter", while fan F Waugh, of Westerhope, wrote to the local Press on the occasion of his hero's death to hail "a great hitter of the ball…the finest player and finest moving athlete I've seen on a soccer field".

The striker's chief bullet-maker, Bobby Mitchell, remembered: "The indefatigable Jackie Milburn, that express of a human being with a shot in both feet to strike terror into the hearts of all goalkeepers", while the Scottish winger also offered a rare insight into one of his team-mate's unorthodoxies. Instead of leaning over the ball when shooting, Milburn went against the textbook by leaning back into the shot. Still, the proof the pudding is in the tasting, and while such an approach would lead mere mortals to fire sky-high, his accuracy and goals-per-game ratio should have prevented a controversial inquest from new manager Duggie Livingstone in 1954.

"In a way, I could appreciate the manager's wishes," said Mitchell, recalling an attempted tutorial which helped destroy Livingstone's reputation in the dressing room. "Milburn DID kick the ball wrong. He was invariably leaning backwards and apparently off-balance. Not the most stylish of performances, I admit. But what Duggie forgot was that, in spite of Milburn's apparent faults, he was still getting the goals!"

Goal-scoring, of course, is at the very heart of the Milburn legend. Mitchell believed that "Jackie's job was to hang around and thump the ball into the back of the net. No more, no less", but he added "and how splendidly he did his job." Milburn may have lacked some of the fine play-making craft of a Gallacher, Beardsley or Gascoigne – indeed, some critics felt that his successor as No. 9 hero, Len White, was a better all-round technician. But when it comes down to spectacular goals, few can rival Wor Jackie. And if we are taking about important goals, Ashington's most famous export is standing out on his own. Out of the 239 goals he scored in black and white, 13 stand out for significance – the goals that helped bring three FA Cups to Tyneside in 1951, 52 and 55.

Only Bobby Cowell and Bobby Mitchell can match Milburn's feat in lifting those three trophies – and surely no one person did more than Newcastle's No. 9 to deliver the silverware which established United's reputation as one of the most glamorous clubs in the land.

The emphasis on Cup football here – for Milburn and his team-mates – was quite deliberate, even if the selective motivation put paid to arguably United's best ever post-war side, in 1950-51, achieving the double. Undefeated in their first 10 matches and sitting top of the league, the Magpies would win just once in 11 games between the FA Cup semi-final and the final. Milburn later recalled: "We stopped playing league games after the semis".

The inconsistent, wilful brilliance of that Newcastle side – boasting attacking greats such as Mitchell, Ernie Taylor, and George Robledo, and redoubtable defensive talents such as Frank Brennan and Joe Harvey – seemed perfectly suited to the one-off drama of a competition which was, in Tyneside's eyes, seen at least as the equal of the league title. But there was no doubting who the spearhead was. Milburn scored in every round up until the final – six in all – before writing FA Cup history as the black and white underdogs dominated a final against Blackpool, which was billed as a Stanley Matthews showpiece. In the 50th minute, springing Blackpool's offside trap, Milburn sprinted clear from the halfway line, evaded his marker Eric Hayward and buried the ball past goalkeeper George Farm. It was a classic striker's goal, and he would, in later years, recall it as his favourite strike.

"It was a goal for the connoisseur, the one every centre-forward dreams of scoring," he said. "The trouble with a free run of about 40 yards like that is that you keep seeing imaginary shadows chasing you and you're convinced you can feel the panting breath of half a dozen defenders down the back of your neck. That's why it means so much to score. So many things could go wrong."

Many players would struggle to match such a goal, on such an occasion, for the rest of their career. For Milburn, that challenge took five minutes. Indeed, most observers would differ with the great man and assert that his second strike, from the corner of the box following a clever back-heel from Ernie Taylor, was even better.

Milburn remembered it like this:

"Tommy Walker, our outside-right, pushed the ball to little Ernie Taylor and as he did I yelled 'Backheel it'. Ernie did, but even so I was really too far over the ball. I struck it with all my might and it flew straight as an arrow into the back of the net. Had I been better positioned when I made contact it would probably have hit the crossbar."

For once, and to the great joy and relief of the travelling black and white hordes, Milburn *had* been leaning over the ball when he made contact! It seems incredible to recall now that opponents Matthews and Stan Mortensen – who would combine to devastating effect for Blackpool in the famous 1953 final – were so impressed by Milburn's second effort that they held up the restart for 30 seconds while they congratulated their opponent.

Under the eyes of the nation, a Geordie footballer had dominated the game's showpiece event with two of the finest strikes ever seen at Wembley. Looking back through history, few occasions have ever matched that 1951 final for individual heroic status, perhaps Matthews' own moment of legend in 1953, or in the modern era, Steven Gerrard's single-handed rescue act for Liverpool in 2006. But for many, quite simply, nobody has carried the day in such emphatic, dashing fashion as Milburn did on 28 April 1951.

But the Cup cavalier was only just warming up…

The successful 1952 campaign may have seen only three Milburn goals – but how priceless they were, coming in one of the finest Newcastle performances of the post-war years, a thrilling 4-2 quarter-final win away to a Portsmouth side which was then one of the giants of the English game. Indeed, reports of the time claim there was only one difference between two accomplished and even-matched sides that day at Fratton Park – Jackie Milburn. The player himself – whose stunning hat-trick was added to by a strike from partner Robledo – later described that game as "without a doubt, the best game I have ever played in" and few there to witness it disagreed. It was the display – and result – which gave the Magpies the confidence to go on and retain the Cup, with a semi-final win over Blackburn and a 1-0 win, courtesy of Robledo, against 10-man Arsenal in the final.

That Portsmouth clash was also the game in which Milburn scored a goal arguably even more spectacular than his 1951 cup final double – a strike which personified his unquenchable instinct to go for goal. Team-mate Bobby Mitchell certainly remembered it, not just as Milburn's finest – but the best goal he had ever witnessed. "We were two down when Milburn picked up a ball around the halfway line," said the Scot. "He started a run and just seemed to keep going and going. There was a man goalside of him and one immediately behind, so he was forced to move wider all the time. He seemed to be completely shut out when he produced an astonishing goal from nowhere; he was heavily marked, badly angled and still moving at full pace when he hit a ferocious shot past the goalkeeper's left side that went straight in. It was spectacular and certainly the greatest goal I have ever seen."

It was further example of Milburn's ability as a big-match player – and that knack of rising to the occasion would help bring an unlikely third FA Cup back to Tyneside three years later, as United completed a marvellous treble of Wembley triumphs. Whisper it quietly in these parts, but in truth the crowd favourite's contribution to the '55 campaign had been relatively small – except that is, for one stunning solitary strike in round five away to Nottingham Forest which kept the dream alive. United were two minutes away from going out of the competition when Milburn intervened with a final solo goal after a run from his own half, ensuring a 1-1 draw and the first of two replays before the Magpies finally flew on to the next stage. That rescue act apart, there were few fireworks from a striker struggling with a long-term stomach injury.

Still, even without the weight of history, it is difficult to see then-manager Duggie Livingstone's point when he tried to drop such a proven big-match performer from the '55 final line-up. Livingstone, who was relieved of managerial authority just weeks after that Wembley win, was famously overruled by the Newcastle directors, one of whom, Stan Seymour, declared: "Wembley without Milburn? Nonsense." Milburn had missed a three-yard sitter in the semi-final against York City, and it is true he had competition in the forward line from the likes of Vic Keeble – who had scored five FA Cup goals from the centre-forward's position – Len White, George Hannah and Reg Davies.

Indeed, Bobby Mitchell would later admit: "I felt sorry for Livingstone. In some ways his decision was the right one because

Milburn was not playing particularly well at the time, although I would have put him in the team because he had the ability to rise to the occasion and lift other players around him." Milburn also had 20 strikes to his name going into that Wembley final – second only to left-winger Mitchell's 22 and not a bad tally from a player below par because of injury.

Livingstone had wanted to start the Cup final with a five-man frontline of White, Davies, Keeble, Hannah and Mitchell – who had all excelled in a 5-0 demolition of Sheffield Wednesday four weeks before the big day. The manager, perhaps, had doubts that Milburn's lack of match fitness might count against the Magpies, and Mitchell recalled that the manager delivered his teamsheet with the words "this is the team, but I didn't want it!"

With Keeble's place nevertheless secure at centre-forward, it was up to Milburn to use his versatility and justify his inclusion from the inside-right position – he had been moved across the front line all season, playing in every forward role but outside-left. Perhaps because of the doubts over his selection – although he later claimed he did not discover the full extent of Livingstone's determination to drop him until afterwards – Milburn admitted to feeling more nervous before that '55 final than before any other match of his career.

It took 45 seconds for those nerves to settle and for Jackie Milburn to prove himself arguably the best big-match winner in Newcastle United history. In that time, Milburn put United on their way to victory by scoring the fastest goal in FA Cup history – a record which would stand for 42 years until it was bettered by Chelsea's Roberto Di Matteo against Middlesbrough.

As a header, that 1955 Cup final goal, setting up a convincing 3-1 win over Manchester City, was something of a collector's item, and in truth, Milburn benefited from his own weak reputation in the air. City captain Roy Paul admitted afterwards that he decided at the last moment to leave Milburn alone in the area and instead mark Keeble – a player with a prodigious heading ability. Fate, too, played a part, with White honestly confessing that his corner was actually meant for Keeble at the far post, but had fallen short at the near post where Milburn, a grateful and instinctive opportunist, did not need asking twice. For a player who supposedly could not head the ball, the goal was a masterpiece as Milburn, leaning backwards, directed it perfectly just inside the angle of post and crossbar to beat legendary keeper Bert Trautmann. That fine header belatedly completed a 'hat-trick' of sorts at Wembley – an honour denied Milburn when he had seen a perfectly good third goal ruled out for offside in 1951.

He would later claim the goal as proof that he WAS a decent header of the ball technically – but that years of suffering from chronic fibrositis in his neck had continually deterred him from too much jumping and stretching for the ball under physical challenge. Proof of sorts for that argument would come 12 years later when Milburn scored an almost identical header in his star-studded testimonial game. "Who but Jackie Milburn could race to crowd with arms outstretched in supplication that night as the crowd roared?" asked the *Journal*. "We all knew that despite the years between, he was telling everyone that his Cup final header was no accident."

Rewind back to May 1955 and Livingstone must not have known whether to laugh or cry at Milburn's goal – particularly when the player, looking less than 100 per cent match fit, made little more impact throughout the next 89 minutes. Still, Milburn had already done his part, with that fine early goal, added to the sheer inspiration of his presence (there is little doubt his team-mates wanted him alongside at Wembley) thoroughly justifying his place. Charlie Crowe had insisted that "it was unthinkable for Newcastle to play in an FA Cup final without Jackie Milburn" – while Crowe's own exclusion, through injury, sparked an incident which showed his team-mate's considerate nature, even if it was misguided. Milburn had told the left-half to keep quiet about his injury, insisting the rest of the lads would 'carry him' until his fellow Geordie properly reminded him the FA Cup was at stake!

Of course, crucial as Milburn's soft-hearted nature is to his legend in the North East, it must be pointed out that it only becomes relevant as the flip side of a sporting gladiator who rose to the occasion like no other. Unlike Malcolm Macdonald (two major cup finals, no goals, two defeats) and Alan Shearer (ditto) Milburn proved he could inspire team-mates and take his chance on the big occasion – and how often have United lacked that sort of character throughout decades of under-achievement.

Milburn's legacy as a player stands for more than mere goals, like Shearer and Stubbins, and more than crowd-thrilling entertainment, like Green, Shackleton and Gascoigne. In common with Hughie Gallacher before time and Edwardian title-winning greats such as Colin Veitch and Bill McCracken, Milburn helped put Newcastle

United on the map as a winning team. With Milburn spearheading the attack, United proved the undisputed masters of the most glamorous club cup in world football throughout the first half of the 1950s, and as such, his stature is deservedly massive at St James' Park. Surely nobody has done more in the modern era to establish Newcastle's reputation as a force in British football.

His thirst for success and his knack of producing the spectacular at the right moment have established him as a colossal figure in North East sporting history. "That was the thing about Milburn," said team-mate Mitchell, "you always expected something out of the ordinary from him."

WITH THOSE HEROIC Cup exploits in mind, Milburn's treatment at the hands of the club when he departed as player-coach to Linfield in June 1957 is all the more appalling – even if it remains consistent with the way in which Newcastle United have handled players before and since. The 33-year-old, no longer wanted in the first team, had been led to believe he would be given a free transfer by the club he had served for 14 years. However United had other ideas, and almost scuppered the deal at the last minute by demanding a hefty £10,000 fee plus a player in exchange. It was a massive amount to Linfield, and smacked of a mean-minded gesture to Milburn who later complained: "The day I learned of Newcastle's demands, I was taught a very valuable lesson and that was that football was not just simply the sport I loved playing, but also a big greedy business too."

Milburn went on to win the Irish League Player of the Year award in his first season, tasted European football for the first time and won the Northern Ireland League and Cup in Linfield colours before he hung up his boots. But his heart still lay in Newcastle and he admitted after leaving: "I don't think anyone will ever know how much sorrow I felt the day I actually walked from the players' entrance of St James' Park for the last time."

The feeling was mutual, as the player with arguably the strongest ever rapport with the Newcastle faithful called time on his black and white adventure. Poignantly, he signed for Linfield, on 13 June, just two days after the suicide of Hughie Gallacher; United fans had lost arguably their two biggest icons, one permanently, within the space of two days.

Milburn, thankfully, stayed in touch. Throughout his Northern Irish adventure he remained a keen supporter, flying back at his own expense to watch Newcastle games as and when he could – including one trip to an away game in Manchester when the only available flight was a cargo plane full of live pigs! Now that's commitment! After hanging up his boots, and after that unsuccessful managerial spell at Ipswich, Milburn tried various jobs including driving a crane in a scrapyard, and running a coach tour business, before spending 23 years as a sports journalist on Tyneside, much of them covering the North East beat for the *News of the World*. He managed to combine his work with an unofficial role as advisor or Godfather to a succession of Newcastle managers, with his closest involvement coming during the years of close friend Joe Harvey's stewardship. Yet the hoped-for job offer from United did not come until the end of the 1970s, when Bill McGarry asked Milburn to join his staff – and the pressures of the full-time game by that time no longer appealed to 'Wor Jackie' in his late 50s.

His career in journalism brought many new friends – including long-term *Evening Chronicle* sportswriter John Gibson, who remembered, on the occasion of Milburn's death, a characteristic act of kindness from a strangely familiar face as he encountered the brutal world of the football Press room for the first time as a club reporter. Gibson remembers that only man approached him that day to ease his nerves. "'Is this your first game son?' he said, extending his hand. That fleeting introductory moment perfectly encapsulates the way Jackie Milburn lived his life. The fame and adulation never went to his head. He was genuinely embarrassed at the acclaim his success had brought. He was far and away the most modest sporting superstar I have ever encountered."

Similar stories of Milburn's natural bonhomie abound in his native North East, where he is still remembered with reverence.

HISTORY TEACHES US that we should never say never. Yet it will take a special kind of someone to outshine this man, 'Wor Jackie', the man who scored six goals in his Newcastle trial game, on a pre-match diet of two meat pies and a couple of smokes! His Roy–of-the-Rovers ascent to the pinnacle of club football glory will forever remain a captivating tale in the history of this celebrated club, and one which leaves almost all the other heroes of the Newcastle United pantheon in the shade.

The nearness of time allows us to celebrate the drama of Milburn's 1950s Cup final derring-do perhaps more than the greater team achievements of the all-conquering Edwardian Newcastle United side. It should never be forgotten, after all, that the likes of Colin Veitch and Bill McCracken can boast three league titles each and an FA Cup in United colours (as well as four and two more losing Cup finals, respectively). But for sheer drama, the way Milburn grasped the nettle at the big moment, and his glorious personal influence on three FA Cup wins, he would arguably remain the bigger hero for his on-pitch heroics alone – even if he had not been blessed with such a wonderfully warm personality.

So, pick your own personal favourite hero from the annals, by all means – or the one you feel most deserving of praise – and his initials may well not be J.E.T, but in terms of adulation, thousands of other people have already voted, and have been doing so for decades.

Quite simply, Milburn is the biggest hero, cult or otherwise, in club history.

Kevin Keegan – himself a huge icon in these parts – knew it, claiming: "If I was compiling a list of all-time greats, his name would be at the top." As a dashing footballer and a true gentleman who epitomised the Geordie spirit and brought the genuine pride of a true winner to a region which has too often lacked it, Jackie Milburn is No. 1.

Joe Harvey

1945-1952: 281 games, 13 goals

AMID ALL THE stellar and mercurial talents to have thrilled the crowd in Newcastle United's history, a relative artisan shines through. Joseph Harvey's contribution to the Magpies cause across nearly half a century is almost impossible to measure.

True, he is one of only three uncapped players to make the 20 cult heroes in this book – admittedly he is without the God-given craft of the other luckless contenders, Len White and Albert Stubbins. But Harvey does not make the cut as a terrace legend because of his ball skills – although a useful and respected performer, and selected three times for the Football League XI, he realistically stands at the back of this queue of 20 when it comes to ability. And while he is one of two figures in the list to be included for their contributions as player and manager – Kevin Keegan being the other – Harvey cannot match his successor for individual glory on the pitch.

Yet Harvey, in 10 years as player, 13 as manager and 14 more in various roles such as chief scout or assistant manager, provided inspiration, perspiration, determination, a devoted commitment to entertaining the crowd, and a human touch which made him one of the most loved figures ever to grace St James' Park.

Younger fans wondering why the club named its restaurant after Harvey, who died of a heart attack at home while in conversation with his former team-mate Bobby Cowell back in February 1989, should consider the following:

– Harvey, as skipper, led Newcastle to promotion to the First Division in 1948
– He lifted the 1951 and 1952 FA Cups as captain
– He was coach to the 1955 FA Cup-winning side
– Then he returned and won the Second Division title as manager in 1965
– And masterminded the club's only European trophy success, the 1969 Fairs Cup
– In fact he was intrinsically involved in every major trophy won by the club since 1932

For good measure Harvey also collected two Texaco Cups, an Anglo-Italian trophy, and took his team to Wembley for the 1974 FA Cup final as manager. Never relegated with United as a player or manager, perhaps Harvey's most enduring legacy is a dedication to attacking football which helped to establish a now deeply-held club tradition, and has, more often than not, kept generations of Geordies entertained on their weekly pilgrimage to St James' Park.

Underlying all of those achievements – and helping Harvey prevail during some high-profile failures too – was a strength of character arguably unmatched in the annals of club history.

DESCRIBED BY CLUB historian Paul Joannou as "lean and strong, a tough, uncompromising wing-half who performed best when the contest was at its most fierce," Harvey made an instant impression when he signed for then-manager Stan Seymour just after the Second World War. Putting his background as a sergeant-major in the Royal Artillery to good effect, he was installed as team captain in only his second game, and, as an archetypal tough-guy skipper was loved by supporters for his hard tackling and constant bellowing on the pitch. Newcastle United – for the next decade – could never be accused of lacking leadership. Harvey, despite playing alongside some of the most celebrated players in the British game such as Jackie Milburn, Len Shackleton, Tommy Pearson, Charlie Wayman, Bobby Mitchell and Frank Brennan – always had the self-belief to take charge, with a no-nonsense approach which endeared him to working-class Tynesiders.

Harvey certainly made a lasting first impression on Jackie Milburn, as the latter recalled the response he got when he made a wayward pass to the Yorkshireman in his *Newcastle United Scrapbook*: "Now I was working at the pits and I thought no-one could teach a miner how to swear," said Milburn. "But never in my life have I heard such a torrent of abuse. All the lads heard it too, and got the message. Army man Joe was in charge."

Harvey had his work cut out keeping an even more glittering talent in check in Mr Len Shackleton – a pied piper of a player who liked to dance to his own tune, on and off the pitch. "Some of the Shack skills were unbelievable," Harvey later recalled. "It was nothing for him to give you a short ball inside your own box. I usually gave it back to him as if it was red hot – with a right rollicking when it was eventually cleared."

Harvey's natural toughness would stand him in good stead throughout the dying embers of his managerial career on Tyneside – he stood unflinching in the face of criticism from his once adoring public, prompting the *Journal* in January 1975 to hail "a man – not an imitation". It was the self-same belief in his own ability which had helped Harvey garner his troops into battle in his playing days. Milburn remembered that "it never mattered to Joe how much of a rollicking he got from the crowd; he made his own decisions and he knew that his players were always 100 per cent behind him – and that's not usual, I can tell you."

Not that Harvey received a rollicking from the crowd that regularly. Although overshadowed as a player by the forwards throughout his playing days on Tyneside, he was nevertheless an accomplished and reliable wing-half, and many critics of the time reflected that he would surely have won an England cap, but for Billy Wright's pre-eminence in that position.

The *Journal* sportswriter Ken McKenzie reflected that "Harvey was a great club half-back when too many people were critical of his construction," while the *Evening Chronicle* opined in 1951: "Why Joe has not been capped for his country is a football mystery. Maybe it is not too late, for Harvey is still numbered among the best right half-backs in the game."

Yet despite his undoubted playing talents, it is unquestionably leadership which lies at the core of the Harvey legend. Having led the Magpies back into the First Division within three years of signing for the club, Harvey would go on, as a captain respected by arguably the best United side of the modern era, to marshal his talented troops to victory in the 1951 FA Cup final. His playing style, his belligerence on the pitch and his infectious determination added the steel to a side glittering with talent in the shape of Jack Fairbrother, Jackie Milburn, Charlie Crowe, Ernie Taylor, Bobby Mitchell and George Robledo. It took more than shouting to motivate that little lot, and Harvey's positive influence in geeing up team-mates when they needed it was vital to team spirit.

Ernie Taylor once recalled a rare off-day when, for a lengthy spell, most of his passes went astray. Captain Harvey muttered not a word in reproach until finally a Taylor ball fell inch-perfect at a team-mate's feet. "You know, Ernie," shouted out Harvey in praise, "there's no one can pass a ball quite like you." Touches like that from Harvey helped foster a sense of togetherness which made Newcastle – when they wanted to be – a formidable prospect for the opposition, particularly in 1951. "We were resolved to a man that Blackpool would not beat us," said Harvey after the final. "As captain of the side I knew what this spirit really meant and that Blackpool would have to be a super-team to deprive us of the honour of winning the Cup."

But aside from his man-management skills, Harvey's talent as a tactician would also prove invaluable that day at Wembley. With the scores goalless at half-time, the skipper agreed a plan with his side to play long, early balls to the forwards to combat Blackpool's well-drilled off-side trap, and the tactic worked a treat, playing to the strengths of the jet-propelled Milburn, who broke clear of his marker in the 50th minute to put Newcastle on course for victory.

"Offside tactics were Blackpool's undoing," read the following morning's *Sunday Sun*, while the *Evening Chronicle* was left to reflect that "Harvey is no stylist, but he has a dominating personality that pays a big dividend. And he is a first-rate tactician. Listen at any match and you will hear the voice of Captain Joe Harvey shouting encouragement and, when need be, correcting faults in play."

But Harvey and Newcastle were not finished yet. After a stunning second goal from Milburn had secured the trophy in that 2-0 final win over Blackpool, left-back Bobby Corbett told his skipper he had taken a piece of the Wembley turf as a memento. "You might as well put it back," said Harvey. "I'm coming back next year."

HARVEY AND CO made good on his defiant prediction – and the skipper's motivational skills came to the fore once more during a bizarre FA Cup final win over Arsenal, a game ruined as a spectacle when, in the days before substitutes, the Gunners had to play the final hour of the match with 10 men following full-back Wally Barnes' withdrawal through injury. With 10-man Arsenal putting Newcastle under pressure, a half-time rollicking from Harvey did the trick, with a less nervous United bouncing back in the second half to score the only goal of the game.

Harvey would claim in his testimonial brochure many years later that he had to bully his team-mates into action that day, claiming many of them were too busy feeling sorry for the under-strength Gunners. "My team was full of pity," he said. "I had the hardest job I ever had as skipper. I cursed, I swore, I cajoled, I pleaded. 'You're a set of babies,' I told them at half-time. 'You're feeling sorry for Mercer's lot. You'll feel even sorrier for yourselves if I don't get that cup.'"

Newcastle's superstars got the message, and Harvey's timely intervention galvanised the troops just when they needed it.

SEVEN YEARS BEFORE he would get the official manager's job at St James' Park, Harvey was already effectively in charge on matchdays, with his great friend, manager Stan Seymour, concentrating on team selection, signings and administrative duties. Bob Stokoe, another close pal of Harvey's, who played at Newcastle for 14 years from 1947, was quick to acknowledge the influence of his former skipper. Speaking on the occasion of Harvey's death in 1989, he said: "In those days there was no manager at St James' Park. The skipper Joe Harvey was the man everyone looked to for guidance. He stood out head and shoulders above everyone else. Joe had exceptional leadership qualities. All the young players looked up to Joe. He was our inspiration. He was a bad loser and I think some of that rubbed off on me. Joe would call you everything under the sun to try and get the best out of you."

Harvey officially took over as player-coach – and in the players' eyes, effective team manager – in January 1954, with Seymour, now a club director, insisting: "Harvey is the man who will do all the talking and that includes tactical discussions with the players."

Having helped manager Duggie Livingstone – appointed in December 1954 – and the team to a third FA Cup final win of the decade in 1955 in his role as coach, Harvey took a temporary break from United, managing Barrow and Workington before his return in 1962. But such had been his influence throughout his first 10 years on Tyneside, that the appointment to a club now languishing back in the Second Division was universally welcomed. This was, after all, a player for whom motivation and tactics were always at the core of his game.

Harvey had, after captaining Newcastle to their second FA Cup win in 1952, written a press article detailing some of the tricks of his approach at the club – revealing the serious, win-at-all costs attitude which had long endeared him to the St James' Park crowds. "The will-to-win through must be shown by every member of the team, both on and off the field. On the field there is a motto which must be taken to heart…'no mercy!' Hit them once. And instead of running round the field shaking hands and doing fancy dances of rejoicing, roll the sleeves a little higher and set about the business of hitting them again. Play to the whistle. Concerning at least three of our very important goals there was what the critics called a shadow of doubt… it isn't the time to hesitate. Play on. So long as the whistle hasn't sounded, keep on and bang the ball into the net."

Put that attitude together with Harvey's considerable playing achievements, and it is little wonder that fans, the press and former Newcastle greats queued up to salute his return as team boss.

Frank Brennan declared at the time: "I am very pleased indeed. Knowing Joe of old, I know he will put up a great fight in his new role, and I wish him every success", while Bobby Mitchell added: "Joe is a great guy and given time he must get results – as good as he gained on the field, I hope". The *Evening Chronicle* hailed the appointment as "immensely popular", adding: "He captained Newcastle in their Cup wins of 1951 and 1952 and most people agree he was the inspiration behind both victories".

Supporter Joan Jackson summed up the jubilant attitude on the terraces when her letter to the local newspaper proclaimed: "Newcastle has never been the same since Milburn and Harvey went. The side have been a dead loss for ages and he is just the man to put them back on the promotion trail." And so it proved, with Harvey proving successful in the transfer market to sign Stan Anderson and Jim Iley to strengthen the defence, and Ron McGarry and Dave Hilley up front. That line-up, with John McGrath massively influential too at centre-half, would bring the Second Division title to Tyneside three years after Harvey's appointment – and they would not lose their top-flight status throughout the Yorkshireman's 13-year managerial reign.

Although a much bigger prize would come Harvey's way just four years later, he would cherish that Second Division title as his favourite memory at Newcastle, insisting: "Getting out of the Second Division was crucial because down there you're non-entities. Everything we did stemmed from that Championship. We were a shambles when I took over, but I built something out of nothing and up we went."

Harvey would also wax lyrical over the Anglo-Italian Cup win of 1973, "because we beat a great side, Fiorentina, in their own backyard playing them to death in the process". But for the vast majority of Newcastle fans, an ultimately turbulent reign – yet still the longest ever by a United manager – reached its zenith in the 1969 Fairs Cup win, a competition which, through the one-club, one-city rule, the Magpies had qualified for despite finishing in 10th place in the First Division the season before.

With the mighty Wyn Davies as attacking spearhead, and Bobby Moncur – one of the most accomplished defenders in United's history – marshalling the team from the back as skipper, United shocked some of the biggest names in European football as 33-1 outsiders to lift the trophy. Feyenoord, Sporting Lisbon, Real Zaragoza, Vitoria Setubal and Rangers were all dismissed, before a 3-0 home leg win over much-fancied Hungarians Ujpesti Dozsa in the final seemed to give Harvey one hand on the cup.

But, on an eventful night in Budapest when the Yorkshireman had motivated his troops by putting crates of champagne in the dressing room in readiness before kick-off, Harvey would have to rely on all his inspirational skills in a half-time team-talk which swung the tie back towards the black and whites. Newcastle, as manager and players honestly admitted afterwards, seemed to be staring overall defeat in the face when 2-0 down at the break, having been given the runaround by the Hungarians' swift passing game.

But Harvey was not about to let his team give up. He later recalled his words to the deflated players…

"You're winning, bloody winning, I tell you. Score just one goal and they'll fold. The continentals can't take it. Score one bloody goal, that's all."

Centre-forward Wyn Davies admitted that Harvey's speech had been just what he and his team-mates needed. "He told us to stop feeling sorry for ourselves and remember we weren't 2-0 down, but 3-2 ahead," he said. "Joe raised our spirits, and sure enough we went out and scored three in the second half to sail home." Harvey had risen to the occasion yet again, with his team's victory sparking scenes of jubilation on Tyneside, where more than 500,000 people thronged the streets to welcome United home with the trophy.

The manager's seemingly indefatigable motivational strengths were perhaps all the more surprising, given that, in private, Harvey could be an anxious individual. Even at the moment of his rousing rallying call in Budapest, he was not as confident as he seemed. He later remembered that he "went back to chain-smoking on the touchline – hoping and praying for a miracle". Particularly as a manager, Harvey would endure sleepless nights before even routine league matches, and once admitted: "The hour I really hate is that one before the kick-off, when the lads are all changing, getting ready for the game… and at the end of it, I'll just be sitting there helpless when the whistle goes."

That anxiety was symptomatic of a lifelong devotion to Newcastle United which matched that of even the most hardened supporters. Harvey insisted after retiring as Magpies boss in 1975 that he would never work for another club – and remained true to his word, staying on the St James' Park payroll until his death in 1989 as variously, part-time scout, chief scout and assistant manager to Jack Charlton and Willie McFaul.

Even in his final year as Newcastle boss, Harvey had insisted: "I never switch off from football, never. It's always with me. When I'm playing golf, walking down a fairway, I'm thinking about the problems of one lad or another, the team selection and so on. I just can't get way from it." Perhaps it was the anxious fear of defeat that made Harvey so resolute in his thirst for success. Yet, stern-faced bad loser that he was, the Yorkshireman was also a real character with a sense of humour and always ready to talk up team-mates when they needed it. Newcastle players would fondly recall his peculiar battle-cries as skipper, when he would urge them before kick-off: "Let's go and get the groceries" or "Right mates, baby needs new shoes, let's get in there and get the two quid". If that didn't work, Harvey would, after a defeat, walk to his West Denton home from St James' Park as self-inflicted punishment.

Always searching for innovative ways to bring success on the pitch, Harvey even resorted to tampering with the match ball in his player-manager days at Barrow. "They weren't skilful lads, but they were strong, so I didn't want a lively ball," he explained. "So I put two bladders inside one football case. Blown up with a bit of water on, it was like a cannonball. And while our lads were used to it, there were a few surprised players who came to Barrow and tried to head it!"

Harvey's unconventional approach to the game gave him an anxious moment before his first Football League appearance – his fondness for a Guinness bringing fears that his representative career would be over before it had even begun! "When the waiter came in with the tray my dark glass stood out," said Harvey, remembering the team meal at which all but one player had ordered orange juice. "But all the time I played I used to have a Guinness on a Friday night. I've never been averse to a player having a bottle of beer or a smoke. Jackie Milburn used to smoke half a tab in the bog before a game. If the opposition thought it would help them catch him they'd have smoked a full packet each!"

Harvey's approach was always to give his players a bit of leeway – and although never a soft touch, his human approach to management made him a smash hit with some of the biggest stars of their day. It was, perhaps, the key to a 13-year managerial reign unmatched in its duration at St James' Park. Harvey's ability to soothe the domestic unrest which has traditionally surfaced at Newcastle United won him friends among supporters and players alike – even if, the Fairs Cup apart, his teams never quite achieved what they promised.

Bobby Mitchell remembers, "He was the boss on the field and off it as far as the players were concerned. He was a shocking loser and never flinched from letting us know. But at the same time, if we had any grouses, we just had to see Joe and he would sort them out."

And as a manager, Harvey's nature made him a dream to play for, according to Malcom Macdonald. "He was undoubtedly the best manager I ever played under. Joe was a gem – a man's man. He knew how to treat players and get the best out of them." Put that together with an impressive tactical awareness, religious commitment to the cause and an eye for a good player and perhaps it is not that surprising that skipper Jim Iley – who played under 12 different managers – rated Harvey the best of the lot, even ahead of Bill Nicholson, who famously managed Tottenham to the double in 1961.

The way Harvey looked after his players meant they were all ears when it came to his famous motivational speeches. As full-back David Craig recalls: "Quite simply, we would have run through a brick wall for him." Harvey's unflinching public support for Albert Bennett when the striker's move to Charlton broke down on medical grounds was typical of the manager's style, and left the *Journal* declaring: "Harvey's gesture must surely rate as the most human act seen in North East football, a notoriously unsentimental world, for a good many years.

"A manager who will stick his neck out, as Harvey has done, deserves 100 per cent effort, and more, from his men."

But do not let these testimonies paint a picture of a caring, sharing manager who went easy on his players – Harvey could be ruthless when he needed to be, sharing the supporters' obsessive devotion to putting Newcastle United first. This his former team-mate Alf McMichael found to his cost – the highest-profile casualty of Harvey's return as manager in 1962, when the Northern Ireland full-back's quest for a club appearance record did not save him from the axe. "I only needed to play a few more games… but I never fulfilled my ambition," said McMichael. "I was upset about it at the time. But when I look back now, I realise Joe was doing the right thing for the club. He was never one to beat about the bush. He was a typical Yorkshireman, and if there was anything that wanted saying, he'd say it."

You'd be tempted to raise the question, had Harvey been in charge in the summer of 2005, would he have curtailed Alan Shearer's career before the defining moment of breaking Milburn's goalscoring record?

Kind, but tough, ruthless, determined, loyal to the cause and, of course, successful to a degree – they were all qualities which helped turn born-leader Harvey into one of the most popular managerial figures ever seen on Tyneside. Longevity too, must come into the equation, since only Stan Seymour, as player, unofficial team manager, director and chairman, can boast a longer association than Harvey's 37 years of service to United. But there is, perhaps, one aspect of Harvey the manager which stands out as his lasting legacy – perhaps the X-factor which elevated him from the respect usually afforded managers, to the love normally reserved for star players, was his love of the entertainer. Harvey's devotion to exciting football came as a welcome surprise for those older Newcastle fans who had watched him, as a hard-working and fierce team skipper, battle to get the fancy dans around him to play to a team ethic. But, in a succession of glamorous signings and with his attacking philosophy, Harvey ensured that the Tyneside public were, if still generally unaccustomed to success, at least royally entertained on a Saturday afternoon.

OF COURSE, NEWCASTLE had a tradition for attacking football even before Joe Harvey signed for the club – but history suggests he has done as much as anyone to uphold a proud tradition on Tyneside. Indeed, looking back at some of his public declarations on tactics, it is like listening to Kevin Keegan some 30 years later. Just after winning the Second Division title in 1965, he explained: "I used to say to the lads: 'Don't worry about winning the ball. The other teams are so bad they'll give it to you. The important thing is to be able to play when you get it.' I'd players who could do that."

And he was about to get more.

Harvey signed three of the cult heroes elsewhere in this book: epic crowd-pleasers in Malcolm Macdonald, Wyn Davies and Tony Green. His other signings included the mercurial 'Jinky' Jim Smith, Terry Hibbitt and Terry McDermott – while he showed he had an eye for good defenders by picking up Bobby Moncur and David Craig, two of the very best in the modern era at Newcastle. In his role as chief scout after retiring as manager in 1975, Harvey also strongly urged Gordon Lee to sign a young Partick Thistle defender called Alan Hansen, a year before he joined Liverpool. Lee, however, lost confidence in the deal and that episode, he later declared, reminded him of the importance of acting on impulse as a manager. "The secret is to make up your mind quickly and act on it before someone else does. That's how I pinched Terry McDermott from under the noses of Liverpool when he was at Bury."

But, although he had an eye for a defender too, entertainment was never far from Harvey's mind – hence the quickening of the pulse when he watched a young Chris Waddle play for Tow Law in 1979, a player he successfully recommended to then manager Arthur Cox – whom he'd also help appoint! "It's all about entertainment and I always bore that in mind when I bought a player for Newcastle," he said. "I thought 'Will the crowd like him?' and more important, 'will they put down good money to watch him?' I hate sides full of robots and managers who say they don't like stars. Hell, stars are worth their weight in gold. A team of nonentities never won an egg cup never mind anything else."

Harvey's understanding of what makes Newcastle fans tick – of what made them worship all the heroes who went before him – men like Gallacher, Stubbins, Milburn and White – helped the blunt Yorkshireman himself break into that legendary inner circle. He once explained: "Whether a bloke works down the pit, in a shipyard, or in an office all week, he needs to watch players on a Saturday who can give him something to talk about the following week, players who can excite."

But despite his empathy with United supporters, there is no doubt that Harvey's popularity was at an all-time low as Newcastle boss by the time he retired to concentrate on scouting duties in 1975. Three years earlier, he had survived one of the worst results in club history – the infamous 2-1 FA Cup replay defeat at Hereford in 1972. But his side's pathetic display in the 1974 Cup defeat to Liverpool arguably hurt his managerial reputation more – and he would later name that as his biggest disappointment in the game, insisting he was baffled by United's meek capitulation.

Unlike almost all of the cult heroes in this book, he had to weather a storm of criticism and abuse from Newcastle fans, coming in the final months of his managerial career. The unrest was worsened by another FA Cup defeat, this time to Walsall in a mudbath in January 1975, after which the Newcastle board suggested he bring in a No. 2. By that stage, a small band of supporters had organised a campaign against their manager, and had won press coverage for their printing of 250 free "Harvey Out" stickers, which they gave out to fellow disgruntled fans. "Newcastle have the strongest playing squad in the country, but they don't get results," bemoaned campaign organiser Ian Watson.

For his part, Harvey insisted at the time that injuries that season – he lost midfielders Tommy Cassidy, Jim Smith and Terry Hibbitt within three weeks of each other and at one stage had all five full-backs on the treatment table – had robbed him of the chance to fulfil his promise, made at Wembley in '74, to make up for that embarrassment. "The injuries have broken my heart," he said. "I thought we were going to repay the fans this season and it hasn't happened and I'm sorry."

It was not the first time that injuries had broken Harvey's heart – the manager was reduced to tears at the early demise of the club's most influential player, Tony Green, in 1973. But injuries apart, Harvey's reign had doubtless run its course two years after Green's devastating diagnosis – and the team he had hoped to build around the Scottish genius never quite materialised.

OVERALL, HIS RECORD as a team boss will never match the title-winning achievements of 'secretary' Frank Watt in the early part of the last century. But for his passion, commitment, 'roll-your-sleeves-up-and-get-at-em' leadership on the pitch, and the exciting brand of football his sides produced as manager, his claims as a bona fide cult hero are undeniable.

Indeed, taking into account his ability as a player, his influence as captain and his contribution as manager – involved, remember, in all four of Newcastle's post-war major honours and playing a leading role in three – Harvey lays a strong claim to the unofficial title of United's most important ever signing. Never has £4,250 been better spent by the Magpies.

His death in February 1989 came just four months after that of Jackie Milburn – and the sudden loss of the two biggest icons from the 50s Cup-winning years, the most glamorous era in club history – hit Tyneside doubly hard. The tributes poured in, with team-mate and long-term friend to the end Bobby Cowell simply declaring that "Joe was a great player and a great man". Club chairman Gordon McKeag, meanwhile, insisted that Harvey's soubriquet of 'Mr Newcastle' was well deserved. "Joe Harvey epitomised all Newcastle United stood for," he added.

But the final word should go to his favourite signing, Malcolm Macdonald, a player whose relationship with Harvey was at the core of the Yorkshireman's credentials as a Newcastle United hero. While many managers would have blanched at the cocksure antics which helped turn Macdonald into a legend in his own right on Tyneside,

Harvey proudly admitted that he actively encouraged them – to give the fans some much-needed entertainment. "I used to tell him every Friday to go out and announce to the Press how many goals he'd score the following day," said Harvey. "He did, too, and the punters rolled up. They loved him."

Harvey's pay-off for 37 years of devotion to the club came at a lavish celebration dinner in his honour organised by the Newcastle United Supporters Association in 1981, and attended by a who's who of the Magpies, past and present. Jackie Milburn, Charlie Crowe, Bobby Cowell, Bob Stokoe, Albert Stubbins, Bobby Corbett, Frank Brennan, Stan Anderson, Jim Iley, Frank Clark, Malcolm Macdonald, Ron McGarry, Dave Hilley, John Tudor, David Craig and Tommy Craig were among the stars in attendance. Harvey said afterwards: "It's been a night I'll never forget. To see all the old faces again was marvellous. Moments like this make everything worthwhile."

Just as at Harvey's funeral eight years later, the tributes poured in thick and fast for a man who could make a mighty claim to captain or manage an all-time Newcastle XI. But perhaps no homage that evening better captured the essence of 'Mr Newcastle' than these words from the man he described as his No. 1 signing. "Joe brought excitement and charisma to Newcastle," said Macdonald. "He gave the public what they wanted, and football can never close its doors to a man like that."

Frank Brennan

1946-1956: 349 games, 3 goals

BIG FRANK IS widely regarded as the finest defender in Newcastle United's history. He also happens to have been a renaissance man-of-the-people who demanded respect on and off the pitch. In a region obsessed with strikers, and at a club steeped in attacking tradition, it takes a special defender to become a cult hero. Brennan was such a player.

For nearly a decade, the gigantic Scot with his size 11 boots was the rock upon which countless waves of opposition attacks foundered. His career coincided with a golden age for British centre-forwards – yet some of the biggest ever names in the game found themselves snuffed out by Brennan; legends in their own right like Stan Mortensen, Tommy Lawton and Trevor Ford.

Brennan's contribution to two of the most famous achievements in United's history – the 1951 and 1952 FA Cup-winning teams – was mighty. He was also pivotal in the 1947/48 promotion team – a side which, surprisingly, he rated as better than either of the victorious Wembley line-ups. But the bare facts of Brennan's honours list do not come close to capturing the man's legend on Tyneside. Brennan enjoyed a superb relationship with his adoring Geordie public during nearly 10 years of sterling service, and so many of the qualities of the player were qualities all his supporters aspired to.

Brennan was a born leader; he was strong, inspirational, in control, composed, even-tempered – but aggressive as a bull when he needed to be.

He was, at least off the field, a perfect gentleman. He was also firmly devoted to his beloved black and whites, a Lanarkshire lad who, like many Scots before him, found the North East region and its people easy to fall for.

And they fell for him. But his love affair with the Newcastle United hierarchy ended acrimoniously in the mid-1950s in one of the most controversial episodes in club history. It was a row which would rob Brennan of the chance to pick up a third FA Cup winner's medal in 1955. And the fall-out was so severe that one of the true Newcastle greats was forced to play his testimonial at Roker Park, the home of bitter rivals Sunderland, when United refused him permission to use the St James' Park pitch.

The fans sided almost to a man with Brennan throughout a power struggle which effectively ended his league career – but he had long since become a living legend on Tyneside and, looking back, it is not difficult to see why. The Press Association library notes on Brennan, registered just 12 months into his Newcastle career, capture the very essence of a remarkable man:

> "BRENNAN, Frank: Newcastle United and Scotland centre-half. Native of Annathill mining village, Lanarkshire; age 23. From junior club, Coatbridge St. Patrick's, he joined Airdireonians aged 15, standing 5ft 11in in size 11 boots. Newcastle paid Airdrie £8000 for 6ft 3in 14 and a half stone solid giant, May 20 1946. A born captain, he skippered Newcastle, February 1947. Has represented Scotland v England, Ireland, Wales. Takes minimum hour's sleep before every game, has big match temperament; worth goal start to any side any time. Works at Hartley Mains Colliery, Northumberland, as electrician. Excels at Badminton; golf; sprints to win. Trained tenor, sings with sister Agnes at piano; enjoys amateur theatricals."

And in his spare time, he also played a bit of football .

BRENNAN HAD A lion's heart in his 6ft 3in frame, and he arrived at St James' Park with a burgeoning reputation as one of the hardest defenders in the game. He had been turned down by Albion Rovers as a 14-year-old, and told to come back in three years' time. He was back, 12 months later, as a member of Airdrie's first team. Seven years on, at the age of just 22, Brennan earned rave reviews by snuffing out the great Tommy Lawton in his debut for Scotland – the unofficial 'Victory International' at Hampden Park on 13 April 1946. Lawton's scoring record for his country, including wartime and Victory Internationals, stands at 46 goals in 45 games – but he drew a rare blank at Hampden, where Brennan's performance was instrumental in a shock 1-0 win for the home side. Newcastle United, among many clubs, had taken notice, and weeks later Brennan was a Magpie, following the route of another black and white great in Hughie Gallacher, by swapping Airdrie for the Magpies "It was right out of the blue," Brennan later recalled. "I was happy at Airdrie at the time, but there were a few clubs in for me and Mr Seymour suddenly turned up… It was a decision I never regretted. My years at Newcastle gave me memories which will never be forgotten."

At 14st in his stocking feet and with an appetite to match, the young Brennan made quite an impression on his team-mates. His captain Joe Harvey later recalled: "Many's the time on the morning of matches I have seen him demolish grapefruit, cornflakes, three or four eggs, bacon, sausage, tomatoes, fried bread, toast and marmalade – and then polish off the mixed grills other players left."

He was soon devouring centre-forwards for breakfast, as well, as Newcastle resumed their Football League career after a six-year break during World War Two.

Seven games into the 1946/47 season (three wins, three draws and one defeat), the young Scot had well and truly settled in to his centre-half's berth – and he stole the show with a commanding display in a 1-1 draw in front of 34,192 at Barnsley. The *Sunday Sun* newspaper headline the next day read 'Brennan Brilliance', as Newcastle United correspondent Ken McKenzie purred:

> "The second half display of Brennan against storming Barnsley attacks – to an increasing extent carried out through the centre as they became more and more anxious for a winner – brought down the house. He never made an error with foot or head, and several times made vital recoveries."

A star had been born that day on 28 September 1946, but Brennan's sparkling display was about to be overshadowed in remarkable fashion when debutant Len Shackleton scored six in the very next game, the famous 13-0 home win over Newport County. Under manager and former player Stan Seymour, the club was looking up, but would miss out on promotion in Brennan's first season – a mistake he and his team-mates put right the following season, securing second spot and a return to the top flight. And 'Shack' the showman would later pay due recognition to the role played by Brennan – a very different type of footballer – in Newcastle's success.

A direct, combative stopper-style centre-half, Brennan was not the sort to take risks at the back – and his concentrated devotion to defensive duties gave the team a solid platform, giving free rein to the likes of Shackleton – who rated his team-mate the best defender of his era – and a young winger called Jackie Milburn. "Brennan takes the field for every match with one idea on his mind," Shackleton later recalled, "the subjugation of all attacking moves down the centre of the field – and what a magnificent job he makes of it."

A man utterly devoted to the art of defending was also well equipped to handle the sort of physical exchanges which would see striker and marker red-carded in the modern game. Milburn later told a tale about his team-mate playing cricket and, while running between the wickets and seeing a thrown return come his way, laughingly heading the cricket ball away. "That's the sort of teak-hard fella he was," added Milburn, "a man who, unlike a lot of centre-halves, never squealed for cover. He'd tell his full-backs: 'Piss off out of the way and let me get on with the job'."

In the days before substitutes, Brennan would frequently play on with injuries, whilst sporting bandages, while his collision with an iron drainage pipe in the 1951 FA Cup semi-final replay has passed into club folklore. Health and Safety officers would have had a field day at Huddersfield on 14 March 1951 as piping used to drain the waterlogged pitch lay scattered around the touchline. Sure enough, an accident happened, and Brennan was the unlucky player as he came down to earth after heading a corner clear. The crack rebounded around the stadium, and things did not look good for Brennan or United, who were 1-0 down and being subjected to rampant Wolves attacks. Yet a clearly concussed Brennan, white as a sheet, shocked the crowd by determining to play on after lengthy treatment – but under strict instructions not to head the ball again. Immediately, he broke his promise, jumping to launch one of his typically massive headed clearances towards the halfway line, before flashing a winning grin at his astonished team-mates. 'Bren Gun', just one of his myriad of warrior-like nicknames, was back and a rejuvenated Newcastle launched their comeback, equalising through Jackie Milburn before Bobby Mitchell scored the winner which booked their place against Blackpool in the Wembley final.

Brennan's Lazarus impersonation in the semi-final proved conclusively that he was the man for the big occasion, and his personal contribution to the three successful sides of his era – the promotion team of 1948, and the Cup-winning teams of 1951 and '52, was massive. The *Sunday Sun* described the value of his performance in the 1-1 draw at Tottenham on 24 April 1948 – the point which clinched promotion:

> "A very valuable effort this from Brennan, for in the last quarter of an hour when United organised a purely defensive concentration bar Milburn, Spurs took a tremendous amount of keeping out."

Brennan played more games (43) than any of his more experienced team-mates in that promotion side. But three years later, his steely eyes were on a greater prize as he masterminded the defence against Cup favourites Blackpool to help bring United their first trophy for 19 years. Brennan and his defensive colleagues, Bobby Corbett and Bobby Cowell, weathered the Blackpool storm in the first half, allowing Milburn and George Robledo to steal the limelight with the second-half strikes which won the Cup for United. United's centre-half had been up against the great Stan Mortensen throughout – and his superb man-marking job had not gone unnoticed. The *Sunday Sun*'s correspondent, Ken McKenzie, picked Brennan along with Milburn and Cowell as the three biggest factors in Newcastle's win. Under the heading 'Brennan Master', he wrote: "Stan Mortensen, from South Shields, dynamic against United in the League recently, opened well, but was negatived (sic) by Frank Brennan after 20 minutes of resounding conflict with Blackpool calling the tune."

Two years later, Mortensen would run amok in the FA Cup final at Wembley, scoring three in a 4-3 win over Bolton who, sadly for them, had no one quite like Frank Brennan in their line-up

But before the tangerine dream would finally become reality, Newcastle would be back to successfully defend their trophy – a swashbuckling team full of star name attackers, with Brennan as its strong-beating heart. Arsenal were the 1952 victims and Newcastle warmed up for the task, having taken their foot well and truly off the pedal in the league, by putting it back down in a 6-1 win over Aston Villa, which included a rare headed goal by Brennan. The then 27-year-old dedicated his goal sarcastically to fellow Scot Hughie Gallacher, who had offended Brennan in a recent newspaper column by questioning his all-round footballing abilities.

There were no Brennan goals against the Gunners at Wembley, indeed he scored only three times in 349 appearances for the club – but there were still plenty of heroics from United's man-mountain. In truth, Newcastle had the odds overwhelmingly stacked in their favour when Arsenal right-back Wally Barnes hobbled off injured after 24 minutes, reducing his team to 10 men on the massive, strength-sapping Wembley pitch. A solitary George Robledo strike proved enough to retain the Cup, on a day when United had undoubtedly shown nerves against a spirited Arsenal side. "Thankfully for Newcastle, Brennan stood firm," wrote the *Sunday Sun*'s Ken McKenzie. "Indeed, it must have remained an almost complete stalemate, with Brennan seeming invincible against the quick, skilful Arsenal thrusts… Only the exceptional power of Brennan averted a possible sensation. If Holton or Cox could have got any change out of him, the Cup might well have stayed in London."

The *Sunday Post* chose the three Scots Brennan, Bobby Mitchell and goalkeeper Ronnie Simpson as the pick of Newcastle's side that day, while the *Newcastle Journal* hailed his "redoubtable efforts". Yet again, Brennan had risen to the occasion.

IF THE 1952 final was Brennan's finest hour, then the quality which proved most crucial to the side was his famous unflappability. Fans and team-mates adored Brennan because he was a man to rely on in a crisis. "Brennan from the early minutes was striding like a giant to chop off dangerous Arsenal thrusts," read the *Sunday Sun*, "and essayed nobly, though vainly, to spread his air of ease to the rest of the side." It was this rare mix of aggression and insouciance which helped mark out the Scot as a hero to the Geordie masses, and earned such respect among one of the greatest line-ups in the history of the club.

Brennan seemed outwardly to have everything under control, and his laid-back, happy-go-lucky attitude off the pitch is shown by this pre-match verdict on the 1951 final. While others were suffering big-match nerves and sleepless nights, he trilled: "This game will leave no regrets, however it ends. We are 11 players, fighting fit, happy together and playing as a side. We hope we do Tyneside and ourselves proud."

Yet it was not unknown for Brennan to lose his famous cool. The way he dealt with an unsociable and very large German tourist when on holiday in Spain once made the local newspapers when an *Evening Chronicle* correspondent happened to be present – and this was in 1977 when the great man was 53! "Frank picked up the obstreperous Teuton by the scruff of his neck with one huge hand and shook him as a terrier shakes a rat," read the report.

And Brennan was certainly far from laid-back on the pitch – although his opponents often were – laid flat on their backs on the turf, or worse, if you were Trevor Ford. Brennan recalled, after his playing days were over, bumping into the legendary Wales striker at Leeds-Bradford airport in 1973. "Hello Frank – I'm still getting bits of red gravel out of my body," said Ford, remembering the St James' Park clash between the pair which had left the then Aston Villa player sprawling over the shale track which surrounds the pitch."

Allied to Brennan's aggressive on-pitch approach was a lifelong dedication to fitness and a natural enthusiasm for the game which rubbed off on all who played with him. The Scot was far from the typical lumbering centre-half, and would work privately on his sprint training to make sure he kept up to speed with the strikers of his day. That philosophy would stand his North Shields side in good stead throughout their 1969 FA Amateur Cup win – and on the morning of the final itself, when, as manager, he led his team on a full training session in Hyde Park!

The tactic looked questionable when the Robins went 1-0 down to Sutton United, only for Shields, possibly buoyed by superior fitness, to rally in the second half and take the trophy 2-1. Brennan would be truly moved when the club sought FA permission to have a winner's medal cast for Brennan – the first ever presented to a manager – and he would later pick that FA Amateur Cup win as his favourite moment in football. "This Wembley win has given me a bigger thrill than appearing in Newcastle United's victorious FA Cup sides in 1951 and 1952," he said at the time.

Newspaper reports of the time paid tribute to Brennan's motivational qualities as North Shields boss – the same driving force behind the Newcastle side of the early 50s.

On 3 August 1969, the *Sunday Sun* reported: "In two FA Cup finals, Brennan was the powerhouse centre-half who drove Newcastle to two successive victories. And it was the same zest, the same iron-fisted drive that brought North Shields their success."

BRENNAN COULD BE forgiven if his choice of favourite footballing memory had been at all influenced by his bitter departure from St James'. One of the region's most celebrated footballing sons – a defender oft credited with carrying the team on his massive back – bore the brunt of one of the most shameful episodes in the club's history. There is no doubt that Brennan adored playing for United – describing the Cup-winning Newcastle as "a team in a million – it was an honour simply to play in it". He also declared, years later, that his years at St James' "gave me memories which can never be forgotten". Yet Brennan's heroics off the pitch, and his dignified demeanour on it, did nothing to protect him from the whims of the Newcastle boardroom.

In the days when footballers did not receive their just desserts when it came to pay, Brennan had worked as an electrician at Hartley Mains colliery, Northumberland, to supplement his playing wages during his early days as a United player. There was no objection to this practice from St James', but it was a different matter when Brennan opened a sports shop in Blackett Street, Newcastle, in June 1953.

Brennan's problems were just beginning. Manager Stan Seymour, who ran his own sports shop in the city in Market Street, took a dim view of this development, and the row would rumble on until Brennan was transferred out to non-league North Shields at the age of just 31 on 7 March 1956. In between, Brennan saw his £15-a-week maximum wage (plus bonuses) effectively halved to just £8, while he would make just 10 league appearances in his final two seasons for the Magpies, as the club, now chaired by former manager Seymour, with

Dougal Livingstone installed as team manager, turned to his defensive understudy Bob Stokoe.

The fans were in uproar at their hero's treatment – Stokoe was a solid player, but not in Brennan's class, and he himself had described his mentor as "phenomenal". Brennan's case, as he was cast out into the black and white wilderness, was even raised by Players' Union chairman Jimmy Guthrie at a Trades Union Congress meeting in September 1955, when the issue was highlighted as an example of footballers being "bought and sold like cattle". Chairman Seymour, for his part, claimed the wage reduction reflected the player's dip in performance since his newfound business 'distraction'. "It is not easy to do well in two spheres at once," he told the same TUC meeting. We had to take this into account at Newcastle concerning Brennan. Last season he just could not provide the football he had done in the past. He seemed on his way out as a player, though active in business."

United eventually upped Brennan's pay in the October before he left, but he was still no closer to a regular first-team recall, and in the eyes of the supporters, he had been made to pay dearly for going into business competition with his manager. Although perhaps no consolation to him at the time, Brennan's treatment merely turned him into more of a hero, and cast the St James' hierarchy in the familiar role of pantomime villain. United had long since established a reputation for ingratitude towards their players – culminating in the row after the 1951 FA Cup win when the team's win bonus was a handbag each for the wives and girlfriends!

The local media were not slow to spot the difference in attitude when lowly North Shields made Brennan honorary life vice-president in 1978. The *Evening Chronicle* reported: "North Shields, a little part-time club, know how to look after their former stars, while United patently didn't…. at the very height of his powers he was driven out of United and banished into non-league soccer. His treatment by United was disgraceful."

At the time fans held protest meetings aimed at getting their defensive rock reinstated in the team, while newspaper offices were inundated with letters of complaint. The saga caused a split in the Newcastle boardroom when Seymour released a statement in January 1955 declaring that Brennan was on the transfer list – and stating this was nothing to do with his business interests, but because "we do not consider that he fits in with our scheme for the development of younger players". Director William McKeag was incredulous when the *Evening Chronicle* asked for his response:

> "This is news to me – there must be some mistake somewhere. I have no knowledge of any decision by the directors to place Brennan on the transfer list... No one would have authority to determine a major issue of policy like this without the approval of the board of directors. I have asked the chairman, Mr Stan Seymour, to call a special meeting forthwith so that the whole matter can be clarified. So far as I am concerned, Frank Brennan is still a Newcastle player. He has given yeoman service to the club and if he were to go in this atmosphere and in these circumstances, I would feel ashamed and humiliated at the treatment accorded to him."

As the row over whether Brennan was or wasn't officially for sale rumbled on, the player demonstrated his determination to weather the storm by turning down moves to first Middlesbrough then Leeds and Plymouth, the first of which had already been ratified by Seymour. "The first, second, third or fourth team will do for me, so long as I am playing," Brennan said of Boro's approach. "I still have no desire for transfer." The row certainly ended an international career which had already been hampered by the Scottish FA's legendary reluctance to select 'Anglos' or English-based players. Brennan won just seven official caps, the last two against England and Ireland coming in 1954.

But if he had given up on wearing the blue jersey of his homeland again, he did seem hopeful of wearing the black and white of his adopted Geordie nation once more. Explaining away his initial refusal to accept a reduced Newcastle contract, he declared: "I do not want to part company with United. Although I have refused to re-sign, I am still hopeful of being able to negotiate terms with United that will satisfy me and allow me to remain a Magpie." But those hopes included playing regularly and they were in vain, despite a public meeting at Newcastle's City Hall, designed to bring matters to a head. That meeting, attended by around 2,000 supporters, was organised by Mr

EC Pringle, chairman of the Shareholders' Association, who asked, in vain, for Stan Seymour to attend and answer the supporters' concerns about "the Brennan business and other unsatisfactory factors in the management of Newcastle United". Seymour's response was dismissive: "The gratuitous intervention of Mr Pringle in an obvious effort to use the Brennan affair for his own purposes is to be deplored," he said in a club statement. "The so-called Shareholders Association, principally organised by Mr Pringle himself, is not, and never has been, recognised by the board of directors."

Seymour, the manager who had led United to the 1951 and 1952 FA Cup wins, but had since acquired a reputation for high-handed treatment of players as chairman, weathered the storm, and Brennan would remain in limbo, playing just one 'A' team game for the club in the two months leading up to his departure.

The *Evening Chronicle*, reporting his shock move to North Shields, described the long-lasting feud as: "One of the greatest controversies of the North East". If Brennan had shown, in his refusal to leave United, the same stubborn streak which made him such a great on the pitch, then the supporters simply loved him all the more for it – but the premature end of his league career leaves a sour note in the tale of arguably the club's finest-ever defender.

UNITED ADDED INSULT to injury six years later when, in the spring of 1962, they refused him permission to hold a benefit game at St James' Park. Bitter rivals Sunderland – though they had no connection with Brennan – stepped in, and a crowd of just under 14,000 paid to watch some of the biggest names in British football turn out in tribute. Len Shackleton, Jackie Milburn, Bobby Mitchell, Don Revie, Jack Charlton, Tommy Lawton and Johnny Crossan were all in attendance to show that Brennan demanded respect almost everywhere in football – if not in the United boardroom.

But if that snub hit Brennan hard, his exclusion from United's third victorious FA Cup-winning team seven years earlier had hit harder. 1955, his final year as a player at Gallowgate, was perhaps the lowest point of Brennan's career. Usurped by Bob Stokoe at the heart of defence, he had made just one league appearance – at Portsmouth – when the team lined up to beat Manchester City 3-1 at Wembley on 7 May.

But, on a personal level, worse was to come. The following month, Brennan accidentally hit and killed a cyclist while driving through Wallsend at night. Two street lamps were out at the time, and the United defender was cleared of any blame, except for a subsequent prosecution for driving without road tax. United director William McKeag – a staunch Brennan supporter – represented the player's interests at the inquest of the death of Lawrence Buggy, a 32-year-old miner. Sadly for United, McKeag could not resurrect the United career of a player who still had much to offer.

After his spell playing for and managing North Shields and an abortive three-month stint as Darlington manager, Brennan, who had settled just a few miles from Newcastle in Whitley Bay, put his drive and enthusiasm to good use as a roving coach for the British Council. He spent time in Singapore, Sarawak, Guyana, Thailand, Trinidad, Borneo, Canada, Saba, Malaysia and Hong Kong preaching the British football gospel – and the gigantic, tough-tackling Scot must have made quite a stir among the natives.

As a lifelong United fan and occasional media pundit, he would create a stir of a different kind when, in 1978, in the depths of the Magpies' underachievement, he called for supporters to boycott the club. It was a rational enough argument – but one that did not go down too well with the most passionate supporters. Despite criticism of his words on Tyneside – and the local newspapers calling instead for fans to get behind a team struggling, unsuccessfully, to stay in the First Division – Brennan typically stuck by his words. He said: "I am the greatest supporter Newcastle have and it grieves me when they lose a match. But I think things have got to the stage where a boycott by supporters is the only way to make the club realise what the fans really want."

His assertion – that United's board came nowhere near to matching the ambition of their supporters – was a common, and correct one, but, like many others, he was hoodwinked into thinking the long barren run without a trophy was nearly over under Kevin Keegan's managerial era in the early 90s. Predicting a title win for KK's side in their first season in the Premiership in the summer of 1993, many supporters thought Big Frank had taken leave of his senses – but with a third-placed finish, a buoyant United side so nearly proved him right. "I can feel the resurgence of optimism in the town which was the hallmark of our great days when the likes of Wor Jackie, little Ernie Taylor and Joe Harvey ruled the roost," he declared.

But for Keegan, trophies there were none. He noted in his autobiography, although not strictly correctly, that Newcastle finished higher in the top flight in every season under his stewardship, than the FA-Cup winning sides of the 50s ever had done (in fact, the 1951 side finished fourth, while Keegan's team finished sixth in 1995). But in any case, Keegan missed the point. The FA Cup in the 50s WAS the big one and Newcastle's players – as Jackie Milburn would later admit – saved themselves for the cup clashes, ever more so as a run progressed.

Also, the team of the 50s won trophies – and that simple fact means the shadow of legends such as Milburn, Mitchell, Robledo and Big Frankie Brennan still loom large in this, the next century.

BRENNAN HIMSELF WAS always too modest to accept his own heroic status in his adopted homeland, once declaring: "Och, I wasn't as good as all that. Anyone could have played in that marvellous team – it was easy to be one of them." But don't allow yourself, like countless of the day's finest centre-forwards, to be fooled by Big Frank – the man was a colossus, who rose almost straight from the Scottish pits to become a fearsome, bone-crunching defender in black and white.

Goalkeeper Jack Fairbrother, of the 1951 cup-winning side rated by contemporaries to be the best of United's 1950's line-ups, once admitted that "75 per cent of my success was down to Frank."

The man's workrate, amazing consistency and positive demeanour made Brennan a joy to play with and a hero on the terraces throughout arguably the most glorious chapter in Newcastle's chequered history. A strong, big-hearted tackler with brilliant timing and a supreme motivator, Brennan the destroyer of reputations was commonly regarded in his prime as the equal of two mere mortal defenders.

As the club's No. 1 stopper, a player's player, and for eating six-course breakfasts before playing, Frank Brennan takes his place as one of the biggest United heroes of them all.

George Robledo

1949-1953: 166 games, 91 goals

BEFORE Nobby, Ginola and Tino, Mirandinha and Benny Arentoft, came the first big money foreign import in Newcastle United history... and surely the best. George Robledo rivalled Jackie Milburn in the goalscoring charts – and the popularity stakes – during four glorious years on Tyneside. The warmth of his welcome back then and the deep resonance of the Robledo name on these shores to this day, more than half a century later, is proof positive that Geordie fans can be among the most hospitable in the land.

In the days long before the Premiership's League of Nations, Chilean Robledo was something of a novelty. But any doubts about his credentials to mix it with the Brits on the pitch were quickly dispelled. By the time Robledo left his adopted homeland to return to his birthplace in 1953, he had scored 91 times in 166 games. To put that in perspective, it is a goalscoring ratio – at 0.55 per cent – which Jackie Milburn, Malcolm Macdonald and Alan Shearer cannot match.

Indeed, many United No. 9s throughout the decades can only eye Robledo's statistics with envy – and it is worth stressing that his prolific output came not as a No. 9, but an inside-forward.

The Chilean became only the second inside-forward in 25 years to top the First Division goalscoring charts with his haul of 33 League goals in 1951-52. Even more significantly for United fans, Robledo's overall 39-goal total that year – six coming in a second successive FA

Cup-winning run – equalled a club record set by Hughie Gallacher a quarter of a century earlier. That mark would last another 42 years unbreached, before Andy Cole made a sensational impact on club history with his 41-goal tally in 1993/94.

But the likes of Milburn, Shearer, Macdonald, Kevin Keegan, Len White, Wyn Davies, Micky Quinn and Les Ferdinand – specialist goal-scorers one and all – would each fail to match the scoring standards set by a man who had been signed primarily as a foil to Jackie Milburn. Robledo succeeded in that regard too, of course, and the players would feed off each other as they developed one of the most dangerous partnerships United fans had ever been treated to. Team-mate Charlie Crowe admitted: "Jackie was a better centre-forward when George Robledo came. They were the perfect pair." It cut both ways. Giant centre-back Frank Brennan was quick to point out Robledo's 'sniffer' instincts around the penalty area. "Jackie would have a crack from 20 or 30 yards," said Brennan, "they would come off the woodwork or a defender's body, and there would be George to put them away. He was always poaching around the goalmouth."

ROBLEDO BECAME THE first player in five years to outscore Jackie Milburn in that 1951/52 season, finishing 10 goals ahead of the celebrated United No. 9. But goalscoring explains only part of the high affection in which the Chilean is still held on Tyneside, now fully 17 years after his death from a heart attack. Burly, hard-working, yet a clever player with an uncanny positional sense, George Robledo was as idiosyncratic an inside-forward as Newcastle had ever unearthed. And perhaps the clue to this unique blend of abilities really does lie in his cosmopolitan background, and an unusual mix of European endeavour and South American style.

Wor Geordie's rise to superstar status in Newcastle – 3,700 miles from home – is certainly one of the most unlikely tales in this book. The sad yet adventurous story of his beginnings in British football is worth re-telling, since it was fundamental to the mystique of a colourful character whose energy and passion for the game made him an instant hit on Tyneside. George's legend is also irrevocably linked to the tale of his brother Ted, or Eduardo, another one of Newcastle's 1952 FA Cup-winning heroes, whose life would end in circumstances so murderous, tragic and mysterious, they were worthy of an Agatha Christie novel.

But the beginning of the Robledos' story is almost as dramatic. The boys were born to an English mother and a Chilean father – head cashier of a gold and copper mine – and spent their early childhood years in the Pacific port of Iquique. It's safe to assume that neither had ever heard of Newcastle United, let alone harboured any ambitions of playing for the club, when – fortunately for football-loving Tynesiders – a violent socialist uprising in Chile took a decisive turn in 1932. The boys' mother, Elsie, who had been in South America teaching English since the end of the Great War, decided to make a short-term retreat to her native Yorkshire with five-year-old George, three-year-old Ted and baby Walter. The return trip was cancelled when her husband fell ill and died before the rest of the family could set sail for Chile, and the two eldest Robledos soon found they had a talent for football which helped them settle in their new, unfamiliar Yorkshire surroundings.

Yet of the two, George was always the one who stood out, adding craft and guile to his brother's hard-working half-back game, and the former's goalscoring debut aged 16 for Barnsley lit the spark on a career which would never be short on fireworks. Just seven years later, 'Pancho' as he was almost instantly known to Newcastle fans, was lighting up Tyneside as one of the most expensive players in the history of the game. Barnsley received – according to varying reports – anything from £23,000 up to £26,500 for the pair, when Elsie, backed up by George, insisted that the latter was going nowhere without his little brother.

United, alerted to the striker's potential by his hat-trick display in a War Cup tie against the Magpies, readily agreed, with George making up around £20,000 of the joint fee. Newcastle director Stan Seymour – who was to take over managerial duties too within 18 months – was the man credited with pushing through one of the most successful transfers in club history. Admitting that his one-man rescue act in that cup tie for Barnsley had sparked United's interest, Seymour added: "In the second leg at Barnsley the Yorkshire side needed three goals to beat us. They scored them and the man behind the win was George Robledo. It was the first time I had ever seen him and I was greatly impressed."

What Newcastle got for their money was a 5ft 9in fair-haired and handsome striker with the muscular build of a middleweight boxer. Robledo was strong, naturally fit, hard to knock off the ball, superb in the air and with the ability to pass his way through a defence; he seemed to complement Milburn's fast running game perfectly. Throw in a poacher's eye for goal, a powerful accurate shot and a willingness to try his luck from anywhere, and United fans never knew quite what to expect when Robledo was in possession.

So impressive was Robledo's workrate, it is tempting to regard him as the labourer to dribblers such as outside-left Bobby Mitchell and playmaker Ernie Taylor – his fellow inside-forward, but in reality he was a very different type of player. Manager George Martin used to tell Robledo: "We didn't buy you to play football – just get in the six-yard box," while a feature on the player by the *Sunday Sun* newspaper referred to him as "The Grafter", adding: "There was no standing on ceremony with George. He used to blast them in from all directions, and no matter what the distance, even six yards, they used to go in like a bullet. George took a lot of weight off Jackie [Milburn] in the air, and revelled in his high leaps with the opposing centre-halves."

But if dribbling tricks were not really in Robledo's reportoire, it is unfair to label him as an artisan among artists. It certainly was not the Chilean's style to run with the ball – but contemporary observers remarked that he had a superb football brain to go with his unquestioned aerial power, and an ability to read the play, which explained his uncanny knack of being at the right place at the right time.

He also took a modern, forward-thinking approach to the game – trying, in vain, to persuade the club to wear the new lighter, more flexible football boots in their 1951 Cup run, before such footwear became commonplace later on in that decade. On the pitch, Robledo's approach – quick passing, with an economy of effort and letting the ball doing the work – was ahead of its time and perfectly suited to a team full of talented technicians. His ability to spot an opening early, and react accordingly, meant that one of his few perceived flaws – a lack of blistering pace – never hindered him at the top level.

"For a time George was regarded as somewhat slow as he gathered in the goals by inspired poaching," wrote sports journalist Ken McKenzie in 1972. "But unflappable finishing refuted any such criticism, especially on the heavy grounds when his immense strength made him seem ever faster as others slowed. In addition he was a grand club man. Always well turned out, on and off the field, he looked even then every inch the prosperous mining executive he has now become back home in South America."

If Robledo could not match the jet-propelled Milburn for pace (who could?), then not everyone agreed that he was slow. Indeed another newspaper profile of the player declared: "He was brilliant with his head, his approach was direct and thrustful and, despite his stocky build, he moved with elegance and speed."

ROBLEDO WAS CERTAINLY in a hurry to get his United career off to a good start – and who better, in the eyes of Newcastle fans, to score against than Sunderland – in his third game for the black and whites? Robledo's winning strike in a 2-1 victory got the new boy off to a flyer with the crowd, and, with Milburn grabbing the first, the game marked the start of a long and fruitful partnership. That derby win was also significant for another reason – it marked the debut of left-winger Bobby Mitchell, signed just three weeks after Robledo in what must be the most productive spell of transfer activity in the history of the club.

Robledo's 11 strikes in 30 games that first season was an impressive return for an inside forward – but there was much more to come; the South American, in tandem with M & M (Milburn and Mitchell) would cement their place in Tyneside folklore with two FA Cup wins in the next three years.

So many legends were created in that golden spell in the early 50s, and so too much of the tradition, the very fabric of Newcastle United as an engaging, attacking, divided, glamorous and inconsistent club. Robledo, as a master finisher and busy creator, was at the very heart of all that jazz. As McKenzie wrote in the *Journal* in 1972: "Every mature Geordie of even modest sporting memory knows that the handsome Chilean heavyweight played a tremendous role in those Magpies glory years of the early '50s. George Robledo was one of the so-merry Magpies for a comparatively short time – but in that period he helped to carve out golden figures of United history… and riotous goal-getting in which he played a momentous role."

The most obvious example of Robledo's influence is his goal – the only one of the game – in the 1952 final against Arsenal, a game marred by the early withdrawal through injury of Gunners full-back Wally Barnes, and a final in which the Londoners earned many plaudits for their brave resistance. That late header – coming in the 83rd minute – was a godsend to a tiring United, and was testimony to the craft of the

Robledo and Mitchell – the former reading his winger's true intentions when feigning to shoot, to move into space on the back post to receive an inch-perfect pass before finishing with typical aplomb.

The *Sunday Express* correspondent, Alan Hoby, described the contest as "one of the toughest, grimmest and most gruelling Cup finals I have ever seen" before heaping praise on "the bronze bull from Chile" for breaking the deadlock.

His report takes up the tale:

> "From a tackle-collision between George Robledo and Don Roper, the ball spun away to Newcastle's wizard from Scotland, outside-left Bobby Mitchell. Mitchell, who has one of the most educated left feet in the business, crossed from the left to the far post. Robledo, always a master at subtle positioning, waited for the ball. It shot down and glanced off the foot of the inside part of the post and into the net."

Any player who scores a late winner in an FA Cup final is going to have hero status immediately conferred upon him and receive adulation not to mention the odd sot of hyperbole. The *Evening Chronicle* told its eager readers that "the unmistakable mahogany skin of Robledo reacted with the reflexes of a cat... first a move that was an odd combination of spring and crouch, then a quick stab of the head. The ball struck the inside of the post and glanced into history."

But there is so much substance behind this hype. That header was Robledo's ninth FA Cup goal in two seasons – he had scored in the '51 campaign and failed to get on the scoresheet only once in '52 – when Bobby Mitchell's lone strike secured a hard-fought fifth round away win over Swansea.

A brace in the 3-0 fourth round away win over Tottenham was another personal highlight for the terrace hero, while Robledo was also instrumental in the epic third round home win over Aston Villa, when the Magpies recovered from 2-1 down with nine minutes to go to win 4-2. With his side 2-0 down after 15 minutes, Robledo created United's first for Billy Foulkes, then watched Mitchell equalise before playing the Scots winger through to make it 3-2 – and then adding a fourth himself at the death for good measure.

Even when he was not on the scoresheet personally, the busy Robledo seemed almost always involved in Newcastle's most telling moves. His was the through-ball to Milburn in the 2-0 1951 FA Cup final win over Blackpool which set the No. 9 off on his famous charge for goal and the Magpies on their way to their first major trophy in 19 years. Milburn later recalled: "Matthews wriggled through to the byline and pulled the ball back, but it went straight to a defender who immediately fed George Robledo. He whipped it on to me, just inside my own half. I got past Eric Hayward and was away like the wind…"

Nearly 12 months later, Milburn repaid the favour when he crossed for his team-mate to head home in the 2-1 semi-final win over Blackburn Rovers which sent Newcastle back to Wembley. The two had also shared the goals – Milburn three, Robledo one, in the 4-2 quarter-final win at Portsmouth, which has become widely regarded as the greatest FA Cup performance in the club's modern history.

Like fellow cult heroes Mitchell, Brennan and Harvey, Robledo and Milburn grew in stature through the club's Cup adventures – and there seems little doubt that the latter pair in particular spurred each other on to great heights. As Milburn said in 1981 on the occasion of Robledo's flying return visit to the North East: "George had a magic knack of hitting the back of the net. I couldn't have wished for a better partner and it's wonderful to see him again after 28 years."

Robledo had paid the £2,000 air fare out of his own pocket that year to attend a reunion of Newcastle's 1951 FA Cup-winning team. He received a special award from the Newcastle United Supporters Association on his only return to the region and told the North East press that the loving feeling was mutual. "The best years of my life were spent with United," he declared, "and I've kept in touch with how they were doing through friends on Tyneside."

Ironically, he was returning at a time – the end of the 1980/81 season – when the Second Division Magpies had just set a new record for the fewest league goals (30) ever scored in a season. Bobby Shinton had finished as United's top scorer with seven goals – a total once matched by Robledo in one game, when he set a club record of the more welcome variety in a summer tour win over Border Province back in 1952.

In the season after that sensational friendly display, 18 goals (all in the league) were enough for the Chilean to finish as United's top scorer for the second successive year, before Robledos Senior and Junior would depart English shores almost as dramatically as they had arrived. Despite suggestions that he was eligible to play for England, George had long since honoured his dead father by opting to play for the country of his birth – and his 34 international caps, taking in the 1950 World Cup, mark him out as one of the most successful players in this book on the world stage. But it was still a shock when the brothers decided to go "home" to sign for Colo-Colo, especially since George was at the height of his fame on Tyneside and the joint fee – at £15,000 – was substantially less than the price United had paid Barnsley for their services.

Press reports suggested that the Chilean government had ordered the Robledos' return to boost their flagging domestic game – and it was true that the Ministry for Sport partly-funded the players' contracts, installing them as government-sponsored coaches on top of their playing duties.

However, United were forced to put out a statement denying any coercion from South America, and insisting that both players were happy to return to Chile – even if the joint transfer was anything but an unqualified success. Newcastle chairman Dr Robert Rutherford declared: "It is incomprehensible to me that such straightforward business proposals can be made the jumping-off ground in a number of newspapers for mischievous unconfirmed statements and suggestions."

Stories of the players' unrest – difficulties with the language (they had spoken English since childhood) and the hot weather, and rumours of a return to England with United, Arsenal or Barnsley – would surface regularly in the English press over the next few years. "Here we play all year long, and too much sun is doing us harm," Robledo told an English newspaper in 1955, while in that same year Barnsley chairman Joe Richards declared "I am still willing to fly to Chile if there is a chance of bringing them back to Barnsley".

Weaned on the laissez-faire management of Stan Seymour at Newcastle, neither brother adapted well to the more disciplined regimen of the South American game. George, it was said, found it particularly difficult being restricted to five cigarettes a day and being told to be in bed by 10pm every night! But Colo-Colo, desperate to keep George in particular as the most famous face of Chilean football, slapped unrealistic price tags on the brothers to keep the Robledos in harness, and prompted a mini-riot when they dropped the unsettled pair to the reserves in January 1955. The fans' reactions showed that – hero though George was on Tyneside – his stock was probably even higher in the land of his birth.

The *Sunday Sun* reported that: "The press, radio and supporters all took their side. Supporters organised public demonstrations in protest against the club's decision and one night there were two torchlight parades that resulted in the traffic being held up for half an hour in the main avenue in Santiago." Sweetened on such fervour, lucrative contracts and a lavish family home complete with servants for the entire Robledo clan (which still included mother Elsie), George knuckled down to win a Chilean Championship in 1956, and become one of the country's leading football amabassadors before following his late father's footsteps into the mining business after hanging up his boots.

Newcastle director William McKeag visited the player 11 years later, and came back to the North East to tell the striker's still-adoring fans: "George still coaches his works team, but takes no part in big-time sport now. He is very well known and much respected throughout the country."

RESPECT HAD FOLLOWED George Robledo closely throughout his career – and his latter role as a smart, successful mining executive would have come as no surprise to those who knew the player away from the field during his Tyneside days. Widely regarded as a model young man, and secretary of a youth club, the eldest Robledo was surely ideal son-in-law material, except that he had promised never to marry! That vow was broken as a more solemn one was made to Chilean woman Gladys (honestly) in 1959 – and she, as George's widow, would make an emotional trip along with the couple's daughter Elizabeth, to Tyneside in 1991, two years after her husband's death. Returning his medals to the club museum, she was welcomed by Robledo's former team-mates Bobby Cowell, Bobby Mitchell, Frank Brennan, Bob Stokoe, Charlie Crowe and George Luke – but sadly not by skipper Joe Harvey or talisman Jackie Milburn, who had both passed away before him. "I can never forget this day – or this wonderful welcome," said Gladys. "The medals belong only in one place. I treasure them, especially since George's death, but I know that they should go on display for the people of Newcastle to see. George always talked about the happy times he had at Newcastle United, and the special players he played with. They were names that meant so much to us. Now we are able to meet them and know them, which is a great honour. But there is a sadness that Jackie Milburn and Joe Harvey are not here today. George talked so much about them, and I remember how upset he was when he heard of Jack's death."

Yet neither Milburn nor Harvey's passing was as shocking as the death of Ted Robledo. George's spectacular story in Newcastle colours had always been entwined with that of his more slender, younger brother, who had battled his way into the 1952 Cup-winning side as an industrious left-half. And no summing-up of George's enduring status on Tyneside – which is at least partly based on a fascination with his dramatic life – can be complete without touching upon the sad and mysterious disappearance of Eduardo.

Ted, as he was known to Magpies fans, had made a belated return to English football with Notts County in the late '50s, before taking a job on the oil rig Discover One. On a week's leave in December 1970, Ted accepted an invitation from a West German oil tanker captain, Heinz Bessenich, to join his 350-ton coastal tanker *Al Sahn* on its passage from Dubai to Muscat. Setting sail on 5 December, Ted went missing the following day and was never seen again. The captain was charged with his murder amid prosecution claims that he had used an ornamental dagger – missing from his cabin – to stab the ex-player before throwing him overboard. Some of the ship's staff told the British Agency Court in Dubai that Ted had been drinking with Bessenich on the night he disappeared – and further claims were made that the captain had made no effort to find his passenger, nor phone in an SOS once his disappearance had been made known. However, Bessenich was ultimately acquitted, and George would later tell the *Newcastle Journal* that the tragedy broke his mother's heart. "Ted was my mother's favourite," upon returning to Tyneside in 1981. "I believe his death shortened her own life."

But if Ted was Elsie's favourite, big brother George was indisputably No. 1 on Tyneside. In an assorted crew of braggarts and hermits, mavericks and shrinking violets in this book, George Robledo was a man – like Len White and Peter Beardsley – who kept his passion for the pitch. Indeed, so reserved was the Chilean that Jackie Milburn once revealed that, in the aftermath of Newcastle's 1951 FA Cup win, only Robledo and Bobby Mitchell seemed unmoved.

Capturing the mood of an ecstatic dressing room, he said: "There were tears of laughter, jokes, shouts and songs. Only Bobby Mitchell and George Robledo, who are two strong, silent men, showed little emotion. They just sat to watch everybody else's reactions."

If Robledo was surprised by the emotion of his team-mates, he would be even more bemused by the rapturous welcome he received back at St James' Park when he returned to the city in 1981 – 28 years after kicking his last ball for the club. "I am quite overwhelmed," he admitted, "but so happy to be back among old friends."

Passion, though, was shown in abundance by Robledo on the pitch throughout four and a half sensational seasons on Tyneside. The strong, silent type he may have been, but on the pitch, Robledo was a hard-working maestro, whose energy and astute play helped beckon arguably the most glamorous era in the history of the club. "He became a hero among heroes in those glorious years with Newcastle United," wrote sports journalist Paul Tully in the *Evening Chronicle*, while another scribe, Ken McKenzie, captured the Chilean's infectious enthusiasm by revealing he once turned out for the club – and scored – while injured and with a bellyful of fish and chips! "George was injured and out of the team to play Liverpool, and as he wasn't playing he sat down to a hearty meal of fish and chips," wrote McKenzie. "Then he got an SOS. 'You're wanted after all,' he was told. George was rushed to the ground and, despite his injury and the heavy meal, he banged in two fine goals."

It is perhaps that heart – the spirit which British football fans more often see in their own players rather than foreign imports – which is the biggest clue to Robledo's enduring legend. More than the wonderfully gifted David Ginola and Tino Asprilla, Robledo put his heart and soul into the club, earning 'honorary Geordie' status among Tynesiders higher than any foreign player before or since.

The *Evening Chronicle* provided Robledo with the ultimate accolade in 1962, insiting the Chilean had "rapidly established himself as 'Wor Geordie' – as popular as 'Wor Jackie'." It is, as Newcastle United's chequered history with foreign imports shows, a rare trick to win over such a partisan crowd so completely.

Perhaps, before he hangs up his boots, the smiling, trumpet-playing figure of Nobby Solano will rival his fellow South American for popularity, but sadly, it seems the Peruvian will never match the Chilean for honours. Robledo's heroics in two epic FA Cup wins – and in particular his match-winning efforts in 1952, a year in which he was arguably the biggest driving force behind the Magpies' march to silverware – mark him out as a player who rose to the big occasion.

His relatively short United career may mean, ultimately, that he must take his place behind the likes of Milburn, Mitchell, Beardsley and Shearer in United's Hall of Heroes – while he did have the natural infectious charisma of a Kevin Keegan or a Malcolm Macdonald. But once those names have been spoken, whose is bigger than George Oliver Robledo? And remember that, unlike Beardsley, Shearer, Keegan and Macdonald, the 'bronze bull' actually won major trophies at United.

For that, he remains widely loved in this region, 7,000 miles from his homeland. For being a winner, for bringing a touch of Samba magic to Tyneside and for proving so eloquent in goalscoring – a language treasured as much in Newcastle as in Santiago – the quiet man of Newcastle's golden decade will never be overlooked.

Bobby Mitchell

1949-1961: 410 games, 113 goals

"SHOW 'EM YOUR arse!" was Mitch's regular call-to-arms from his first Newcastle manager George Martin. And, for 13 seasons in a black and white shirt, the Magpies No. 11 did just that – bamboozling the finest full-backs in the land with a dazzling array of dribbling skills.

The greatest winger in Newcastle's history is proof positive that you do not have to be a centre-forward to become a Tyneside icon. Indeed, if nicknames are the measure of a footballer's esteem among supporters, then Robert Carmichael Mitchell, and his many monikers, might just overshadow them all. Variously known as Bobby Dazzler, Mitch the Magician, Maestro Mitchell, Wor Bobby and The Matthews of the Magpies, Mitchell was one of the most powerful of wing wizards in an age when Scottish sorcerers were much prized south of the border for their fine ball skills and close control. Indeed, he became the most expensive winger in British football – and the highest transfer between English and Scottish clubs – when he made the switch from the now-defunct Third Lanark to United for £17,000 in February 1949. His arrival on Tyneside came just three weeks after that of Chilean inside-forward George Robledo – and the two were destined to make an indelible mark on club history. Playing alongside fellow legends such as Jackie Milburn, Joe Harvey and Frank Brennan, Mitchell was the natural stylist of the team, a born entertainer and a player whom skipper Harvey used to joke was in the side "to give the rest of us a breather".

Only a handful of men have ever been worshipped as much by United fans. Writing upon his retirement in 1961, sports journalist Ken McKenzie – who covered them all from Gallacher in the late 20s through to Len White in the early 60s – declared that Mitchell was "installed on a pinnacle as high as that erected in Tyneside eyes to his great pal and ex-team-mate Jackie Milburn".

We need say no more in support of Robert Carmichael Mitchell – since, in these parts, there is no higher praise.

AMONG THE TRIBUTES which poured in upon Mitchell's death, at the age of 68 on 8 April 1993, so many of them concentrated on his captivating dribbling skills – an aspect of his game which sent the Geordie crowd into raptures for more than a decade. "Mitch was in a class of his own. His ball control was wonderful to watch, and wonderful to play alongside," said stopper Frank Brennan, while Charlie Crowe added: "What a magnificent player. We used to say he could open a can of beans with his left foot!" To Bob Stokoe, he was, quite simply "the finest left-winger I ever saw" while full-back Bobby Cowell, echoing skipper Harvey's sentiments, added: "Mitch was a lovely fellow and a magical footballer. No one could match his skill on the ball. We could give him the ball he would keep it for five minutes while we had a breather."

But Ronnie Simpson paints the most vivid picture with his portrayal. "Mitch would have defenders not knowing what was happening," said the former Newcastle keeper. "He had marvellous style and balance about him, and was also very brave. He was a wonderful player, and unique in the truest sense of the word." Sir Alf Ramsey, then a Tottenham full-back, was on the receiving end of Mitchell's mastery on more than one occasion, and the Magpie once admitted he loved facing the future England manager, because of Ramsey's tendency to drop off when marking.

Giving Mitchell the space to twist and turn could be fatal – as Huddersfield's England right-back Ron Staniforth also discovered in an FA Cup sixth round replay in 1955. Mitchell would later recall his mesmerising performance that day as "the best game I ever had in a black and white shirt", adding: "I could do nothing wrong. I feinted, tricked, dribbled and streaked past poor Ron. He was completely lost. I have since talked to Ron about that game – and to Mrs Staniforth, who told me that, for a week afterwards, Ron was having nightmares about that game!"

But as well as delighting supporters and giving defenders sleepless nights, Mitchell's eye for weaving elaborate patterns on the pitch would lead to one or two problems with managers over the years – most notably Charlie Mitten, whose arrival at St James', in the player's own view, hastened his own departure on a free transfer to Berwick in 1961. The problem for coaches wanting to make their mark at United was that Mitchell could, for some, be a frustrating player to work with – since he was already the finished article, and so much of his game stemmed from his innate natural ability, and his willingness to take players. As former team-mate Crowe once commented: "He never liked the principle of coaching. He used to pull my leg and call me a con merchant because I was one of the first qualified coaches in the area. But Mitch never needed coaching. You just had to let him play his own game." Thankfully, in the main, Newcastle's management team let him do just that – Stan Seymour's laissez-faire style in particular suited Mitchell down to the ground – and the result was an enduring love affair between player and crowd which has hardly ever been matched before or since in its strength and duration.

THE SHEER JOY of watching Mitchell play may well lie at the heart of his legend, but there is more – much more – to his weighty claim as a Newcastle United cult hero…

> - Mitchell is one of only three players, alongside Cowell and Milburn, to play in all three victorious 50s FA Cup-winning teams
> - No forward has made more than his 410 appearances for the club ...
> - Only six players in total have played more games for the Magpies
> - Only six – all strikers – have scored more than his 113 goals at United
> - He finished joint-top scorer with Milburn on 23 goals in 1955
> - And he is the third highest FA Cup goalscorer in club history

Indeed, Mitchell's one-in-four scoring ratio is truly remarkable for an outside-left and his record in black and white is one that many No. 9s can only envy. Gifted as he was in the creative arts – with the ability to deliver pinpoint crosses for the likes of Milburn and Robledo – the 5ft 11in curly-haired wonder was just as effective when he made a beeline for goal ... And a player snubbed as a youth by a clutch of clubs north of the border, due to a lack of physical stature, would enhance his massive reputation on Tyneside by scoring some sensational – and priceless – goals.

Like so many of the iconic figures in United's history, Mitchell had an on-pitch presence that inspired team-mates – and an uncanny knack of rising to the occasion. Nowhere was this more in evidence than in the FA Cup – a competition which brought the best out of United's merry band of all-star cavaliers.

Mitchell's impact was huge in a tournament which, in three epic years in the 1950s, did so much to forge the glamorous reputation of Newcastle United in the modern era.

The yarns trip off the tongue for old-timers. Perhaps the favourite of all was the "Gie us the ball" semi-final replay when Mitchell, having never taken a penalty in English football before, stepped forward to score the spot-kick which secured United's place in the 1952 Final – when star names such as Milburn, Robledo and Harvey refused the challenge. United had drawn 0-0 with Blackburn in the first semi at Hillsborough, and honours were even at 1-1 in the replayed tie at Elland Road when Mitchell answered the call, under the severest of pressure, to show he had guts to go with his fancy-dan skills. "No one dared to take such an important kick," he remembered years later. "Jackie, who should have taken it, said he was injured after a foul a few minutes before. Joe Harvey was standing with the ball in his hand and everybody was walking away.

"Joe offered the ball to George Robledo and George went white – the colour just drained from him. I went up to Joe and said 'Why don't you take the bloody thing?' and even Joe said no. So I thought 'this is crazy', grabbed the ball from Joe, put it on the spot and thumped it into the net. Only then did I think what it would have meant had I missed it."

The bottle Mitchell showed in taking that penalty meant his stock on Tyneside rocketed – and he later learned that his manager Stan

Seymour and trainer Norman Smith were so nervous they, along with most of the Newcastle side, turned their backs to the action until they heard the roar of the Geordie crowd.

Mitchell's massive on-pitch influence – unusual in a winger – came to the fore again in one of the most dramatic FA Cup turnarounds in club history against Aston Villa. The Magpies, as holders, were 10 minutes from going out of the competition in the 1952 third round tie at home to the Midlanders. At 2-1 down, thousands of disgruntled fans had already headed for home when Mitchell took the game by the scruff of the neck and single-handedly turned the tables in a competition United would go on to win for the second year running at Wembley. Mitchell treasured the precious memory in an interview with the *Sunday Sun* back in 1961. "Nothing was going right," said the Scot. "Then Bobby Corbett got the ball on the halfway line and swung it across field to me. I swear to this day I didn't really expect what happened. I was at the corner of the penalty area, swung my foot and was flabbergasted when it flashed into the net.

"So were Villa's defenders – they were still arguing about whose fault it was when the same thing happened again – straight from the kick-off. Across came the ball – and whoof! I slammed it into the net. I'll remember the look of disbelief on those Villa defenders until my dying day. Right on time, Robledo notched a fourth."

In the days before *Sky Sports*, *Ceefax* and text messages, many of the numerous departees in the original 56,897 crowd needed some convincing afterwards that the Magpies had, indeed won the match, prompting some amusing tales around the city. Mitchell himself enjoyed one such story.

> "St James' Park was half-empty because everyone had gone home in despair," he remembered. "In fact – and this is a true story – one bloke had gone home a quarter of an hour from the end, rowed with his missus, stormed off to the pub, grumbled at his mates all night and refused to listen to them when they told him we'd won 4-2. He went home again, still furious and moaning, and only found out the truth when he picked up his newspaper next morning!"

Mitchell's two goals had come within the space of 60 seconds, and provided long-term North East sportswriter Ken McKenzie with one of the highlights of his journalistic career. "Few memories give me a greater thrill than Bobby Mitchell's two Cup goals in a minute against Aston Villa," he wrote in the *Journal* in 1961.

"What a pity there is no film strip to record the faces of Villa keeper Con Martin and pivot Frank Moss, as those goals won that tie at Gallowgate which seemed all sewn up for Villa."

That game may be the most dramatic example of Mitchell's big-match temperament – but there were many others. United's No. 11 scored a spectacular winner in the 1951 semi-final against Wolves at Huddersfield, which, together with his famous penalty against Blackburn in '52, meant he scored the goal which booked United's place at Wembley two years running.

A 25-yard rocket shot in a muddy fourth round battle with Tottenham in 1952 was another example of Mitchell's eye for the spectacular, during a Cup-winning campaign which many believe was the zenith of a glorious Magpies career. The Scot came up with the winner again away to Swansea in the fourth round, scoring the only goal of the game – and his determined performance that day, rising above the clatter to prove his class in the face of a murderous physical onslaught from the Welsh side, was testament to a courage not usually found in gifted wing wizards.

Perhaps that determination, that strength of character, helped Mitchell pass the Cup final test with flying colours three times in a black and white shirt. Having scored 11 times in three triumphant FA Cup campaigns, his performances in three victorious FA Cup finals – 1951, 1952 and 1955 – arguably put him on a higher level as a cult hero than more modern-day icons such as Kevin Keegan, Peter Beardsley and Alan Shearer. In the 2-0 final victory over Blackpool in 1951, Mitchell earned praise from the following day's *Sunday Sun* for, along with Ernie Taylor, "injecting the defence with their respective brand of tremor inducement" and for showing various "gems from his artistic reportoire".

Twelve months later, Mitchell took centre-stage at Wembley, as he had done en route to the twin towers, creating the only goal for George Robledo which sunk a valiant effort from 10-man Arsenal.

The *Sunday Sun* declared that Mitchell's "incisiveness was responsible for disturbing a rearranged Arsenal defence to the extent of opening up one final flaw in marking – and this decided the game". The Scots winger had played with a strapping to support a hushed-up midweek training injury, but it did little to curtail his performance.

Robledo would later give Mitchell much credit for setting up that match-winning goal, in a typically crafty fashion. "I saw Bobby's pass coming over as I moved in," said the Chilean striker, "and there was only one place I could nod it. Bobby fooled them. They thought he was going to shoot and tried to anticipate it."

Fast forward three years later, and the Scottish winger enjoyed probably his finest Wembley performance in a 3-1 win over Manchester City, scoring a glorious second goal and creating the third for George Hannah after Jackie Milburn's first-minute opener had been cancelled out by City.

The *Sunday Sun* hailed "maestro Mitchell's knockout goal in 53 minutes", adding that "five minutes later, Mitchell, who had very nearly done a Stan Matthews act in response to delightful service from Scoular and Hannah, said, 'thank you' by laying on the final score for his inside partner."

Mitchell's twisting runs, fed on superb service from Jimmy Scoular in particular, proved the scourge of the City defence, and he even contributed to United's numerical advantage when City right-back Jimmy Meadows limped off with ligament damage in the 18th minute, sustained while trying to follow a body swerve from his opposite number.

In 1952, Mitchell's Arsenal marker Wally Barnes had also injured himself and had to leave the field before half-time – meaning two out of three of his direct Wembley opponents failed to last 45 minutes! "But I claim 100 per cent responsibility on only one of them," said Mitchell, 35 years later. "Jimmy Meadows of Manchester City in '55. I went as if to cross the ball, then feinted the other way and Jimmy tried to turn with me, but his knee turned the wrong way and his ligaments went."

MITCHELL'S GOAL IN '55 capped an awesome display, and all the winger's native cunning was in evidence as he became one of the few players to beat City's legendary German keeper Bert Trautmann on his near post. The *Sunday Sun* match report read: "White made a fine cross to Mitchell, who beat close-marking Spurdle 'on a sixpence', deceived

Trautmann into expecting a cross, and from within a foot of the byline rammed in an eight-yarder between the keeper and the near post".

It was a case of cometh the hour, cometh the Flying Scotsman – and Jackie Milburn apart, nobody did more to bring that famous FA Cup to Tyneside three times in the glorious 50s.

But the reasons for Mitchell's enduring esteem on Tyneside do not end in May 1955, even if that Wembley win over Manchester City would be his last taste of silverware. Five and a half years later, he was still wowing the crowds as a 36-year-old, stealing the show as he made two (for Gordon Hughes and Len White) and scoring two himself to bring United back from behind to clinch an epic 4-4 draw with Wolves. "Here," read the *Journal* match report, "on the rain-soaked Gallowgate turf, we saw him perform as dramatic a left-wing rescue act as fiction could endure." Mitchell's feats that day, 15 October 1960, prompted a spontaneous pitch invasion in which the hero of the hour was mobbed by United's delirious fans.

The player's battle for a regular starting berth under Charlie Mitten – a manager who never fully took to the talented Scot – had by then long been a subject of frustration to supporters, and they made a powerful demonstration of where their loyalties lay on the St James' Park turf.

The following day's *Sunday Sun* takes up the tale: "What a scene it was after that second goal. More than 100 youngsters swarmed on to the field. Mitchell went on to the floor under their rapturous celebrations. But the sight at the final whistle was even more stirring when the crowd stormed on to the field to pay homage to his skill... Such a happy ending for Mitchell – the man described by a manager (who shall be nameless) as 'that high-stepper'. If it had not been for him, I doubt whether Newcastle would have been in the hunt. For the truth is that they just did not click, except when Mitchell was weaving the patterns."

The paper was prompted to ask: "Just why is Bobby Mitchell being cold-shouldered so much at St James' Park?"

Mitchell, although suffering at times with an ankle injury, was also frequently dropped in the last two years of his United career. And, like that of so many of the club's feted stars over the decades, his reign on Tyneside did not have a happy ending – after that Wolves match, he would last just eight more months in a black and white shirt before being given a free transfer to Berwick Rangers. Despite being just two months shy of his 37th birthday at the time, he still felt betrayed by Mitten's decision not to offer him a new deal – and the fact that the Press were told of this before he was. "I thought I was used to shocks until I read the news last weekend that Newcastle United will not stand in my way if I can get another job in soccer," he told the *Journal* in March, 1961. "I don't mind confessing that this information came as a complete surprise and really rocked me. For only 24 hours earlier I had turned down offers from York City and Halifax Town, pretty confident that I could still be of further service at St James' Park."

That refusal to join York prompted the first proper fall-out with Mitten – but Mitchell would later claim that he knew the writing was on the wall for him as soon as the new manager had been appointed in the summer of '58. "It was when Charlie Mitten arrived that I knew I was at the end of the line," said Mitchell, who for the first time in his career would be regularly moved out of his favoured left wing role to play in midfield and at wing-half during his final seasons on Tyneside.

Mitchell – never a big fan of tactics or managers who 'interfered' too much on the playing side – did not warm to the modernist, thorough approach of a team boss full of innovative coaching ideas, whose success never matched his energy during three years at St James'. The low point – although Mitchell would later laugh at the memory – came during an away match against Cardiff in 1961, when Mitten's new 4-2-4 system, tried out once in a training ground win over the United juniors, brought chaos and a two-goal deficit within 10 minutes.

"This 'victory' was enough to convince Mitten that we had found the secret of the new style overnight," said Mitchell. "It was announced to a party of mystified players that we would be employing the new 4-2-4 at Cardiff.

"We kicked off and after 10 minutes, when we were 2-0 down, and reduced to a complete shambles, there were frantic signals from the bench to revert to the normal way of playing. It was an incredible experience. Nobody knew who was marking who or who was supposed to be playing where. It was complete confusion." The game ended in a 3-2 defeat.

Mitchell, who had played such a pivotal role in the most successful Newcastle spell of the modern era, could have been forgiven for wanting out as United finished 17th, 19th and 21st in three of his final years on Tyneside. But his loyalty, and love of playing for United, kept him motivated to the end. Like local lads Jackie Milburn and Alan Shearer, pulling on the black and white shirt every week was reward enough in itself. Indeed, the Glaswegian was the last survivor of the famous Cup-winning heroes when he finally joined Berwick on a free in 1961.

AS A CLUB, Newcastle has long held a reputation for getting under the skin of its players – with the almost unique experience of playing in front of such a passionate crowd providing the highlight of many a footballer's career. Indeed, all 20 players in this book have relished the challenge of performing in a region obsessed with the beautiful game – and their self-confessed love of Newcastle United has endeared them all to supporters. Most recently Irishman Damien Duff has cited that passion for the game, and the need for him to rediscover it after a spell at robotic Chelsea, as the reason why he swapped the glamour of West London for Tyneside.

However, there are surely none who loved the club more than Mitchell. After all, this is a man who believes his obsession with everything black and white even cost him a successful international career. The stature of Liverpool winger Billy Liddell is often hailed as the number one reason for Mitchell's paltry return of two Scottish caps, but Mitchell himself, although he scored on his debut against Denmark in 1951, believes that his failure to impress was largely down to the fact that he could not settle away from Newcastle United. He played two years at Berwick, then spent three as player-manager at non-league Gateshead, and told the *Evening Chronicle* in 1990: "My career was over when I finished at Newcastle. Emotionally, I couldn't play anywhere else. After what I'd had at Newcastle, there was no other place to be at all. I didn't enjoy Gateshead, but that wasn't Gateshead's fault. I simply could not enjoy football anywhere else. The same thing happened on the couple of occasions I was picked for my country. I didn't feel right emotionally – because it wasn't Newcastle. It didn't seem right. And the Scottish players looked on me as an Anglo, because I was playing south of the border, and hardly spoke to me. I felt like a stranger up there…it was the old Anglo thing, but I didn't enjoy international football. I used to get out on the pitch and say 'God, I wish I was back at Newcastle'."

Indeed, Mitchell's heartfelt happiness at United, and living in his adopted Geordie homeland, is not only the key to his iconic status among fans who shared his love of all things black and white – it also provides a clue to the secret behind the Magpies' glorious 50s heyday.

Long after he finished playing, having settled in North Tyneside, the ever-approachable Mitchell would make himself available to the local media, providing some fascinating insights into the culture of the club in their FA Cup-winning years. With 'manager' Stan Seymour largely leaving team-talks up to skipper Joe Harvey, and a very close knit bunch of self-motivating, larger-than-life characters, Mitchell revelled in an all-star team for the 1951 and '52 Cup wins and he thrived in a relaxed atmosphere in which ball-playing superstars were allowed a bit of freedom on and off the pitch. It's an approach – like the spontaneous joy of celebratory pitch invasions, or Jackie Milburn's regular motorbike trips to work at the pit with Len Shackleton riding pillion – which now seems outmoded and even foolhardy in the 21st century. But in the 1950s, this managerial philosophy worked a treat – with United, quite deliberately, saving their best performances for the trophy they won three times in five years.

"Being at Newcastle United in those marvellous 50s was an honour, a joy and a privilege," he said, three years before his death. "A wonderful team developed – the sort of team you will only see once in a lifetime. There was no weakness anywhere in the side. The football we played was second to none. Off the field, all the players were great friends. No animosity, no troubles. Everyone at Newcastle United laughed a lot. Every player was a character in his own right. The crowds we attracted were huge – and magnificent. What I got from playing for Newcastle then is something to be treasured forever. And I do treasure the memory. In the 50s, Bernard Joy, the great Arsenal player, tried to persuade me to join them. He went on at me all through a Chelsea FC dinner in London and finally said: 'You'd be playing for the best club in Britain'. I turned to him and said: 'I'm already playing for the best club in Britain', and I meant it."

Newcastle fans have grown used, over the years, to being patronised by players paying lip service to their sterling support – but those words from Mitchell strike a deeper chord than most. This was a man who simply adored the club, and served it for 13 seasons as proof, even though – like Shearer four decades later – he could have enjoyed his pick of the biggest clubs in the land.

BUT LOYAL SERVANT though he was, Mitchell was no goody-two-shoes – some of his escapades would make the likes of Milburn and Shearer blush. Indeed, despite his even temper and natural modesty, he was, behind the scenes, a fully-paid up member of the Magpies' maverick club – adding his own colourful ingredients into the mix of strong characters which he regarded as crucial to the team spirit and success of United in the early 50s.

Mitchell once nearly found himself recruited for the Romanian Secret Police team in 1957 when, on a close season tour, he verbally agreed the move after enjoying too much of the strong local brew! Shocked club director Stan Seymour had to stand firm the next day when Romanian officials came to finalise the deal, insisting there had been a misunderstanding.

Seymour by then had become used to getting players out of scrapes – and Mitchell, together with Bobby Corbett, had in particular caused him grief just two days before that first triumphant FA Cup final appearance at Wembley in 1951. The pair had gone out drinking without permission – avoiding an official evening of entertainment in the team's Buxton hotel – and many clubs would surely have reacted more sternly, by dropping the pair from the Cup final line-up. Mitchell, though, believes such high jinx merely helped team spirit – as he told the *Sunday Sun* in 1961. "Stan Seymour was threatening me 'You can ruddy well go back to Newcastle.' I was replaying: 'Who cares? What's an English Cup final to a Scotsman?' Even now I see that scene as clearly as when it happened 10 years ago. I can see it – and laugh. Just as Stan Seymour will do…And why not? Laughing was one of the things Newcastle United did a lot of during my happy years there. Newcastle's players and management weren't just footballers – we were cavaliers. And like all adventurers, we were frequently getting into scrapes. We lived hard, and played harder. We were great in ability and more importantly, greater in spirit."

Mitchell decided to face the music head-on that night in Buxton – unlike Corbett, who crept up to his room, where Seymour and trainer Norman Smith found him 10 minutes later lying in bed and pretending to be asleep!

Having duly recovered to win the Cup – alongside Corbett – Mitchell also fondly recalled taking the field in the last league match of the 1950/51 season at Wolves, having "celebrated in every local hostelry" the night before the game. He added: "When we took that Wolves field the next day, I'll swear not one of us was a true example of sobriety. But what a fantastic game! Wolves attacked and attacked and attacked, but they couldn't score…Then, to rub things in, we went up and scored, minutes from the end, and won!"

Further testament to the carnival-like atmosphere of which keen crooner Mitchell was a part, came in the team's regular singing sessions on away trips. "We were always singing," said the Scotsman, "with Bobby Cowell leading in 'Keep right on to the end of the road', Joe Harvey in 'Blaydon Races' and Stan Seymour in 'Inky Dinky Do'."

If only *Celebrity Stars in their Eyes* had been around in the 50s…

INTERESTINGLY, MITCHELL WAS, in retrospect, keen to stress the important part played by Seymour in fashioning such a determined, all-star line-up, highlighting what a few critics in retrospect have earmarked as a managerial weakness – his lack of tactical involvement – as one of the secrets of United's success. Before the 1951 final, for example, Mitchell remembers that the manager simply said in the dressing room: "I'm not going to tell you how to play – that's your job. You wouldn't be playing for Newcastle today if you weren't good enough. Now go out and do your stuff!"

It certainly seems a far cry from Jose Mourinho's detailed dossiers, but Seymour's stand-offish style was tailor-made for those players and those times. Professionally, and despite six barren years without a trophy from 1955 onwards, Mitchell could not have been more fulfilled at Newcastle, insisting he was as privileged as any footballer could be to play in front of the St James' Park crowd for so long. But those supporters' hearts would twice go out to their hero after tragedies in his private life.

Mitchell himself had already survived three car crashes – one which also involved Jackie Milburn and another when he had to be rescued from a mangled phone box after being hit by a car while using a pay phone – when his 22-year-old son Alan was killed in a collision on the Felling by-pass in 1970. Ten years later, his five-month-old young grandson Wayne, son of Mitchell's daughter Julie, was found dead in his pram, a suspected victim of cot death syndrome. "Wayne's birth helped me get over the death of Alan," the ex-player said at the time. "We just hope we can slowly get over this loss now."

When Mitchell himself passed away, aged 68, he left many thousands of fans with cherished memories. He was a keen golfer, crossword addict, singer and family man – but, for United supporters, most of all he was a brilliant, and brilliantly effective, footballer. Touched by the same brush which painted the genius of Len Shackleton, Mitchell proved a superior big-match player to the Yorkshireman, and stands with only a handful of United idols who managed to deliver when it mattered most. As the *Sunday Sun* said upon his death in 1993: "Glasgow-born Mitchell was a supreme entertainer with mesmeric ball skills. But three FA Cup wins were testament that on the big occasion he had nerves of steel."

In terms of service, Mithcell's 13 years on Tyneside means he stands second only to Jackie Milburn (14 years) for longevity among the 20 cult heroes in this book. His loyalty – ignoring overtures from the likes of Arsenal to forego silverware in the second half of his career – also contrasts sharply with the choices made by the likes of Paul Gascoigne and Peter Beardsley in the mid-80s. Of course, football was a different game by then, with transfers ever easier and more frequent and loyalty a dying concept.

But still, it is a fact that Mitchell was much lauded on the terraces for the way in which he accepted – indeed relished – playing for a side which, as often as not, was fighting at the wrong end of the table in the late 50s. He readily acknowledged that, with the break-up of the 1955 Cup-winning side, he knew the glory years had, for him at least, gone for good. Yet he still found intense pleasure in pulling on the black and white shirt and playing for a team whose chances of success were wrecked by rivalries and in-fighting – in the dressing and boardrooms, almost throughout the second half of his Tyneside sojourn.

IN HIS POST-PLAYING years as a publican on Tyneside – landlord of the Cradlewell in Jesmond and the Lochside in Heaton – and then as an occasional media critic, Mitchell remained a much-loved figure in the region up to his death. In 1973, a *Journal* feature on the former Magpies favourite revealed that he was regularly regaled with pub-goers' memories of his finest moments in a black and white shirt – even if Mitchell himself could not remember them all! "There are many moments which he forgets," read the piece. "When a fan drops in at the Cradlewell to recall some Mitchell majesty which his firmly imprinted on his mind, he often discovers that his hero cannot recall the moment or the movement the fan is reconstructing."

There were, after all, so many.

A massive 41,000 crowd, and a plethora of all-star United players, turned up for Mitchell's St James' Park testimonial in 1961 – a massive figure for a benefit game and testament to the affection in which the Glaswegian was held. Much of that affection was afforded the player in return for magical memories of a man who played the game with style and flair. "All right, so I fiddled!" joked Mitchell once in response to the occasional criticism that, in his individualism, he could occasionally be a frustrating player. "Seriously, however, I have always preferred the purists of soccer. The game is an entertainment and the spectators want to see clever work."

Clever work, goals a-plenty, laughs galore – Mitchell provided all of that, and despite the odd brush with management and his fondness for the odd pint, he did so with a committed approach and modest outlook on the game which endeared him to the faithful. The man who presented his testimonial cheque in 1961, Sir James Bowman, declared: "Your popularity on Tyneside rests not only on your performances on the field. You have been able to carry your popularity and greatness with modesty and dignity off the field. Newcastle fans are very discerning, and I think the way you have carried yourself entitles you to be described as 'Ambassador of Soccer'."

Another nickname for the collection, then.

Len White

1953-1962: 270 games, 153 goals

IN NEWCASTLE UNITED'S Hall of Fame, a stocky miner lurks in the shadows – ready to spring forward and grab the limelight, as he did in his epic playing days. So many of the Magpies' legendary figures are strikers – names such as Gallacher, Milburn, Macdonald and Shearer spring readily to mind, of course. But to many of those who watched and adored White in his pomp, none can match him.

As a person, the uncapped White was far from typical cult hero material and as a deep-lying No. 9, very different to the traditional battering-ram British centre-forward. But his strength, determination, pace and prodigious footballing gifts put him on a pedestal on Tyneside, and provided him with the sort of iconic status which amazed and moved him.

A full 29 years after his departure from United, White admitted he was stunned by the fervour which greeted a belated North East testimonial, played at the ground of non-league Whitley Bay in 1989. He told the *Journal*:

> "I'm a Geordie at heart and I feel like a king when I come up here. I started coming up three years ago for talk-ins and the reception I got was fantastic. I thought I would be a forgotten man.

"It was the same at my testimonial dinner a few weeks ago. The reception I got – I've never known anything like it in my life. There were so many things I wanted to say but couldn't because I had a lump in my throat the size of a football. I was so overcome at the welcome."

If Len White was stirring emotions of older Newcastle supporters in the late 1980s, they were only repaying a favour from the 1950s. After a couple of others had tried and failed, White was the man charged, after being brought in from the wing, with the unenviable task of filling Jackie Milburn's boots in the No. 9 shirt – and he rose to the occasion in dynamic, crowd-thrilling style, scoring 105 goals in 131 games as a No 9, before injury effectively wrecked his Magpies career. That strike-rate, of over 80 per cent and without taking penalties, goes a long way to explaining White's legend on Tyneside.

Including his early days as a winger, White scored 153 times in black and white – a total only bettered by Shearer and Milburn in the club's history. Consider, too, that so many of those goals were spectacular efforts – the result of long, mazy dribbles and long-range rocket shots, and it is not difficult to understand the adulation this modest Yorkshireman was afforded at Gallowgate. Had TV been around in sufficient proportions to capture White's stupendous striking power, Malcolm Macdonald may have found himself branded 'the new Len White'.

WHITE'S EXCITING BRAND of irrepressible attacking football was just what the Geordie paying public have always craved. United's highly-rated inside forward Ivor Allchurch – one of the most celebrated Welsh players in history and, along with George Eastham, provider-in-chief to White – picked him as the best player he had ever encountered, while long-term Newcastle United correspondent Ken McKenzie, who covered the club over five decades for the *Journal* and *Sunday Sun* newspapers, even put the 5ft 7in striker above two giants of the past in Gallacher and White's direct predecessor Milburn.

"I have been reporting United football for about 45 years," McKenzie wrote in 1973, "and say deliberately that White, while at his peak and playing in the No. 9 shirt, can fairly be nominated as the finest centre-forward and goal-getter in Magpie history." McKenzie added:

"Sweet memory recalls the late Hughie Gallacher of the 1920s as the greatest... And, of course, I am not forgetting the immense claims of Jackie Milburn... But I doubt if I'm alone, among United supporters of the 50s and early 60s, in rating Len White as worthy of very close comparison to these two greats."

For McKenzie, White got the nod "for his bee-line for goal and confidence to take the ball past one, two, three rivals by sheer balance and craft". Team-mate Charlie Woods was another who rated White even ahead of Milburn, explaining: "Jackie Milburn would go past opponents with sheer pace, but Lennie did it with pace and skill."

Like his friend and mentor Milburn, White had begun his career as a winger and this background, though it meant a slow start in his ascent towards superstardom at United, undoubtedly added greatly to his unique striking tactics. Shunning the goal-poaching style of many out-and-out strikers, White would often outsmart rather than outfight defenders by ranging deep and wide to collect the ball. Good with both feet, although naturally right-footed, White's prodigious leap made him a surprising force in the air, while his vision, passing and sublime finishing marked him out as one of the most complete footballing centre-forwards in the game.

But perhaps most tellingly, the pocket dynamo had the pace, confidence and ball skills to run right at the heart of defence – a knack which would quicken the pulse of his many thousands of United followers. With a smooth hip swerve and prodigious change of pace, his ability to create goals out of nothing had the St James' Park crowd on the edge of their seats. Like Peter Beardsley 30 years later, White is fondly remembered for a legacy of sensational goals – and the excitement he brought to his near-decade in black and white has been fondly remembered by contemporaries ever since. Lifelong United fan Steve Smart, 58, who now resides in Somerset, is one believer: "During his peak for or five seasons at No. 9 White was, and remains, for me not just the best NUFC striker of my time (I only saw Milburn a couple of times at the end), but the best centre-forward I've ever seen. He was miles better than the likes of Macdonald and Shearer. You have to appreciate his all-round abilities and entertainment value as a striker. He could score any type of goal you could possibly imagine –short-range, long-range shots (he once scored a stunner from the left wing with the from about 25 yards against Wolves), and headers of all kinds as he had a prodigious leap for a short man. But most of all he was loved for his brilliant individual goals scored after amazing, weaving, dribbling runs past defences."

The strike Smart refers to against Wolves, which bounced back off the stanchion, was hailed at the time by opposition manager Stan Cullis as the best he had ever seen. But a string of contenders would come to mind for regular White-watchers.

"I once saw him score a goal against Spurs," said Smart. "Where he started off with the ball in the centre circle and proceeded to go past the entire Spurs defence before shooting past the advancing keeper. Unforgettable!" Even allowing for nostalgic exaggeration, it is indisputable that White was capable of creating wonderful goals from nothing – a talent which stirred echoes of Gallacher to older supporters in the 50s, and would bring White's name up when Peter Beardsley worked his magic three decades later. They were three strikers linked by genius across eight decades.

White's goal at home to Manchester City in April 1958 is another which earned rave reviews. That 4-1 win helped Newcastle to avoid being sucked into relegation trouble, and *Journal* correspondent McKenzie was in no doubt who was the star. "A solo dribble by Len White from 15 yards inside his own half ending with a great 12-yard shot into the net past the advancing Bert Trautmann – the best goalkeeper in football – made memorable the burial of the relegation blues in the St James' Park floodlights," he wrote. "In the 55th minute, the crowd's roar positively tore holes in the atmosphere as White came away for his wonder-goal."

The *Evening Chronicle* declared: "Over 50,000 spectators roared their appreciation and in a football flash, Len White became a Magpie hero."

GIVEN HIS AWESOME reputation, it is astonishing looking back to note that White was never capped once by his country. He was famously and often referred to as the greatest uncapped centre-forward in English football – a claim backed up by contemporaries such as Jackie Milburn and Johnny Haynes. Milburn believed White's lack of height was the reason, but plain old-fashioned anti-northern bias from the England selectors proved a more popular theory. Former team-mate Vic Keeble once said: "I swear that if he had been playing in the south, he would have been an England regular."

Anti-North East bias was seen by many observers as the reason why the legendary Jackie Milburn earned only 13 England caps, and it certainly seemed easier to catch selectors' eyes in London back in the 1950s.

Journal writer McKenzie, pointing to White's impeccable goal-scoring form between 1957 and 1961, commented: "No one could convince me that over those four years little Len was not worth capping. In a London team he's have walked into the England side."

White would later blame the horror tackle which put him out of the game for six months – and robbed him of some of his legendary pace – as critical in wrecking his England chances. But in truth, he should have been capped much, much earlier. A seven-minute hat-trick for the Football League against the Irish League should have strengthened his chances, after all! That feat, with goals in the 50th, 53rd and 57th minutes, came in a 5-2 win at Anfield on 12 November 1958, and White, like all true showmen, had saved his best till last - a 30-yard dash through the heart of defence finished off with a firm shot on the run.

White would later recall that his great friend Ray Wilson – who went on to win the World Cup with England eight years later and who would sadly preside over White's cremation in his capacity as a Huddersfield funeral director – described the Yorkshireman's performance that day as the best he had ever seen.

White did play one more time for the Football League, a 1-0 win over the Scottish League, and he had two FA appearances under his belt – against the Army and RAF – from his days with Rotherham in 1951, but his lack of due international recognition caused him regret long after his career was over. "Even one cap would have done me. It would have meant so much," he said.

Those words reveal so much about the true motivation of a player who simply lived to play football. Indeed, White's lack of a cap seems incredible in the 21st century, when players such as Kieron Dyer have found the doors to international football open so easily despite question marks over their own form, fitness and approach to the game.

White stands as one of only two players – alongside Joe Harvey – in this book who failed to win full international honours, yet his lack of international status did nothing to dull a stellar career on Tyneside. White's other misfortune – although this is a common one among

Newcastle cult heroes – was lack of silverware. His one trophy win in black and white – the 1955 FA Cup – is still one more than many terrace heroes at United and his individual achievements, coming as they did against the backdrop of a stuttering club side, are all the more remarkable because of that.

Although his greatest success as a striker would come later, White still played a major part in that 1955 success. White had been part of the Second Division Rotherham side which had knocked out United, as holders, in the third round of the FA Cup in 1953 – and had arrived at St James' Park the following month when Newcastle boss Stan Seymour was rebuffed in his attempts to sign the Tykes' senior winger, Jack Grainger. But Grainger's young understudy was destined for much greater things on Tyneside than even Seymour can have imagined – starting with some vital contributions to that 1955 Cup win. White scored a priceless equaliser in the quarter-final against Huddersfield, then added United's second in the 2-0 semi-final replay against York to book the Magpies' place in the Wembley showpiece.

Those efforts seemed enough to guarantee White's involvement in the final, but he only made it by the skin of his teeth. Manager Duggie Livingstone had White in his original line-up, but not Jackie Milburn, and he planned to drop the Yorkshireman when the Newcastle directors insisted Milburn must play. In the end White was given a reprieve when a sudden attack of tonsillitis ruled out Reg Davies on the eve of the final. United fans had early reason to be thankful for the presence of both players when White provided the corner for Milburn to head home after just 45 seconds. It was the fastest goal in Cup final history at the time – and an early springboard for a 3-1 success, with White also providing what the *Sunday Sun* described as "a beautifully placed cross" for Bobby Mitchell to score Newcastle's second.

White, who had to play most of the final with an ankle injury, would later admit that his apparently pinpoint ball to Milburn had been an underhit attempt to reach Vic Keeble at the far post! The modesty of that confession was typical of the man. An exciting crowd-thriller though he was on the field of play, White's approach to life off it was in stark contrast, and the warmth of affection he generated in the North East long after his playing days was in no small part down to his affable personality. A quiet man who could barely fathom the adulation he encountered on Tyneside, White was a very different animal to the likes of Gallacher and Macdonald – and was an altogether shyer figure than his immediate predecessor in the fans' affections, the warm and witty Jackie Milburn.

However White did once evoke memories of Gallacher's pre-match fondess for a pint when he – unwittingly – took the field with a bellyful of ale to face Arsenal in April 1954. Incredibly, he regards his performance that day as critical to his United career, insisting: "After that, I became more of a regular". Not expecting to play, the then 24-year-old had nipped to the Windmill Arms, a pub near his Fenham home, for a few pre-match beers with his brother, before heading to St James' Park to watch the action – only to find that an injury to Jackie Milburn and the non-appearance of stand-in Billy Foulkes had unexpectedly pushed him up the pecking order. "There I was, full of beer and getting ready to play Arsenal. From the dressing room, you could hear the team being announced over the loudspeakers and when they came to my name, I heard the crowd grumbling and murmuring. "So I thought I would show them what I could do and went out really determined. If I say it myself, I played pretty well that day and we murdered Arsenal – mighty Arsenal – 5-2."

WHITE SCORED IN the game (the other goals coming from George Hannah and a Reg Davies hat-trick), and his on-pitch achievements would soon make it all the harder for him to avoid the limelight. Indeed, the more this homespun superstar shunned the playboy lifestyle, the more the crowd loved him for it.

Journal features editor Tony Henderson, a childhood disciple of White's, would write in adulthood that "Len holds a special place in the affections of tens of thousands of fans because of his outstanding footballing ability, modesty and dignity". His working-class background certainly helped. White, although not a Geordie, settled seamlessy into North East life as a miner at Burradon colliery in Northumberland. In the early part of his Newcastle career, before the advent of full-time professional wages, White's hard-grafting lifestyle gave him an instant affinity with those on the terraces. A family man and father of six, White may have been a quiet man off the pitch – yet the physical resilience he showed against the country's roughest defenders could come in handy when his famous patience was stretched to the limit. Team-mate Charlie Woods was on hand for one such occasion and he later recounted the tale of how White dealt – rather emphatically – with a troublemaker on the bus home from training from Newcastle to Fenham.

Yet if White was tough, he could also be insecure – and self-doubt may help to explain why his Newcastle career had been such a relative slow-burner until the winter of 1957. Having made his debut against Liverpool in the latter part of the 1952/53 season, he would make just 13 more appearances in the following campaign, and after four and a half years at the club spent largely as an out-and-out winger or inside-right, had scored less than 40 goals. Compare and contrast that with seasonal tallies of 25, 25, 29 and 29 when White was firmly ensconced in the centre-forward's role from 1957 to 1961.

The player himself – far removed from the cockiness of striking successors such as Malcolm Macdonad, Kevin Keegan and Alan Shearer – would later claim that his slow start was down to a lack of self-belief Asked by *Sunday Sun* sportswriter Geoff Whitten to explain why he did not show his exceptional ability earlier, he said: "I don't know, lack of confidence as much as anything, I suppose. I seemed to play quite well in practice matches, but as soon as I got out in front of the public things seemed to go wrong." Whitten had written in early December 1957 that "his displays had been lacking in spirit and confidence".

There were other theories. *Evening Chronicle* sportswriter Harold Palmer, upon White's selection for the Football League in 1958, noting it would be a first representative game since an FA XI appearance seven years previously, wrote:

> "If there is any explanation for this strange interval in the wilderness, it may lie in the fact that for 10 years after leaving school at the age of 16 White worked in the pits. Only in the last two years has he been able to apply himself to full-time training. The result? He doubled his scoring rate last season and has doubled it again this season."

Yet plenty of scribes believed White's hard-working background as a miner was integral to his success on the pitch – helping to forge him into one of the fittest, toughest strikers in the game. "White was not born, but mined", was a common reflection among supporters and although not a violent player, he was certainly difficult to shake off the ball. The result was that, despite occasional flashes of brilliance from the right wing – including a four-goal first-half haul against Aston Villa in 1954 – few Newcastle fans deemed White capable of filling Jackie Milburn's considerable boots when the Geordie left Newcastle for Linfield in the summer of 1957.

For the next few months White was involved in a four-way battle for the No. 9 shirt with Arthur Bottom, and local lads Alex Tait and Bill Curry – and he would hail a two-goal showing in a 3-0 win over West Brom just before Christmas as the turning point in swinging the fight his way. White also hit the woodwork three times in a scintillating display and would never look back in four spectacular goal-laden seasons until an untimely intervention by Tottenham's Dave Mackay cut him down in his prime. The tackle which wrecked his ankle ligaments was, by all accounts, a shocker – and White admitted he was never the same player again.

Jackie Milburn – watching from the stands as a fan on that fateful London night – declared: "I reckon that Mackay's tackle was the worst I have ever seen".

White himself recalled: "I nipped in for a short corner and Dave Mackay came from behind and felled me. I ended up in a heap and had to be carried off and have my boot cut off. Everyone was delighted my ankle wasn't broken but in hindsight it would have been better if it had been, because the torn ligaments were a mess. I was out for a long time before making a comeback after we'd gone down to the Second Division and even scored a hat-trick against Bristol Rovers, but it never felt the same again."

White believed he had been on course at the time to beat Hughie Gallacher and George Robledo's record 39-goal haul for the season, and his biggest fans insist that, had he not been felled at White Hart Lane, he would have left the club as indisputably its best ever striker. For struggling Newcastle, who had pulled off THE shock of the 1960-61 season by beating Bill Nicholson's double-winning Spurs side 2-1 at White Hart Lane in that fateful game, White's injury had a more immediate, and devastating effect. Robbed of their star striker, United lost momentum in their battle against relegation, and broke the hearts of their supporters – still furious to a man at Mackay's tackle – by dropping into Division Two. "Dave Mackay was a good player and had no need to play like that," said White years later, remembering the tackle from behind which ruptured his ankle ligaments. "He later wrote in his book it was an accident, but let me just say when I was being carted off to hospital at Tottenham that day, their manager Bill Nicholson came up to me and said: 'I'm sorry Len, I didn't tell him to play like that'. Sadly it was never the same again, Newcastle went down and things broke up. But nothing can ever take away the memories of the great days at Newcastle United."

WHITE HAD PROVEN to be the United fans' saviour from relegation once before, in the 1957/58 season when, after that pivotal December performance against West Brom, he rattled in 19 goals in 16 games, and 22 league goals in total, to leave United clear of the drop zone on goal average. Fittingly, he completed the job by scoring the goal against Manchester United that finally ensured survival. "Stocky Len White is the hero of Newcastle United's successful relegation struggle," declared the *Evening Chronicle* on 24 April, "his amazing scoring sequence has been largely responsible for United finishing in the clear."

White's disciples had no doubt he was on course to repeat the trick three years later, having scored 29 goals before being carried off the White Hart Lane pitch.

But United won only twice in their last eight games without their talisman. Despite the unhappy ending of relegation, that bizarre 1960/61 season was as memorable as any for the stocky Yorkshireman, as he almost single-handedly battled the inadequacies of the worst defence in Division One.

A hat-trick in a 3-2 home win over Preston started Newcastle off as they meant to go on, then White found the net again in a 7-2 win over Fulham, twice in a 5-0 win against Cardiff, once in a 4-4 home draw with Wolves and bagged a brace in the 4-3 defeat to Tottenham. In all Newcastle scored a respectable 86 goals, but conceded 109, and defeats such as 6-1 to Chelsea, 6-0 to West Brom and 5-3 at Burnley left one newspaper lampooning the United backline by depicting the Magpies' goalposts, complete with automatic goal meters fitted.

Like Paul Gascoigne a quarter of a century later, White was finding that his best efforts were constantly hampered by the ordinariness of many of the players around him. But if circumstance prevented him matching the trophy haul of United's Victorian greats, or even early 50s heroes such as Milburn and Bobby Mitchell, the crowd loved him none the less for it. Indeed, hopes were high that White's goals would fire the Magpies back into the top flight and herald a new era on Tyneside. His recovery from injury, after six months on the sidelines, however, was never quite complete. Six goals from 19 Division Two appearances in 1961/62 might have been respectable enough for some, but it was clear to those who had followed White's career closely that he had lost some of his legendary sharpness. "Since his injury in March, the free-scoring centre-forward has failed to strike anything like his true form," said the *Evening Chronicle* in December, and two months later, White and his supporters were heart-broken at an inevitable parting of the ways.

IT SEEMS INCREDIBLE now to recall that White, aged just 32, went to Huddersfield for the now little-known Scottish inside-forward Jimmy Kerray – and United had to pay £10,000 in cash to make up the deal. "I don't mind admitting I shed a few tears when Newcastle let me go," White said later, while the *Journal* declared: "All of Tyneside will regret that United were not in a position to bring off a Kerray deal without parting with White".

After Huddersfield, White moved to Stockport, Altrincham and Irish side Sligo Rovers. Spurred on by a lifelong enthusiasm for the game which proved one of the key ingredients to his legendary status on Tyneside, he played on into his 50s for a string of amateur sides in his native Yorkshire and his capacity for hard work and family life never left him either – he took a job with tractor manufacturers David Brown then worked at a chemical dye plant in Huddersfield before finally succumbing to the stomach cancer which claimed his life.

Falling a year short of the decade's service required for a testimonial match, White's earnings from the game were pitiful by today's standards – and some fans believe it was to Newcastle United's discredit that a 1989 benefit game in the North East, organised by Radio Tyneside sports presenter Barry Hindson, was held at non-league Whitley Bay's ground rather than at St James' Park.

White earned £9,400 from that and a series of talk-in events – less than half the gate receipts collected by utility player Kenny Wharton when his testimonial was hosted by United in the same year. Perhaps this fan's letter to a local newspaper 13 years earlier should have been heeded: "White made peanuts out of the game and wasn't granted a testimonial by United although he thrilled thousands like myself with his goals and sportsmanship," wrote J Hulme. "If White was granted a testimonial by United now I'm sure there would be a great turnout. How about it United?"

However, White, like so many of his era, was not strongly motivated by money – nor even the pursuit of silverware. As a loyal club servant for nine years, he admitted to feeling a touch bemused by the desire of players such as Chris Waddle, Peter Beardsley and Paul Gascoigne to leave his beloved Magpies in the 1980s. "I was really disappointed when they were relegated," he said after United dropped into Division Two in 1989. "When you look at the number of players who have been through their books, like Beardsley, Waddle and Gascoigne, who are now playing for England, it's tragic. But can you keep unhappy players in the team? I was never unhappy at United – we played for the love of it then, but I'd still love to be a player today."

White's biggest regret – even more, perhaps, than missing out on an England cap – was that Mackay's tackle brought his love affair with Newcastle to an end too soon. "I think I got some black and white blood in my veins when I was there," he once said, "memories too, the sort you never forget." The feeling was reciprocated, and Newcastle fans today – even those who have never seen him play – remain in thrall to White's legend, now 11 years after his death from cancer in 1994.

When it comes to star quality and heroic status, White, as one of the quietest of Newcastle's cult heroes, may just be edged out by the glamour of Gallacher and the charisma of Milburn, not to mention the self-assurance of Shearer.

But as an elusive, will-o-the-wisp striker, the purists adored his technical skills, and his rip-roaring dashes for goal delighted the masses. His misfortune – and another key reason why his name has never quite topped the summit of Newcastle giants - was to hit his personal peak in a very ordinary Newcastle team, which finished in the First Division's top ten only twice during his nine years at Gallowgate.

With better all-round class behind him, White's claims to being the best ever might just have become indisputable. As it is, put White with Green, Gascoigne, Beardsley and Gallagher as one of United's most magical on the pitch – yes, ahead of names like Milburn, Keegan and Shearer when it comes to pure ability. Fans were captivated by his desire to take players on, and few in United's history have brought such raw excitement to St. James' Park.

Finally, if you want any more convincing – White was my dear late father's favourite Newcastle player, and boy, did that man know his football.

Wyn Davies

1966-1971: 216 games, 53 goals

THE strange case of Wyn Davies is an absorbing tale which sheds light on the riddle of what makes a Newcastle United cult hero and it surely proves conclusively that it takes more than football ability.

Not even his biggest champions would claim that Davies was a true all-time great as a player; in truth he is easily overshadowed, in terms of his ability to master a football, by a whole host of names elsewhere in this book. And the likes of Hughie Gallacher, Albert Stubbins, Jackie Milburn, Len White, Malcolm Macdonald and Alan Shearer may all lay far stronger claims to the No. 9 shirt in Newcastle's mythical all-time XI. And yet, look closer at the enigmatic Welshman's United career and you may well agree that few names in the club's history have formed a stronger emotional bond with the black and white hordes.

The measure of the man in Tyneside's eyes is shown by the 85 per cent of fans who voted against his departure in a national newspaper survey in 1971, as their favourite son was about to leave for Manchester City – this despite the fact he had scored only two league goals the season before!

No, we will get nowhere if we measure Davies' weight in goals. The power of numbers may strengthen many a legend on Tyneside – Andy Cole being perhaps the purest example of an icon built almost purely on scoring success – but a return of 53 goals in 216 appearances from Davies does little to set the pulse racing.

If a picture is starting to emerge of an unlikely cult hero, then consider too:

- That Davies was a complex man, full of insecurities
- That he hated the limelight and was described by his own team-mates as "a loner"
- His ball control was at times much derided, even by Newcastle supporters
- He had a mercenary reputation and admitted he would go anywhere if the money was good
- And he had turned United down once before after haggling over a signing-on fee!

The case for the prosecution rests, and it is already clear that Davies was far from an identikit dream striker – or if he was, it was a strange sort of dream. Yet Davies, one of the most idiosyncratic centre-forwards ever to play for the Magpies, was perfect for his times, with the 1969 Fairs Cup win providing one of the most bizarre – and unexpectedly joyful, episodes in club history.

Here was a man struggling for league form who led a mid-table side (Newcastle had qualified for the Fairs Cup by finishing 10th, due to a one-club, one-city rule which meant all the teams above them could not qualify) to European glory. And they did it, despite the club's reputation for skilful attacking football, by resorting to route one.

UNDOUBTEDLY, THE SIMPLEST explanation for Davies' enduring esteem is the part he played in that trophy success – still United's last major trophy and their only continental honour. And it is true that all the major attributes of the Welshman's game were put to devastating effect across the continent that season, with club chairman Lord Westwood declaring that "Without Wyn Davies, United would never have won the Inter Cities Fairs Cup". But delve a little deeper into the Davies' on-pitch psyche and it is clear that those attributes – bravery, workrate, aggression and true brilliance in the air – would have turned him into a terrace hero irrespective of silverware. Throw in an innate ability to attract trouble, to spark incident, which lies at the heart of the Davies legend and the fact that, like Hughie Gallagher before him and Paul Gascoigne nearly 20 years later, things simply seemed to happen around Davies on the pitch, and he was never far away from a flashpoint. But out of that trio of mischief-makers, Davies stands alone as a man who seemed to undergo a dramatic transformation when he took the field.

While Gallacher and Gascoigne could create hell on and off the pitch, Davies was a quiet, at times anxious figure who saved his rabble-rousing for 3pm on a Saturday, his personality ballooning as he donned his striking white boots. Ruthlessly competitive, wildly emotive and painfully committed, Wyn Davies was the sort of player you could not take your eyes off – even when he was having a bad game. Whether he liked the attention or not (off the pitch he certainly didn't) Davies was a natural star on it, with real presence twinned with a religious work ethic. And opponents who were not ready to rise to the war-like challenge of containing this colossus were in for a rough ride.

Team skipper Bobby Moncur once declared: "It is not only a matter of what he can do with that head of his, but what influence he has on the other team. Often he destroys them almost before a ball is kicked." Davies was a master of engineering the sort of confrontational moments which get a crowd off the seats of their pants and passionately embroiled in a football encounter – and how the United fans loved him for it. This capacity for playing pantomime villain enlivened countless afternoons and evenings for Newcastle fans – and reached its zenith in a two-legged Fairs Cup tie in the autumn of 1970 against a mighty Inter Milan side chock full of Italian internationals who had helped their country to the World Cup final just a few months earlier. Men such as Roberto Boninsegna, Alessandro Mazzola, Tarcisio Burgnich and the legendary Giacinto Facchetti stood in United's path.

Davies had taken a battering from his marker Mario Giubertoni in the away leg, including one thigh-high tackle which led to a booking for the Italian and a United free-kick, from which Davies scored a header described in press reports as one of the best ever seen at the San Siro. United's crowd favourite then warmed up for the return leg by giving as good as he got in a running battle with Coventry's Ernie Machin at St James' – with Machin being sent off for one challenge on the Welshman, and Davies himself booked for retaliation.

But if one game encapsulated Davies the player, it was surely the home leg against Inter, where, in a furious and epic encounter, the Welshman lit the blue touch paper on those infamous Latin passions, resulting in a melée in which the referee was pole-axed and three policemen had to enter the field of play! Fouled by Inter keeper Lido Vieri, after Davies had feinted to charge him, the Welshman's reward was an indirect free-kick to United, while Vieri lost his cool and knocked the referee to the ground. With the Italian supporters – and players – rounding furiously on Newcastle's No. 9, Vieri was sent off for his trouble, while Davies' marker, Facchetti, decided to take his revenge with repeated and blatant kicks on the Welshman. The home crowd could barely contain themselves when one assault was followed up by team-mate Boninsegna, who punched Davies in the face, bloodying his nose. At this stage, even United's skipper Bobby Moncur thought things had gone too far – as Davies later recalled, "The great Facchetti marked me in the second leg – and what treatment he dished out," he said. "Bobby asked Joe [Harvey, manager] to bring me off at one stage for my own protection, but I told them I was staying on to see the job through . . . Bob and I both scored and we won 2-0."

The roar which greeted Davies' sweet revenge goal – completed despite a rather blatant body check from the Welshman inside the box – shook St. James' Park to its foundations, and left even the player's media critics, and they were numerous, paying fulsome tribute. "Wyn Davies is the type of soccer personality who will always steal the thunder and the cash from the more classic, but reserved players surrounding him," read the *Evening Chronicle*'s match summary. "Controversy courts Davies in a way which sets the cash register jangling and the fans talking. When so much happens to you so regularly, the amount of actual soccer skill you possess is not that important. You are a star, a personality, in a game with fewer and fewer personalities."

The supporters' love for Davies – an affair, perhaps, of the heart rather than the head – had never been more intense than after that wild Italian conquest.

Lifelong fan Rhys Younger was on the terraces that night, and he recalls it now as one of his most memorable games ever at St James' Park "Fachetti was as tall as Wyn and supposedly as tough - as well as notorious for dirty tricks. But Wyn played him off the park, winning everything in the air and never once reacting to the treatment he received. Wyn was a marvellously consistent player, and had much better close control than he was given credit for – I remember him winning a penalty in a derby with Sunderland at Roker Park after nutmegging Charlie Hurley. But that night against Inter Milan was his finest moment. He scored a great goal, despite all the abuse, and I recall a tear in my eye that night as I stood there clapping, watching him exchange shirts with the big Italian."

Despite such adulation, the player himself– 6ft 1in and 12 and a half stone of contradictions – actually contemplated jacking it all in at the height of his popularity. "I'm fed up with taking knocks," he said after the Inter Milan result. "I'm sick of it all."

Tyneside was not ready to lose its icon so quickly, though, and in manager Joe Harvey, they had a kindred spirit – a man who regarded Davies, with his wild crop of hair and distinctive Roman nose, as vital to the Newcastle cause. Harvey would later reveal that a player whose energy could barely be controlled on the pitch, needed a lot of cajoling off it. "He used to come into my office every week and plead to be dropped because he wasn't scoring goals," said the manager. "But he won us the Fairs Cup on his own – foreign teams were scared to bloody death of him."

There were, in truth, many long spells without goals – especially in the league, where his return of 40 in 191 games is comfortably the least impressive of any Newcastle striker in this book, but Davies' ability to hold the ball up and his combative playing style – often keeping two defenders busy to open up spaces for the likes of Albert Bennett and Pop Robson – created many more United openings. "Wyn did a great job for us," said Harvey, "and it isn't strictly fair to judge him on his goals record alone."

Yet many of the critics – even some of the club's own supporters – did, and Davies remains to this day a cult hero who can divide opinion like no other. Davies was hailed by the *Journal* in August 1971 as, "one of soccer's most controversial characters… he split the fans, who either wrote him off as a player who promised much and delivered little, or revered him as 'the king'."

One of Davies' problems – particularly among the press, who like to praise the artists who elevate the game they cover to a higher level – is that the Welshman was no purist. His aerial domination and physical style was largely responsible for the club adopting a route one approach which, while proving especially effective in the Fairs Cup, brought them few friends in the English game. Defender Frank Clark would later describe it as "the direct, journeyman approach to the game which had been so roundly slated by the press".

Even one of the players who, by all accounts, had profited most greatly from Davies' unselfish play, Bryan 'Pop' Robson, who scored 55 goals alongside the Welshman in two seasons, cited Newcastle's long-ball approach to Davies as one of the reasons for his leaving the club in 1970.

"I'm sick and tired of it," he said.

The style had been adopted by Harvey to maximise Davies' unique abilities – and even the player's greatest detractors had to admit he was at least master of one of the footballing arts – heading the ball. Indeed, quite a few of his contemporaries – including Manchester City boss Malcolm Allison and England midfielder Bobby Charlton – rated him the best in the business. "Davies is the greatest header of the ball in the world," said Allison of a man he would later lure to Maine Road, while Charlton declared: "You can have Denis Law, Ron Davies and the others, but for me Wyn climbs better than all of them. I would like to know the percentage of Newcastle goals that can be attributed to his presence."

It was this special ability to outjump his marker that had first attracted Harvey to Davies in the first place – when the Welshman terrorised the United defence in a Second Division clash between Bolton and the Magpies in 1965, the match which clinched promotion for Newcastle. "I hit the bar a number of times before big John McGrath clobbered me and I was carried off," Davies remembered years later. "Perhaps that made an impression on Joe."

That ability, coupled with a prodigious workrate – Davies would often be seen clearing balls from his own penalty area – quickly seduced the United crowd, even as rumours of a transfer away from Newcastle started almost as soon as he arrived in the October of 1966. The player's domination of the opposition back four gave confidence to team-mates and supporters, even on those plentiful days when Davies himself did not find the net.

In May 1969, the *Journal* tried to explain the pervasive influence and strong appeal of "a strange, aloof character". "To older spectators, nourished by the all-round ability of Gallacher, the craft of Wayman or the sight of Milburn bearing down on goal, Wyn Davies' attempts to play the ball around or chance his luck from 25 yards must draw reminiscent signs," said the newspaper. "But to watch the tall Welshman win his first challenge in the air and then strut, peacock-proud, knowing he can get a defence going, gives you the sense that all is going to be well with United up front."

And by the time those words were written, Davies had found a competition – and opposition – tailor-made for him to shine. Before the 1969 Fairs Cup adventure, Davies had to ride out a storm where his unusual playing style was blamed for United's decline. A top-five challenge from Harvey's men had petered out in the second half of the 1967/68 season, with United's eventual 10th-placed finish, bringing justifiable suggestions that the Magpies had reached the Fairs Cup through the back door.

Indeed, many reporters – such as the *Evening Chronicle*'s John Gibson – felt that Davies would even not be around to taste Continental competition the following season. "I know that several United directors, while accepting that the sight of Davies hurtling through the air is both exciting and stimulating, are bitterly disappointed in the net result, both in the number of goals he scores and the number which come from him," wrote Gibson. "There is, of course, another disturbing aspect. United's alarming decline, in which they won only one of their last 12 games, had a lot to do with the complex Davies situation. Players find it hard to read Wyn, an unorthodox sort of player who is also basically a loner. There have been difficulties in tactical talks. They were also annoyed because near the end of the season Davies deserted his penalty area beat to go wandering." Yet tellingly, Gibson added: "United are a little afraid of the fans' reaction, should any deal be done."

His supporters, thankfully, got their way, and allowed Davies to embark upon an adventure which would cement his place in Geordie folklore. Used to playing a more sophisticated game, with the ball played in to feet, European defenders had never seen anyone quite like Wyn Davies before, and Newcastle, as they marched towards their one and only European trophy, profited greatly from the ensuing panic he generated in and around the box.

IF MONCUR WAS the calm and steady guiding hand of the Fairs Cup-winning team, Davies was its strong beating heart, terrorising defenders in the air, and frustrating them with his uncanny knack of soaking up any amount of physical abuse. "Wyn is the most courageous player I have ever seen," said Harvey after the cup was won. "To us he was a walking free-kick. He was hacked down that often it was incredible how he remained all in one piece."

The litany of injuries is frightening. Davies suffered a broken nose in the semi-final win over Rangers, a fractured cheekbone in the home leg of the final against Ujpesti Dozsa and a leg injury away to Feyenoord which left him hospitalised for a week and was described by club physician Dr Salkeld as "the worst I have ever seen". Davies also took the field against Sporting Lisbon in the second round with a splint for a broken finger, a cut eye and a badly swollen right arm – sustained in a clash with Liverpool days before – then had to be sent for X-rays on a suspected broken toe after the 1-1 draw!

Fans were aghast to read about how their hero, his face covered in blood, had his broken nose re-set in the dressing-room after the 0-0 semi-final away leg at Ibrox.

But perhaps Davies' most courageous act was to play in the second, away leg of the final against highly-rated Hungarians Ujpesti Dozsa, despite fracturing his cheekbone in a collision with his own skipper, Bobby Moncur, during the 3-0 first leg win at St James'. United tried to keep a lid on news of the injury to their talisman, after Davies had defiantly insisted: "I'll be in Budapest for my medal". Club coach Davie Smith was amazed by the striker's attitude. "How on earth does this man play with a broken nose and suspected fractured cheekbone? I've never known anyone with more courage," he said. "Without Wyn against Ujpesti, I don't think we would have won by three clear goals. He murdered them in the air."

Newcastle fans were united in awed appreciation of Wyn's battling attitude. Little wonder the *Journal* reported that "if he missed a match they wouldn't send for a doctor – they would bring a priest". But Davies was more than a Fairs Cup warhorse – he also found his goalscoring touch, hitting the net in the first round against Feyenoord, the away leg against Real Zaragoza and both legs of a tight 6-4 aggregate quarter-final win over Vitoria Setubal. "The Continentals couldn't cope with the high ball in the air," he would later recall. "It was alien to their style, and I had great freedom."

His aerial prowess also turned him into a creator. He made two goals agains Feyenoord and created the winner from a long ball against Sporting Lisbon in the second round, heading on for Pop Robson to volley home. In a stormy semi-final second leg at home to Rangers,

Davies outjumped the defence yet again to head an Ollie Burton free-kick on for Jackie Sinclair to fire into the net.

The breakthrough in the 3-0 home leg win over Ujpesti Dozsa also owed much to Davies, when his fierce shot was parried to skipper Bobby Moncur, who opened the scoring. And the Welshman showed his creative influence in a topsy-turvy second leg which saw the Magpies trailing 2-0 at half-time. Substitute Alan Foggon was the beneficiary this time, latching onto a Davies' flick-on to run through and kill the tie off with Newcastle's third goal of the night. Nobody had given more to the cause than the Welshman – who missed the after-match celebrations on Tyneside when he was immediately whisked away for overdue surgery on his fractured cheekbone – and he later recalled feeling overcome when that see-saw second leg ended in Hungary. "When the final whistle went, I remember just dropping to my knees out on the pitch. It was very emotional and had been a long haul. I was in tears."

Manager Joe Harvey was left in no doubt that Davies – above even Moncur, who scored three times in the two-legged final – was the driving force behind a trophy success for the 33-1 outsiders which sent Tyneside into delirium. "Bobby Moncur was a great skipper and showed it by captaining Scotland," said Harvey. "But if any player did more than anyone else to win us that Cup it was big Wyn Davies. Quite apart from the fact that he played so often with injuries that would have kept anyone else out for a few games, he frightened them all with his power in the air. I can remember one game on New Year's Day in Zaragoza and the way the big Spanish centre-back Santamaria went confidently for the first ball we tossed up to Wyn. I can see the look on the Spaniard's face now when big Wyn climbed about two feet higher and knocked it down!"

THE IMPORTANCE OF that Fairs Cup win – and the massive role Davies played in it, evoking memories of Hughie Gallacher's massive influence in the 1927 title success – cannot be overplayed when it comes to analysing his credentials as a Newcastle United icon. Thirty-six years later it is still the club's last trophy success, and, having brought a 14-year barren run to an end, Davies and his team-mates were rightly hailed as conquering heroes back on Tyneside, where supporters thronged the roadside throughout the players' seven-mile route back to St James' Park from the airport.

Then club director Squadron Leader Jimmy Rush later recalled that everyone connected with the club was blown away by their reception. "Never in our wildest dreams could we have imagined the crowds and the size of the enthusiasm which greeted us on our return," he said. "The day we came back with the Fairs Cup must go down as the greatest reception the team has ever had." Davies had joined a select band of Newcastle terrace heroes by lifting silver in black and white – an achievement which players such as Malcolm Macdonald (his immediate successor as United No. 9) and Alan Shearer can only covet with envious eyes.

Nine years after leaving Newcastle, Davies would stress the trophy factor in a tacit comparison with Macdonald, the man bought to replace him. "I had some wonderful times up there and for a while I was 'King of the Tyne' until Macdonald came along," said Davies. "I'm pleased to say that I did at least win something when I was up there!"

But before the love affair came to an end, Davies and Co, while never taking the First Division by storm, threatened to make a successful defence of the Fairs Cup in 1969/70, seeing off Dundee United (the Welshman, in a man-of-the-match display, scoring with two headers in three minutes), FC Porto and Southampton before losing out agonisingly to Anderlecht on the away goals rule in the quarter-finals – a two-legged tie in which Davies again found the net.

His menacing contribution in Europe – where he scored an impressive 10 goals in 24 games for the Magpies – continued in that infamous two-legged tie with Inter Milan in the Fairs Cup first round at the start of the 1970 season. Davies headed home both goals in the 2-0 second round home leg win against Hungarians Pecsi Dozsa, with the *Journal* declaring that "Wyn Davies rose majestically to power home two brilliant headers".

But with Davies still at the peak of his powers in Europe, Newcastle would go on to lose their way in the return leg and find themselves knocked out of the competition on a penalty shootout. And without the motivation of his favourite competition, Davies' form hit a slump as he bowed out with just two league goals in his fifth and final season on Tyneside, before a move to Manchester City in August 1971. The deal left City's joint managers Malcolm Allison and Joe Mercer salivating – Davies never had any shortage of admirers within the game – yet a *Manchester Evening News* feature on the new boy, written by journalist

Haydn Berry, wondered how a player who had never scored more than 12 league goals in a season for Newcastle had amassed such a cult following.

Marvelling at the survey which showed 85 per cent of Magpies fans to be against the sale, he wrote: "How did Davies generate such fanaticism? How did he win over some of the most knowledgeable fans in the country? The answer is not immediately apparent."

If the riddle has a one-word answer, then 'passion' is as good a try as any. Davies was an emotional, committed, honest player – attributes which went down as well in working-class Tyneside as in the North Welsh village of Caernarfon where he was born. The *Evening Chronicle* summed up this appeal back in January 1967, declaring: "All Tyneside has taken to the big flame-haired Welshman, who rises like a guided missile whenever the ball is pumped into the penalty area. His contribution at Burnley was really fantastic – one minute he was heading away a free-kick in United's penalty area, the next he was testing Thomson at the other end."

DAVIES' GENUINE LOVE for playing in front of the Newcastle fans – which made his eventual departure painful for both sides – was another key factor in the player's enduring recognition. He would later describe his five years at St James' as the best of his life, and, in a 1990 interview with the *Evening Chronicle*'s Paul Tully, he went misty-eyed at the memories, remembering: "They used to sing: 'You've not seen nothing like the Mighty Wyn'. It was brilliant – there was no better place."

An honest, heart-on-his-sleeve approach somehow allowed Davies to live down a couple of massive PR gaffes with the Tyneside public. First, he had angered manager Joe Harvey, Newcastle United and the fans by refusing a move north from Bolton in 1965 because the £6,000 signing-on fee – a massive amount in the mid-60s – was not deemed good enough. One disgruntled United fan told the *Journal*: "On Davies' gold-digging admissions, and his contemptuous treatment of Newcastle and their manager, he can go anywhere else he likes for me." Davies already had a sizeable faction against him on Tyneside, then – even before he cheerily admitted, after finally agreeing to join the club in October 1966 – that he would have preferred to stay in the north west and join Manchester City! And, making no secret of his desire to cash in on a lucrative transfer, Davies declared: "If there is not reward to be earned in Newcastle, then where else? I'll give them everything I have. I would have gone anywhere where the money and top-class distinction was to be gained."

But perhaps the most significant words in that startling admission were "I'll give them everything I have" and Davies, a naturally fit player who had earned a reputation as a committed trainer, was as good as his word. That commitment, coupled with a headstrong nature, would carry the fans' backing as Davies fell foul of the football authorities with a series of on-pitch rants against refereeing decisions. Former United skipper Jim Iley – Davies' first captain and unofficial 'minder' – would later smile at the recollection of how busy the job kept him. "I've seen myself run 60 or 70 yards to get in between him and the referee when he has started arguing," said Iley. "It's just Wyn's nature to lose his temper quickly. It would be no good trying to curb it, because this is part of his make-up... the trouble is he will sometimes not let a matter drop."

Local legend has it that manager Harvey asked his star man to swear at the official in his native Welsh tongue to avoid a booking – a plan that backfired on more than one occasion when officials, not surprisingly, managed to get the message anyway! There is another, equally likely tale in which Davies got himself erroneously booked for swearing when he absent-mindedly slipped into the Welsh tongue. Yet it is doubtless to Harvey's credit that a player widely recognised as difficult completed five years at United without a major row. A fall-out with manager Tommy Docherty would end Davies' career at Manchester United in 1973, while a walkout from the Wales squad – Davies was angered at continually playing understudy to Ron Davies and John Toshack – would create a storm in the player's homeland in 1971.

Davies departed days before a match with Northern Ireland in Belfast and asked not be considered for an upcoming European Championship qualifier with Finland, leaving Welsh FA secretary Trevor Morris declaring: "Walking out like this is not the attitude of a professional footballer. As a fellow Welshman, I am disgusted by it all."

With characteristic bluntness, Davies simply told the media: "I just want to go home to North Wales and play golf." Still, 34 caps for his country puts Davies in a select band of Newcastle heroes to have become a success at club and international level. Indeed, upon his signing for Newcastle United, Manchester-based sports journalist Peter Keeling declared that "his appearances for Wales have already firmly established him as the most dangerous centre-forward in the four home counties."

Newcastle seemed to get the best out of the temperamental former quarryman through Harvey's legendary man-management skills. Yet Harvey had to work hard to keep Davies onside by constantly reminding him how much he was loved and appreciated on Tyneside – particularly when lengthy goal droughts (he once went three months without scoring) left the player in a crisis of confidence. Halfway through his last, most disappointing season in black and white, Davies said: "It might surprise some people to know that I'm a worrier, But this season got so bad that I was unable to sleep at nights, trying to work out just what went wrong." Harvey's response was always unequivocal: "I told him we paid his wages and were happy and the crowd loved him. He got the message."

Indeed the fans seemed to love Davies all the more because of his little insecurities and foibles. He may have played the game as a fearsome target man, but he was openly homesick for Caernarfon and the company of his mother Lily. The press at the time recalled with relish that Lily held the key to Davies' transfer talks, with the player, when he signed for Newcastle, keeping Joe Harvey waiting while he popped out to ring the public phone box outside her house to ask for advice in his native Welsh.

All the idiosyncracies of a complex and fascinating player – and above all, a real character – came under the spotlight as the emergence of TV and radio coverage turned Davies into Newcastle United's first all-round media star. One running media debate raged about how to get the best out of his unique talents – Mercer and Allison believed Newcastle always relied too much on Davies' aerial powers, insisting, like the player himself, that he was under-rated on the ground. But the player's former Bolton boss Bill Ridding – who had helped turn Davies into one of the game's most sought-after players before Newcastle won the race to sign him – urged United to curb his natural tendency to wander deep and wide in search of the ball to feet. "He had a fixation for playing deep and he hasn't the necessary skill for that. We changed him and utilised his fantastic heading ability to the full," said Ridding.

Davies himself always longed to be more involved – and saw himself in the deep-lying centre-forward's role made famous by Don Revie. "I've always felt confident on the ground," he declared. "This business of not being able to work a ball with my feet is just a myth conjured up by people because a lot of emphasis is put on my heading ability. Tony Hateley suffers in the same way."

Yet, in terms of enduring fame and popularity on Tyneside, Harvey and Newcastle did Wyn Davies no harm by playing him as an out-and-out target man. A measure of their success is shown by a national survey in the March 1968 edition of the *Football League Review*, in which Davies was voted the most popular player in the country with 22,938 votes! Skipper Bobby Moncur was in no doubt where the secret to the Welshman's status lay. He once recalled, with colourful exaggeration, his amazement in training at Davies' prodigious and infamous leap. "I don't think that anybody in the world gets as high to meet it as he does. The chances he lays off for others are endless," said Moncur. "Once, when we were training, I remember throwing a ball to him. It seemed high to me, but he got up to it. I did it again and again until the ball, it seemed to me, was just a dot in the sky. But every time up Wyn went and got his head to it. Imagine having to face a man like that and one who is brave enough to go in whatever the circumstances. No wonder the Europeans have a great regard for his ability. They haven't seen anyone like him."

The same goes for Newcastle fans, who have not seen anyone like Davies before or since. Davies' former team-mate Ben Arentoft – himself a goalscorer in that 1969 Fairs Cup-winning final – remains a huge fan. Speaking to me from his Denmark home, Arentoft waxed lyrical over the Welshman's prodigious aerial power – and his legendary bravery. "He was GREAT in the air, and I especially remember a goal against Everton away from home, where he scored with a header outside the box. He was just hanging there up in the air, and then he smashed the ball with his head, nearly as strong as anybody could kick it. And I have always admired him for all the stick he took from all the centre-halves. At that time there was a lot of kicking from behind and the forwards especially had to take that. He was kicked all over the place, but he still stood up and got on with the game. He got lots of bruises and scars and blood on the face, but Wyn kept going. And I think that was why the fans just loved him as well as the great goals which he scored."

YET DAVIES TOOK a while to earn this status and to live up to his club record £80,000 transfer fee. Indeed, after just two goals in his first 13 games, some fans could have been forgiven for wishing the Newcastle University students, who had forced the new signing into hiding on the weekend of his debut at home to Sunderland by threatening to kidnap the new signing in a rag week stunt, had been successful in the venture! Yet slowly but surely, Davies become an inspirational figure as the spearhead of Newcastle's attack, carving out a legend for himself as almost the living embodiment of the fans' passionate will-to-win.

Like a boxer who would not stay down, Davies' immense courage, energy, determination – and the power of his aerial bombardment – would leave fans raucous in their applause, and defenders wondering what had hit them. Former workmate Richard Jones – who toiled in the slate quarry with a young Davies then joined him in kickarounds afterwards – summed it up when he declared: "He petrified me, you see."

As the driving force behind Newcastle's only ever European trophy success, and a player adored, like a favourite, wilful, son, by the United faithful, Davies takes his place as a bona fide Magpies hero to stand shoulder-to-shoulder with many players more gifted.

But the last word must go to United chairman Lord Westwood, so taken with the United's marauding No. 9 that he handed Davies an almost unprecedented golden handshake for his contribution to the Newcastle cause when he left for Manchester City. "What a character," said Westwood, "what a man – what a player!"

Malcolm Macdonald

1971-1976: 258 games, 138 goals

THERE HAVE BEEN – a few – greater players in Newcastle's history. But has there ever been a bigger character?

Malcolm Macdonald sparked jubilation when he arrived in a Rolls-Royce, broke thousands of hearts when he departed in a private jet – and delivered countless thrills and spills in between. This cocky Cockney braggart – not a great start to becoming a Geordie folk hero, is it? – scored some of the most spectacular goals ever seen at St James'. And, with his love of the high-life, outrageous 70s fashions and outlandish sound-bite interviews, he also brought showbiz glamour to Newcastle United, becoming as adored on the Gallowgate terraces as he was despised by the opposition defenders he taunted.

Macdonald's success in becoming one of the greatest icons in club history gives the lie to the notion that Geordies need their heroes to be modest, gentle folk. Unrivalled in the modern era as the Magpies' favourite footballing playboy, Macdonald evokes inevitable memories of Hughie Gallacher for the way he played hard on the pitch and off it. Like Gallacher – though not with the same fatal consequences – Macdonald's lifestyle would cause considerable problems in later life. And, in 2012, as he still graces St James' Park in his role as a radio pundit, there remain few clues that this man was once a heart-throb and one of the most impressive athletes ever to wear the black and white stripes. But Macdonald is nothing if not a survivor – he has braved considerable highs and lows to carve out a successful media career in the North East as one of Century Radio's *Three Legends* – a show which gives North East fans the chance to vent their spleen on the issues of the day.

Many of his listeners are old enough to remember a very different Macdonald in his pomp. "Sideburns like a cowboy, built like a middleweight boxer, possessing the speed of a human Concorde and blessed with an explosive, blistering shot," so read one profile in the *Football League Review* of September, 1972. By that time, after just one season in a black and white shirt, Macdonald was already sparking comparisons with the great Jackie Milburn. But then again, in a manner almost as sensational as Len Shackleton, he did get off to a flyer at St James' Park.

IT IS NOW widely forgotten that Macdonald had drawn two blanks – at Crystal Palace and Tottenham – before stealing the show in one of the most famous games in club history. But, with blanket TV coverage a thing of the distant future, Saturday 28 August 1971 was the first time a home crowd had seen the No. 9 in action – and the stirring pictures of an heroic display against Liverpool would live long in the memory.

Macdonald blasted a first-half penalty high into the net to put Newcastle 1-0 up. So far so good, but his second would raise the roof. "There didn't seem much danger when he got the ball wide out on the left, attacking the Gallowgate End," said the *Sunday Sun*'s report on the game. "But in a flash he brought the crowd to its feet with a glorious left-foot drive which soared across Clemence and into the roof of the net."

Macdonald puffed out his barrel chest and turned, both arms aloft, to salute his new disciples as midfielder Terry Hibbitt jumped on his back; a star was born. Goal No. 3 – a powerful cross shot from the edge of the area – arrived after Macdonald had been played in by strike partner John Tudor. And before the new legend's first chapter was complete he cleared a Liverpool shot off the line in a 3-2 win and, to put the icing on the cake, was later was carried off, unconscious, to thunderous applause, trying to score a fourth goal.

With perhaps a hint of trademark Macdonald embellishment, he would describe being spark out for 20 minutes and then having no recollection of his exploits when he did finally come to in the dressing room: "The next thing I remember was waking up and telling this face in front of me: 'I'm going to score a hat-trick against Liverpool'. The face belonged to Frank Clark, who had come round to see how I was. 'You did, you knacker,' said Clarkie."

Macdonald would later describe that day as one of his greatest 'memories' in football – even if he did have to rely on match reports and team-mates' testimonies to create it! Meanwhile one of the most famous nicknames in football had already been created, with the Gallowgate crowd bursting into a spontaneous chant of "SuperMac, SuperMac" during the game.

Twenty-seven more goals would arrive that season, to justify a self-proclaimed 30-goal prediction, which, considering the player's Second Division pedigree, was hailed as outlandish when Macdonald arrived from Luton.

Indeed, Newcastle manager Joe Harvey's £180,000 deal – the third highest for any player in Britain – had been widely deemed excessive for a 21-year-old converted full-back (then Fulham manager Sir Bobby Robson had first pushed him up front), who had never kicked a ball in the English top flight. Yet by the end of that first season – in which Macdonald finished second behind the mercurial Tony Green as the club's Player of the Season – would-be suitors such as Brian Clough's Derby County, Manchester United and Chelsea, who had rejected the player as a youngster for being too small – would be wishing they had shown Harvey's foresight. (Clough would later admit: "We missed him and it was a bad mistake.")

For the next five years, SuperMac's name would dominate the club and the region, as only a very few have ever done on Tyneside. The fervour he created can very easily be compared to some of the biggest legends in Magpies' history – great names such as Gallacher, Milburn and Alan Shearer.

It is not difficult to see why. Further League and Cup goal tallies of 19 in his second season, 25 in his third, then 27 in 1974/75 and 24 in his last campaign left him with one of the best goals-per-game ratios in the club's history – even without the 17 strikes from Anglo-Italian and Texaco Cup matches coming into the equation. Only four men – Gallacher, Milburn, Len White and Shearer – have scored more competitive goals for the club, and all but Gallacher had more games in which to do so.

Those who doubt the Macdonald legend should also consider:

– He scored in every round (except, infamously, the final) to take Newcastle to Wembley in the 1974 FA Cup
– He scored the fastest goal in club history when he lobbed the St Johnstone keeper straight from the kick-off on the halfway line in a pre-season friendly
– He won the Match of the Day goal of the season award in 1976
– He scored five goals for England against Cyprus, still a national record
– He twice finished as the First Division's top scorer
– He once used his trademark long throw to score for United direct from a throw-in!

But impressive as the facts and figures are, the secret to SuperMac's enduring status lies in memories which cannot be measured. Macdonald's charismatic on-pitch persona, his larger-than-life approach off it and his eye for the spectacular mark him out as a special footballer.

Sporting a long, wild crop of hair (that, according to one newspaper report of the time "seemed itself hungry for goals") and huge lamb-chop sideburns which were, difficult as it is for us to believe now, the height of fashion, Macdonald was difficult to overlook. Not the tallest of players at 5ft 11in, he was nevertheless stocky and powerfully built, and with a naturally swagger on those bandy legs. Friend and then Luton director, the late comedian Eric Morecambe once told the North East press they had signed a gem from his old club, declaring that strength, speed and power were his main assets, before adding in homage to his onscreen partner Ernie Wise: "On top of this, Malcolm's got short fat hairy legs. What more could you ask for?"

Goals, of course, and Macdonald – much like his No. 9 successors Andy Cole and Alan Shearer – simply lived for them. Goalmouth hogging obsessives one and all.

Not, by his own admission, the greatest player technically, Macdonald was nevertheless renowned for his direct approach, his willingness to shoot from any distance and any angle – which produced some extravagant strikes – and feared for his natural speed and bullish style. Once timed at an awesome 10.4 seconds for the 100 metres, Macdonald worked tirelessly on his speed in training, and once declared that he would have dedicated himself full-time to a career as a sprinter if he had failed to make the grade in football. Like Albert Stubbins and Jackie Milburn, Macdonald was blistering over the first few yards – and like Kevin Keegan, he had the build and fitness of a natural athlete. His athletic prowess was shown as he reached the final stages of the BBC's 1970s cult *Superstars* show – a platform which brought him yet more national fame. "He raised a few eyebrows in his heat," wrote the *Journal*, "with a 100-metre sprint which would not have disgraced an international running track, some fancy pistol shooting, and a massive piece of weight-lifting."

It was perhaps apt that such a deadly marksman would win the pistol shooting – the swaggering Macdonald was often compared to a gunslinger, and it was a description he relished. "A goalscorer is like a gunslinger in the old Wild West – he's only as good as his last success," he wrote in one of his regular *Evening Chronicle* columns. "And I'm at my best under that sort of pressure – I need it." In his complete and utter devotion to the goalscoring art – and nothing else – on the pitch, the closest comparison to Macdonald elsewhere in this book is Andy Cole and it is perhaps no coincidence that both of these specialists found England caps hard to come by. Macdonald won 14, and has at least got that stunning five-goal display against Cyprus as the highlight of what was ultimately a frustrating international career. He described it at the time, in April 1975 as "the greatest achievement of my life", but moaned after the game about having a sixth goal ruled out for offside. "But I will settle for five," he added. "Why be greedy?"

Yet even Macdonald's biggest fans had to admit he was! Like Shearer after him, he was renowned for claiming any goal, even if he got the briefest of deflections to a team-mate's shot, or conversely, if one of his own strikes had been diverted in by a defender.

In a joint interview with his legendary predecessor Jackie Milburn, he told the great man: "There was a season when George Robledo scored 33 goals and you, Jackie, scored 28. If Robledo was playing now and he scored 33 and I scored 28, I would smack him between the eyes for his audacity!"

IF SUPERMAC'S GOALSCORING genius had been laid bare against Cyprus at Wembley – he also scored in a superb individual and team display in a 2-0 win over West Germany the year before – so too was that irrepressible knack of rubbing certain people up the wrong way. Kevin Keegan would later make light of his on-pitch spat with his strike partner, joking that "Malcolm scored five – and he pushed me out of the way for two!"

Macdonald was a little more forthright in his revelations – and earned some media criticism for revealing that, after scoring his third goal, "Kevin came up to me and said, seriously, 'Alright, you've got your hat-trick, how about making some for somebody else?' I said 'Kevin, fuck off and get your own'."

Seventeen years later, Keegan would again be the target of some plain talking when, upon his succession to the Newcastle United managerial job, Macdonald described him as "a spoiled brat and a cry baby". Macdonald's ability to antagonise at times undoubtedly contributed to the criticism he received as a player. Frank Worthington – one of his main rivals for an England shirt – once described him as "a glorified full-back", while Celtic and Scotland defender Danny McGrain was even more scathing. "Malcolm Macdonald is another player who has gained a reputation way beyond his ability," moaned the Scot. "SuperMac they call him south of the border, but even a name like that wouldn't get him near a Scottish international squad [No Danny, because he's English]… like many other English players, he only talks a good game."

England managers Sir Alf Ramsey, Don Revie and Joe Mercer, could not agree with such over-the-top criticism. But like respected football journalist Brian Glanville – who claimed Macdonald was not England class and got his timing wrong when he predicted the Cockney would flop before the Cyprus game – they shared a feeling that the national side could not be built around such an individualist player who perhaps lacked creative guile and contributed little to the build-up play.

The stand-off mirrored Andy Cole's England frustrations 20 years later. Cole's supporters would copy Macdonald's champions by asserting that his goals should do the talking. The *Daily Mirror* declared after the player's England debut against Wales in May 1972 that Macdonald had looked sharp and "should clearly be given an extended run". And the player himself could never understand his exclusion at England level. He was aware of his weaknesses, but built his entire game on his strengths, once admitting: "I can only run for three or four minutes, but I can sprint like hell, I can stick it in the net and I'll stick my neck in where I know it is going to get kicked. They are my three strengths – and I've got to play to those."

Goals were always the primary motivation, though, and, in his *Evening Chronicle* column of April 1975 he was not shy in claiming: "There's only one goalscorer in England – and that's me. Come to think of it, there's only two in the world! The other's Gerd Muller... "Jackie Milburn summed up the Macdonald ethos when he declared "He's got the whites of a goalpost between his eyes!"

Freely admitting that he based much of his game on a simple instruction learned from his former Luton Town boss Harry Haslam – "get the ball, turn and shoot" – Macdonald declared that he deliberately chose not to get involved in much of the build-up play, because he wanted to stay fresh and sharp in case a late chance came his way. And it often did – such as in the fourth round FA Cup replay against Scunthorpe in 1974. The two teams had drawn 1-1 at St James' Park in the first game, with Scunthorpe defender Chris Simpkin accusing Macdonald of "not breaking sweat".

Needless to say, SuperMac grabbed two – including one in the 87th minute – in the 3-0 replay win, then strolled back to his marker, grinning, to declare: "You should see me when I break sweat!" But Macdonald's self-styled decision to conserve his energy brought accusations of laziness from certain quarters – and coach Keith Burkinshaw faced a long-running, battle with the star centre-forward to contribute more.

Team-mates too, were not beyond criticising their talisman, particularly for lack of effort in training, but Macdonald's stock retort: "Put your goals on the table!" would usually silence them. Macdonald's image as the lazy gunslinger sparked a lovely little exchange between managers Bill Shankly and Joe Harvey after Newcastle had beaten the Merseysiders 4-1 at home in 1975 – a game in which United's No. 9 had scored twice. Macdonald, Shankly scornfully told his opposite number, had never had a kick.

"He had at least two, Bill," came the reply.

Yet overall, Liverpool undoubtedly retained the upper hand over their would-be nemesis. In Macdonald's first season, they avenged that 3-2 away defeat by thrashing the Magpies 5-0 on home turf – a game in which Macdonald the joker had angered Shankly by mocking the famous "This Is Anfield" sign. "There you are, Joe," he said to his manager, "I told you we were at the right place."

"You'll soon find out you're at the right place," Shankly grunted in reply.

But Liverpool's sweetest revenge came in the 1974 FA Cup final, when boastful newspaper interviews from Macdonald – about what he would do the opposition back four – were infamously pinned to the Merseysiders' dressing room wall in lieu of a team-talk. Macdonald's posturing had never seemed so futile after he and his side figuratively failed to show in an embarrassingly one-sided 3-0 defeat.

Macdonald, always keen to stress his close relationship with the United fans, shouted out to them from the Wembley turf that he would make sure they would be back – and this time to win. They did return – two years later in the League Cup final - but again the No. 9's pre-match boasts came to nought. This was the man, remember, who would frequently declare that defenders would be shaking with fear at the prospect of playing him. "I've got a message for Manchester City," he crowed in the *Evening Chronicle* the week before the final. The last time I walked off the Wembley pitch I had just scored five goals… and if that fact frightens City, then it should."

The result? Macdonald failed to score in a 2-1 defeat for Newcastle – although he did make the United goal, when he crossed for Alan Gowling to slide home what was then a first-half equaliser. Those games were as near as he would come to major silverware – he would lose a third final in 1978 when his Arsenal team were pipped to the FA Cup by Ipswich.

ULTIMATELY, SUPERMAC'S FAILURE to deliver when it mattered most must count against him in the final reckoning of cult heroes. Like Alan Shearer, Peter Beardsley, Tony Green, and Kevin Keegan, the big prize of major silverware would elude him, and it is almost apologetically that we have to mention his goals helped in United's Anglo-Italian Cup victory of 1973 (though he missed the final on England duty), and their two Texaco Cup wins in 1974 and 1975.

Greats such as Hughie Gallacher and Jackie Milburn – bringing League title and FA Cup success respectively to Toon – must therefore stand above SuperMac, although in some respects, such was the ability to create the spectacular, Macdonald arguably had no peers.

Two magnificent goals in the FA Cup semi-final win over Burnley at Hillsborough live long in the memory of those who witnessed them – Macdonald showed raw power to hold off defender Colin Waldron for the first, poking the ball past Burnley keeper Alan Stevenson. In the second, he latched on to a perfect through-ball from his creator-in-chief, Terry Hibbitt, to outpace the defence and stick the ball through the keeper's legs.

Macdonald's second in a 3-3 FA Cup draw away to Bolton in 1976 – a long-range screamer with his weaker right foot – would win the *Match of the Day Goal of the Season* award and leave him laughing at the way his right foot was known as "a swinger – even among my fellow professionals in the game… and I chortle my way up the scoring charts as they fall for the greatest myth in football".

But Macdonald picks his finest strike as a stupendous 35-yard shot which came in a 3-0 home win over Leicester earlier that season – a goal which made his opposite number that day, England rival Frank Worthington eat his critical words about the Newcastle player. "You can say I've changed my tune a bit," said Worthington. "That goal gives me very little alternative."

The title of Macdonald's first book was *Never Afraid to Miss* and that mantra served him well against City as he took opposition and team-mates by surprise by shooting first-time and from a position just in front of the centre circle where most players would not even consider it. "Throughout my career, I only hit one perfect shot," he would later recall, "and that was it".

United devotee Terry Nichol agreed, insisting: "It was the greatest goal I've ever seen…. Terry Hibbitt, who had the sweetest left foot in football, got the ball just inside his own half and played a diagonal pass. Macdonald was on it and, without breaking stride, hit it with his left foot. It flew into the top of the net."

With an eye for the spectacular perhaps matched only by Peter Beardsley in black and white stripes, little wonder the fans loved him.

MACDONALD'S ASTUTE UNDERSTANDING of exactly what made Tyneside tick – exciting, attacking football and showmanship – lies at the heart of his legend in this region. His occasional brushes with the law – taken to court for being drunk and disorderly and for drink-driving – added to his colourful image and he is certainly one of the colourful 'bad boy' heroes of this book, if not quite in the Gallacher/ Gascoigne class when it came to hell-raising. In common with those two Macdonald had that innate charisma, that uncanny ability to spark incident – and court controversy – wheresoever he went.

But what sets him apart is that he was perhaps the first to deliberately cultivate such a larger-than-life image. Not for Macdonald the quiet, almost reclusive image of a Len White, Peter Beardsley or Alan Shearer.

Macdonald, who was judging beauty competitions and opening fetes even before he joined Newcastle, and opened a fashion boutique – 'Exclusive Man', in the city – was happier out on the town in his famous flared suits, holding court with a glass of champagne in hand. Like Gallacher half a century earlier, he found in the main adoration rather than jealousy in an area always happy to treat their football stars like kings – as long as, like Macdonald, they were delivering the goods on the pitch.

Even the public boasting which would eventually fall flat in those Wembley finals against Liverpool and Manchester City, plus the boast that he would pulverise non-leaguers Hereford before Newcastle lost infamously in an FA Cup replay, added more colour to a football personality the likes of which Tyneside had rarely – if ever – seen. Newcastle fans loved Macdonald's straight-talking, heart-on-your-sleeve approach, and lapped up every word of his gleeful goalscoring predictions – especially since, more often than not, he made good on them. It was a media approach which Joe Harvey later admitted he encouraged as part of an approach to entertain the crowd which they both saw as central to the very character of the club and the region.

Macdonald later admitted: "I would be quite happy to put in the newspapers that I would score a goal on the Saturday. People said, 'You big-headed so-and-so . . . I don't know how you've got the front to do it'. I knew what I was doing.

"It was a pretence, and at no time can I ever remember it not being a pretence. At no time can I remember feeling that I was no longer an actor and the part had become me or I had become the actor."

Macdonald's reasoning was two-fold, and here we get to the very heart of the man as a successful sportsman: firstly, he was intelligent enough to know that hogging the headlines would help him become a star and increase his earning power – but there was another more practical motivation. He was also exaggerating his natural confidence in order to try and out-psyche the opposition, and give himself a head start even before the games kicked off. "I had to be headstrong and arrogant because basically I couldn't play," he said, with typical exaggeration. "I had to create this aura about me for people to believe in me. I probably had more weaknesses, technically, than anyone who has ever put boots on in the First Division, and I fought to overcome this by concentrating on my strengths, such as my pace and physical power. I would talk about nothing else. That's why coaches tended to find me difficult to handle. I always had this protective barrier up. I knew my weaknesses were there but I wouldn't let anyone else know."

With an average first-touch and head-down, direct approach, Macdonald was certainly an unusual player, and Jackie Milburn once commented that "he has thrown the coaching manual out of the window". But his success at developing the powers that made him such a dangerous goalscorer cannot be denied – even if his boastful approach looked questionable at times.

Harvey admitted that the Macdonald persona – like Wyn Davies before him – sometimes gave Newcastle a goal start. But against the best and most confident opposition, his attitude merely strengthened their resolve and, at times, could make the great man look foolhardy. It was, as Macdonald later admitted in an interview in which he declared that he modelled himself on Muhammed Ali, a delicate balancing act. "I've styled myself on Ali, not only because he's a unique sportsman but because he's unquestionably the greatest salesman of all time," he told the *Evening Chronicle* in 1975. "I felt I must sell myself as a player. I must do an Ali – shout from the rooftops and if necessary, risk falling flat on my face... You need every ounce of confidence as well as skill to survive. I know what I'm bad at, but I talk about what I'm good at, so that the centre-half feels inferior even during the kick-in. I knew it meant the punters either loved me or hated me."

WHETHER YOU WERE in the former or the latter camp seemed entirely, between 1971 and 1976, down to whether or not you supported Newcastle. But the love affair was destined to end as it had begun – in high drama, when a simmering feud between Macdonald and Harvey's successor as manager Gordon Lee – appointed in June 1975 – climaxed in a high noon showdown in the summer of 1976.

The situation was not dissimilar to the power struggle between Alan Shearer and Ruud Gullit 20 years later – but it had a very different result, with manager triumphing over player. Lee, a pragmatic manager who preached about team ethics and workrate, was exactly the wrong sort to appreciate Macdonald's individualistic approach, and the player had got off to bad start when it was widely publicised that he had greeted the appointment by telling the press "Gordon who?"

Meanwhile Lee made no secret of his disdain for SuperMac's superstar status – or the cult of hero worship on Tyneside – when he quickly declared at a specially-arranged press conference: "I want to build a team, not a one-man band". If Lee's approach had few backers on the terraces, he did have some support in the dressing room from players whose noses were getting pushed out of joint by their No. 9's iconic status.

The Journal takes up the tale: "The background to the conference is that members of his first team have complained to him that their efforts in recent successes have been virtually overlooked, and instead the public spotlight had been turned on striker Malcolm Macdonald's failure to score goals." Lee went on to declare: "People talk about the entertainment of the past? What's entertainment?"

The fans knew – and so did Macdonald, but Lee's Newcastle tactics clearly proved he did not. There was little improvement in terms of results either, with Newcastle under Lee finishing 15th, as they did under Harvey, in his one full season.

But by the time Lee had left, Tyneside hearts had already been broken by the depature of Macdonald to Arsenal for the unusual fee of £333,333.34 – specified down to the penny with United holding out for more than a third of a million. Supporters delivered a black and white wreath to St James' Park in protest at the sale, bearing the words: "With deepest sympathy on your terrible tragedy, 28 July 1976."

Macdonald, who had been pushed into a more withdrawn striking role to accommodate Lee signing Alan Gowling in his final season – and had actually finished, with 24 goals, second to the new boy's 30 strikes in the goal charts – insisted he would have been happy to stay on Tyneside had it not been for Lee (incidentally, there is no mention in the records of Macdonald having smacked Gowling between the eyes for his audacity). In truth though, Lee was not the only reason for Macdonald's depature – there were also signs that United as a club, were not fulfilling his ambition, and that he wanted more, in terms of wages, than the Magpies were prepared to pay. The feeling that certain members of the dressing room were growing tired of his headline-hogging also seemed to play a part. But Macdonald, who left Tyneside for Highbury in a private jet, would later accuse Lee of being jealous of his relationship with the fans, adding: "It was almost as if he had a grudge against anyone with any ability."

Lee did, at least, get Newcastle to the 1976 League Cup final, and, though he left in January 1977, he left a team which was on their way to a fifth-place First Division finish. But Macdonald was reluctant to praise a man he never saw eye-to-eye with. "We got to the League Cup final in '76 despite rather than because of Gordon Lee. But we were playing some dreadfully boring football and the crowds stayed away."

The fans certainly did not stay away when Macdonald exacted some revenge for his Tyneside exit by scoring the opener in a 2-0 win for the Gunners in April 1977 – his first return to St James' Park. 44,677 crowded the terraces to watch their former hero; only 30,967 had watched United's previous home game, a 3-0 win over West Ham. But, immediately after the game, Newcastle's fans were given their first real taste of how hard Macdonald's gloating could be when you are on the receiving end. "When I look at the table, I can't see one reason for them being so high," said the striker, referring to United's fourth place in the First Division. "I've never played in a game like it in my life. It was all so easy it became like shooting practice and it was hard to retain your concentration."

The boot was now well and truly on the other foot.

Macdonald – like many ex-Magpies – had roundly criticised the running of the club when he had left nine months before, and police had been tipped off before the game that a minority of Newcastle hooligans had put money up as reward for one of their number to "have a go" at their former hero during the match. The rumour came to naught, but it did not stop Northumbria police giving the Cockney a personal bodyguard to escort him everywhere he went on Tyneside, right up to kick-off.

Tynesiders could have been forgiven for hoping they'd seen the back of their former hero when, after Macdonald also scored a hat-trick in a 5-3 Arsenal home win against Newcastle that season, had his career short in 1979 by a knee injury.

He managed Fulham – taking them from the Third Division to within a point of the top flight – but then personal problems took hold. The strain of the break-up of his marriage to wife Julie, leaving five daughters to start a new life with soon-to-be second wife Nicky, was held as the reason for his resignation at Craven Cottage in April 1984. As the new era of footballing celebrity took hold, Macdonald hit the headlines when Julie told *Woman's Own* magazine, in heart-rending style, that the girls had pleaded: "Daddy, don't go!" as Macdonald walked out of the house.

A FAILED HOTEL venture in Berwick – which ended in acrimony and a court case when the bailiffs were sent in – preceded another divorce, bankruptcy, and a spell trying to build a new life in Milan, before returning to his adopted Tyneside home in 1996 to face his demons.

A *Journal* feature of the time, announcing his return to work for Century Radio, highlights that "Macdonald, who owned a Ferrari in his playing days, now drives a 26-year-old Volvo". Nothing wrong with that you may say – good sturdy cars – but then the 46-year-old, having admitted he was relishing a fresh start, soon found himself in the midst of a long-running and well-publicised battle with the bottle. "I've got no option but to dry out because I know I'm slowly committing suicide," he declared in 1997, after admitting taking to whisky to cope with the pain of osteo-arthritis in his shattered knees. "Painkillers are no use," he said. There is only thing that deadens the pain and that's whisky. I drink three bottles a day…"

Macdonald's fondness for a drink had caused problems before, of course. He was sent home, with Alan Hudson, from an Arsenal tour after breaking a club curfew to hit the bar, while he had also faced a charge of being drunk and disorderly after a row in Richmond, Surrey, in which police found the England star wandering across the road brandishing a lump of wood. And yet never, as a player, was there any suggestion that Macdonald's drinking had become an addiction, or would impact on his playing performances. The public admission of a drink problem came following his arrest for drink-driving in Jesmond, Newcastle, just after hosting his Century Radio phone-in. A period of suspension from his job followed, one of the low points of a rollercoaster life, before Macdonald faced the challenge the challenge head-on to emerge as one of the biggest media figures in the region.

HE REMAINS CLOSELY linked with Newcastle United to this day, in his role as an outspoken critic, and his willingness to speak his mind makes him a natural on the radio. Yet the truth is that, as ever, Macdonald's views bring controversy rather than universal acclaim, and in judging his place in the pantheon, it is important not to be too distracted by the varying assessments of his punditry. At the time of writing, he sparked headlines in the 2005/06 season with his critical stance on fans' favourite Scott Parker, while he remains ever willing to swim against the tide with his views on team affairs at Gallowgate.

In truth, his relationship with the club has been, ever since the summer of 1976, an uneasy one, and several St James' Park officials have claimed this outspoken critic has not always been fair to his former employers. In his time as a football agent, he sold Brazilian striker Mirandinha to the club and became embroiled in a row over United's handling of the affair, even before the player had put pen to paper.

Frequent public condemnation over the club's lack of ambition (some of it unquestionably deserved) certainly seemed to contribute to United's refusal to grant him an interview when his application for the manager's post was ignored in 1984. "We don't want any glamour boys here," said then chairman Stan Seymour.

Perhaps the words Macdonald uttered after his Fulham side knocked Newcastle out of the League Cup in 1981 also counted against him. "I said it after the first game and I'll say it again. We are a better side than Newcastle and if I had to pick the best 11 individuals over the two legs, I would have the same 11 I started with… if they offer me enough money to go up there as manager I would tell them what is the matter. At the moment, I am manager of Fulham Football Club and I'm not going to give any trade secrets away. All I will say is that I had a very relaxing evening tonight."

Newcastle United's general manager Russell Cushing was certainly speaking for some of the fans, when he declared, a few years later: "Malcolm Macdonald always appears to be knocking Newcastle United, which is a pity for an ex-player and it tarnishes the memory of what he did on the field." Yet Macdonald's devotion to attacking, exciting football – which carried on to his managerial career at Fulham, meant that he was still the supporters' choice to succeed Arthur Cox in '84 – and Jack Charlton in '85.

It was never to be, and there would be further spats with United – over the fact he had to pay for tickets, his inability to get a shirt signed on match day and, a remarkable incident in 1999 when the club was accused of snubbing their former hero by leaving him out of a photographic "display of legends" at the newly-revamped St James' Metro station beside the stadium. The club denied it was a deliberate snub, even though the likes of Jimmy Smith, Jimmy Lawrence and Paul Gascoigne were included. Supporter Alan Weir wrote to the *Journal* "to show my disgust" at the exclusion, yet the truth is that Macdonald was in notable company, omitted along with the likes of Len White, Tony Green and Wyn Davies.

It is perhaps ironic that Macdonald's critics as a pundit sometimes point to his public support for manager Ruud Gullit's failed attempts to sell Alan Shearer during the pair's late 90s power struggle. How prescient of him to see the dangers of one man's persona becoming too big for the club – taking a stance which, less surprisingly, also won backing from Gordon Lee, who immediately recognised the similarities, "Gullit has to take some action because his reputation is being eroded on a daily basis…" Macdonald told the *Journal* in 1999.

YET MACDONALD'S STATUS as a terrace hero is awesome. Only a very few of the contenders in this book can rival the emotional fervour and adulation afforded, in his prime, to the wild haired wonder with his gap-toothed grin. As a youngster growing up in the 70s, I was personally aware that SuperMac was a powerful, magical and omnipotent word in North East life even before I knew what it meant. A vibrant, larger than life personality who put the excitement and fun back into Saturday afternoons, Macdonald – a rare Cockney hero in United's history and the only Londoner in this chosen list of 20 – is one of those players whose cult status was even greater than his nevertheless considerable on-pitch achievements.

Macdonald played the game for goals and for thrills, and his natural sense of fun on the pitch found thousands of like-minded souls on the terraces.

Darts commentator Sid Waddell was one convert to his showmanship. " I have one very vivid memory of Malcolm Macdonald, when he was playing with Stewart Barrowclough. There had been some write-ups praising Barrowclough and SuperMac didn't seem to like it.

It was a very heavy day and he started spraying balls out to his winger and they'd always be five yards too heavy, so Barrowclough would go sprawling in the mud like an idiot or the ball went out of play. It looked to me as if he was just doing that because the winger had had enough publicity!"

Macdonald's sense of mischief, playboy lifestyle, his natural swagger and his capacity for thrilling the crowd with spectacular goals mark him out as one of the most colourful and magnetic characters in the United Hall of Fame. Wine, women and song have always been close to Geordie hearts; Macdonald had a fondness for the first two, and sparked plenty of the third on the Gallowgate terraces. "SuperMac, superstar, how many goals have you scored so far?" sang the disciples, to the tune of Jesus Christ Superstar.

"In the Geordies I found a kindred spirit," said Macdonald, "and I was their kind of player – they were my kind of people. My best years were with Newcastle and my, did we party!"

Tony Green

1971-1973: 39 games, 3 goals

TONY GREEN'S elevation to superstar status, despite playing less than one full season in black and white, is the most extraordinary tale in this book.

Green won nothing at Newcastle, his 39 appearances coinciding with one of those epochs of frustrating under-achievement only too familiar to long-suffering United fans. Bear in mind, too, that this shy family man shunned the limelight, avoided interviews if he could and provided little off-field colour to keep the fans enthralled "I don't like the spotlight," he said after his playing days had come to an end. "It was just a question of me doing a job for which I was being paid."

And yet Green, a quiet, modest figure blessed with rare skills, still commands a wonderful, peculiar affection among supporters. His right to stand shoulder to shoulder with men who impressed consistently over a decade for the Magpies is indisputable.

The key to Green's legend is the sheer wonder of watching him play – he is one of a very few Newcastle players who can lay claim to the title 'Genius'. Green was a master of the creative arts. He had the vision of Paul Gascoigne, the passing skills of Peter Beardsley, the dribbling ability of a Hughie Gallacher or Len White and the determination and enthusiasm of a Kevin Keegan. With his slight build – he was 5ft 7in and just a whisper above 10 stone – chipped tooth grin and choirboy haircut, he may have seemed an unlikely cult hero. Yet Green had the heart, energy, desire and ball-playing gifts to stamp his personality on a game, and his swashbuckling performances destroyed some famous reputations up and down the land.

Dribbling skills – perhaps, for supporters, the most thrilling thing to witness on a football field – were at the core of Green's on-pitch persona. "It was Tony's great gift, to take people on in the congested areas," said United's then first-team coach Keith Burkinshaw. "He could beat two in 10 yards. There are lots who can do it on the flanks, where there's room, but he could do it in the middle where it hurts. In this way he opened up superb space for people like Malcolm Macdonald."

Little wonder the crowd adored him.

"Green was the best I've ever seen at Newcastle," said 47-year-old Alan Scott, of Seahouses, Northumberland. "He could boss a game from start to finish and was such a clever footballer. His ball skills were legendary, and he could ghost past players as if they weren't there. He was always ready to take people on, whoever they were. It was exciting football and the fans loved him for it.

Alan Scott is not alone. Fans who watched some of Green's 39 appearances for United still talk, 34 years later, of how privileged they were. Fifty-four-year-old Graham Patterson, of Chester-le-Street, is a season-ticket holder who remembers the Green days as if they were yesterday. "He was quite simply the best Newcastle player I've ever seen," said Graham. "The sheer vibrancy of his game made him special – he was like an electric current running through the team. He had everything – he was like Alan Ball with skill and he had a tremendous effect on the players around him. He produced some of the greatest performances I've ever seen on a football pitch, and would have the supporters standing there transfixed at times."

Nobody else in the club's history has ever made as big an impact in such a short space of time. With better luck, Green might well have emerged as the biggest cult hero Newcastle United have ever had. Some say that is still a fitting description.

AND YET, STRANGELY, it is difficult to escape the conclusion that Green's enduring legend in the North East is not only despite, but at least partly due to, the poignancy of his enforced early retirement. Like Newcastle United's very own James Dean, the Scot was cut down in his prime – although unlike Dean's car crash, the tackle which wrecked

Green's career was not fatal. Grieving in the North East was no less intense for that.

United manager Joe Harvey famously described the announcement of Green's retirement, in November 1973, following a fruitless 14-month battle against injury, as his saddest day in football. "How can you measure a blow like this?" said a distraught Harvey, who declared the £140,000 insurance money as scant consolation. "It's probably the toughest decision I have had to swallow. Spending money on a new player is something I can scarcely stomach at the moment.

"In a way it's almost like blood money – how do you replace a player like Tony Green? You can't go better than the best in the British Isles, for that's what he was. Even now I am trying to tell myself that this isn't real, because this is a tragedy. Not just for Newcastle and for Tony, but for football as a whole."

GREEN'S NEWCASTLE UNITED story, up until that point, had been one of breathtaking football, irrepressible enthusiasm, lung-bursting determination and unadulterated adoration from the terraces. And, unlike many of the cult heroes in this book, he took no time at all settling in at St James', despite stepping up from the Second Division. Green's meteoric rise to legendary status began with a show-stopping performance away to Everton on his debut. Toffees' skipper Alan Ball declared: "I thought Green did exceptionally well. He is very, very quick and caused us plenty of problems. He'll do Newcastle a power of good."

Newcastle had been struggling badly in the league during the start of the 1971/72 season, and United forward John Tudor saw hope, after just one game, that better times were ahead. "Frankly, Tony's performance was a real eyebrow-raiser for us," he said. "We didn't expect so much from him. He's the quickest thing I've ever seen. When you can take on Ball and Harvey in one go and leave them standing, you're doing well. His skills are obvious – I think he'll prove a first-class signing."

Blackpool fans could have told Tudor in advance what to expect. Green had won the Player of the Year award at Bloomfield Road but, ominously, had then picked up an Achilles tendon injury which kept him out of the game for 17 months.

Still, he had bounced back to full fitness, and Blackpool's Scottish scout Willie Stewart had publicly assured United that their No. 1

transfer target, in the summer of 1971, was the best inside-forward he had ever seen.

Stewart had been the man who spotted the boyish-looking midfielder run the opposition ragged at Albion Rovers in the late 1960s, and he remembered that then-Blackpool boss Stan Mortensen needed only the briefest of glimpses before deciding to sign him. "It took me only 10 minutes to decide that Green was a great player in the making," said Mortensen, after travelling to watch his target in action against Cowdenbeath. His subsequent form for the Seasiders had also alerted Leeds United, who had just finished runners-up in the league and FA Cup the season before, Wolves and Crystal Palace. Leeds were the serious competition, but Newcastle had an ace up their sleeve in former player Bob Stokoe, now Blackpool's manager and was reportedly determined, due to a personal dislike of Elland Road boss Don Revie, not to sell to Leeds.

Green remembered years later: "When Don Revie came to the house to try to get information, Bob never let him over the doorstep. He actually kept him at the door. Bob was desperate for me to go anywhere else but Leeds United. It couldn't happen nowadays." Stokoe, though, was much keener on helping his old club out, and when United baulked at Blackpool's £150,000 cash asking price, he helped to negotiate a compromise – £90,000 cash, plus England under-23 striker Keith Dyson – a deal valued at £140,000, which made Green the most expensive Scottish player in history.

Like many of Newcastle's most legendary players, Green never achieved the same recognition at international level, but he did arrive at St James' on the back of an impressive display for his country against England at Wembley five months previously – and it was not long before the deal was looking like a real bargain. Stokoe himself, despite losing the player's services, admitted he was excited by the prospect of Green providing the bullets for one already established star name at United, centre-forward Malcolm Macdonald. "Green is the fastest mover over the first 15 or 20 yards in the game today. He can beat his man and be away before they can get a second bite," said Stokoe. "This is what makes him a player of flair and fire in the area between midfield and the D of the box. I see him as a great provider for Macdonald... You'll find he is very, very accurate laying the ball off at top speed and clipping the short, sharp crosses the defenders have little time to read close to goal."

Green's impact on a bottom-of-the-league club can be easily measured, thanks to the Newcastle's ultimate 11th-placed finish – and, more pertinently, the man-of-the-match system in operation that season, backed by Kimberley-Clark, the Kleenex tissue firm. It would have been quite apt for Green, whose career would end in such tear-jerking style, to be sponsored by Kleenex, and he practically was, picking up 14 out of 29 Kleenex man-of-the-match awards in the league and cup games he played for United in the 1971/72 season. That staggering statistic goes a long way to explaining the Tony Green legend – although he played only 33 league games for the club, and 39 in all, his amazing consistency allowed him to carry the day and wow the crowd in so many of them.

The man-of-the-match system, with players picked by opposition managers, also gives us an impression of a genius at work from some of the biggest names in the game during his early months on Tyneside. Despite earning the individual award – and £10 in cash – at Everton on his debut, Green had been unable to prevent a 1-0 loss, United's fifth defeat in a row. Green had also promised the fans after Goodison that: "I can play a whole lot better than that, in fact I'll be disappointed if I don't".

He did – in the very next match, masterminding a 5-1 Texaco Cup win at St James' in front of 25,130 fans. If there had been an official man-of-the-match award in this competition, Green, by all accounts would have won it. "Gallowgate buzzed with superlatives," wrote the *Journal's* John Donoghue in his appreciation of Green's display. A 3-1 home win in the league over Southampton brought another individual award – Green scored one and made the other two for Macdonald – and the Scot's extra tenners were soon making up a useful addition to his United wages.

Voted top man in a 3-0 away win over West Brom, Green earned high praise from Albion No. 2 George Wright: "Green was wonderful," he said. "A player with so much natural skill. Newcastle's three goals may have been shared by their two strikers, but Green was the man who made the bullets. He was the player who inspired Newcastle to their second-half deeds." By the time West Ham were dispatched 1-0 at Upton Park in the next game, the Magpies had amassed four wins and two draws in the eight games since his arrival – as opposed to one win and one draw in the eight games before that.

HIS ALL-ROUND GAME was rapidly turning Green into one of the most dangerous midfielders in the top flight and earning plaudits from all and sundry. There was but one dissenting voice – Don Revie, who, in mid-November, swam against the tide by publicly declaring: "Green tends to be inconsistent partly because he doesn't do a great deal of work off the ball." Revie would soon have cause to regret that statement on the one who got away, but first Green reinforced his status on Tyneside by coming through one of the darkest days in Newcastle United's history unscathed – to mastermind one of their finest ever performances. The Magpies had long been known as one of the most inconsistent, unpredictable teams in the league – Jackie Milburn had admitted years earlier that the great FA Cup-winning sides of the 1950s simply decided when and where to turn it on. But if one week summed up that frustrating, yet glamorous trait, more than any other, then it surely came in the winter of 1972.

Green, now firmly ensconced as a terrace idol, had already won successive man-of-the-match awards in the 2-2 home FA Cup tie with Southern League side Hereford United and the goalless league draw at Huddersfield Town. Humiliation, though, was just around the corner. Newcastle's now-infamous third round Cup defeat at Hereford on 5 February 1972, remains one of the biggest shocks in British football history. Yet Green's tireless running and prompting meant he was one of the few United players to emerge with any credit from the harrowing 2-1 defeat to Third Division opposition. "Green ran his blood to water for 120 minutes trying to blast United to victory," wrote John Gibson of the *Evening Chronicle*.

"When I was able to tear Hereford player-manager Colin Addison away from the wild celebrations after the game he told me: 'Green was the only man Newcastle had. He alone seemed determined to stop us winning. He has an enormous heart to go with his considerable skills."

And with the supporters still reeling from their FA Cup exit to a non-league side, gleefully broadcast nationally on *Match of the Day*, [the launch of Motty's career and all that] Green and Co promptly travelled to Old Trafford and played Manchester United off the park in a 2-0 win.

The cocky on-pitch attitude of Green, voted man-of-the-match for the fourth time in a row, in outplaying George Best, Denis Law and

Bobby Charlton, marks this out as his finest ever game for the club – and one of the best individual displays ever from a Newcastle player.

Sports journalist and lifelong Newcastle fan Paul Tully would later write: "The form of Tony Green on that never to-be-forgotten day defied description."

Still, plenty of newspapers had a go at it. Here is a selection…

THE JOURNAL: "Don't just say Green – say super-charger. Tony Green cost Newcastle £150,000. At Old Trafford he looked worth a million."

DAILY MIRROR: "The class of Green contrasted cruelly with the confusion of the Bests, the Charltons and the Laws."

DAILY MAIL: "Green stole the scene from George Best and gave his own skipper, Bobby Moncur, an exciting glimpse of the future."

SUNDAY SUN: "Newcastle fought with all their old fire and verve and had the best player on the park in Tony Green. The little Scot outshone all of Manchester United's big names with a display of real genius."

SUNDAY PEOPLE: "Tony Green looked every inch a six-figure superstar and he attacked the home defence with dazzling bursts."

NEWS OF THE WORLD: "Green was the best player afield and Manchester had no-one to measure up to him."

THE PLAYER HIMSELF, who created both goals that day, for Tudor and Stewart Barrowclough, later picked this display as the highlight of his all-too-brief United career. "Of all the games that I played for Newcastle, that one game me the most pleasure," said Green. "Coming as it did after Hereford, it was a marvellous performance from the whole team."

But Green wasn't finished yet – a fifth successive man-of-the-match award in a goalless draw against Everton then another at home to Leicester left him as United's top man in six of their last seven games. His 11th award came in a goalless home draw with Manchester City which left opposition manager Malcolm Allison hailing him "one of the best in the country" – and the *Chronicle*'s Newcastle United man John Gibson searching for new superlatives. "The incredible consistency of Tony Green continues to astound the soccer judges," he wrote. "Newcastle's sprightly little Scot was voted player of the match again."

Despite giving his main rivals Malcolm Macdonald and Terry Hibbitt three months' head start in Newcastle's Player of the Year competition – based then on the man-of-the-match awards - Green lifted the £250 top prize – and local scribes were becoming apologetic in style as they reported Green's top-man status, week after week.

Single-handedly he rescued United from the abyss of relegation. Often that sort of accolade is falsely given, with one player taking the credit where in truth a team played well with one man featuring. But not on this occasion. Green was inspiration and perspiration as United clambered clear of the drop. First-team coach Keith Burkinshaw was in no doubt who was to thank after United turned an appalling start into a comfortable mid-table finish in 1972. "I'll never forget it," said Burkinshaw. "We were bottom, 15 games played and eight points. Things were going badly. And then Joe Harvey went out and signed Tony - and that was it. From the time Tony arrived we were in promotion form and finished in a good position at the end of the season."

BUT ASIDE FROM providing individual inspiration, Green also had the rare ability to bring the best out of others. His club and Scotland captain Bobby Moncur explained the point in an interview with the *Evening Chronicle* on the eve of the 1972/73 season

> "He has astonishing speed, lightning reaction, brilliant skill and the energy to keep running for 90 minutes," he said. "But the thing that gives Tony that little bit extra is his amazing enthusiasm. Of course, everyone is delighted when we win, but Tony displays an incredible kind of youthful exuberance… something that rubs off on all his colleagues. I vividly remember the look of sheer joy on his face when we beat Arsenal towards the end of last season. I'm sure he couldn't have been happier had we won the pools."

Moncur was also keen to give the lie to claims that Green failed on the international stage – although there seems little doubt that in his limited chances, he never quite rose to his true potential. "The times we've played together he has done pretty well, even if he has not quite reached the dazzling standard he consistently achieves at club level," said the then Scotland skipper.

Green's love affair with the Scotland team – he once picked his cap against England at Wembley in 1971 as his joint favourite memory in football along with signing for United – hit a rocky patch the following year, when he angered national boss Tommy Docherty by announcing he would not travel on a summer tour to Brazil. "The trouble is you can get too much soccer in the summer and it makes you stale," he said. Newcastle fans, seeing the move as fresh testament to Green's loyalty to United, loved him all the more for it. Yet the row threatened to end his international career until Docherty relented and gave Green a reprieve, handing him his fifth cap at home to Wales in May 1972 – after a full year without kicking a ball for his country.

Five Scotland games – against Portugal, Belgium, Holland, Peru and Northern Ireland, had passed Green by while he was wowing the crowds on Tyneside. Perhaps, with Green being called up to the squads for the Holland and Peru games but never picked, Docherty had allowed himself to be put off by watching the player in training.

Joe Harvey could have told him not to fall for that one, having learned that, like Andy Cole two decades later, Green was a work-shy trainer who turned into a world-beater on matchdays.

"I do my best, but I know I lag behind the others," he once admitted. "Training to me is really hard. For example, I can hardly lift the weights some players pick up in one hand.

"And all this business about me being extremely fast on the park over short distances – it may be true but on the track when I'm not chasing a ball I'm not the fastest by any means, even over the first 10 or 15 yards. Over 100 yards, I've got no chance!"

Harvey readily admitted that Green was one of the worst trainers at the club, insisting: "When you watch Tony lapping the track you'd think he was about to die. His head rolls and he looks all in. But I like bad trainers who play like a dream. It's when it's the other way round that I worry." It was a handy characteristic as on the pitch, Green could also fool the opposition into thinking he was not interested – his slovenly, almost lazy stance, not dissimilar to Chris Waddle's laissez-faire 80s look – belied a prodigious work-rate and lightning fast reflexes. "Even on the field Green can look wrong – when he's standing still," said the *Evening Chronicle*. "He wears baggy shorts and as often as not his right stocking is around his ankle." But his attitude was never called into question – by manager, team-mates or fans, with Moncur admitting that Green was the one player in the Newcastle dressing room who never needed motivating. His only problem, indeed, with the diminutive Scot, was putting up with practical jokes from a quiet player who nevertheless had a devilish sense of humour once he felt comfortable in his surroundings.

Green's lack of achievement on the training ground is perhaps the one trait that does not seem to fit with the workaholic model professional – but perhaps he was not struggling quite as much as Harvey thought. After all, Green once hinted, in an interview with the *Evening Chronicle* in the summer of 1972, that the motivation was not always there in training. "Everything just seems to come right on a Saturday," he said. "I cannot get involved in five-a-sides and the like when there's nothing at stake." Green was asked, in the same interview, a question which another Newcastle midfield maestro, Paul Gascoigne, would face more than 10 years later – and answered it the same way… a true football genius, it seems, has no idea what he is going to do next! "I'm not consciously aware of what I'm doing or what I'm going to do," he said. "Once a football writer rang me up from London and asked me what I thought of when I had the ball at my feet. I just couldn't reply. I mean, what a daft question. I don't think of anything. Whatever happens just comes naturally, that's all."

But what came naturally to Green was extraordinary to team-mates, opponents and most importantly supporters, who have placed the Glaswegian on a permanent pedestal on Tyneside.

WITH NEWCASTLE'S RELEGATION ghosts banished, there remained the challenge of making Don Revie eat his words during the 1972/73. United boss Harvey was, by now, ecstatic at Green's contribution, hailing him as "a marvel" and "as good as anyone in the country". Revie was forced to agree after watching Green mastermind a 1-0 win over his star-studded team on Tyneside. "Green was super," the Leeds boss graciously acknowledged. "He was certainly Newcastle's best player – a man with skill, courage and pace."

A rare Green goal came in Newcastle's penultimate game of the season, a 4-2 home win over West Brom, and United's No. 1 player was full of high hopes for the future when he picked up his Player of the Year award in the close season, declaring prophetically: "I honestly believe that, barring injuries, we'll shock a few people next season."

Years later, he would blackly refer to Player of the Year competitions as a curse. A 17-month lay-off had followed after winning the Blackpool version and he would play only six more times for Newcastle after that summer presentation.

The first of those, a goalscoring performance in the 1972/73 curtain-raiser, a 2-1 home win over Wolves, suggested great times ahead for club and player. But three weeks later came that fateful clash with Mel Blyth at Crystal Palace, which robbed Green of the chance of becoming one of the game's all-time greats. Green told the *Sunday Sun* that night: "I went one way and my leg went the other", but still neither he nor the club had any idea how serious the injury was.

The initial diagnosis was that Green had torn cartilage and would be out for a month… then two months… and so it continued.

The long, agonising fight for fitness would last 14 months before Green would finally be forced to retire on medical advice – and in that time he would endure three operations and countless false dawns. Joe Harvey declared in the summer of 1973: "I'm delighted by reports on Tony. He is going well in training and I see no reason why he should not be fit for selection at the beginning of the season." Yet one week later, he was booked back in to Wrightington Hospital in Lancashire, for a third operation under surgeon Keith Barnes – the man who had saved his career once before, when that Achilles injury kept him out of action for a full season at Blackpool.

Even then, having been given the go-ahead to resume training, Green was confident that his career was back on track as Tyneside breathed another sigh of relief. Joe Harvey travelled down to watch his comeback for the reserves at Coventry, and greeted the player like a long-lost son after a seemingly successful return to action.

Harvey drove back to Tyneside in triumphant mood, and on 9 November, the *Journal* announced an imminent first-team comeback:

"Tony Green, Newcastle United's mighty atom, exploded through the Cup depression clouds over the North East yesterday, with the most welcoming news manager Joe Harvey has heard in months." Green, the newspaper reported, was just a week away from a senior return. However unbeknown even to Harvey at first, the player's knee, the morning after that Coventry comeback, had swollen up like a balloon. "My knee was in ruins," Green later recalled. "I couldn't even stand on it, and I was back to square one." Only 10 days later, he travelled down to see surgeon Keith Barnes and was given the news the whole of Tyneside had been secretly dreading.

His career was over.

"I just feel empty inside," he told the *Journal*. "I suppose I am still feeling the effect of the shock. And to be honest I don't know where I am going to go from here. "People must have thought that I expected all this to happen – but I didn't. In fact, I felt sure I was home and dry and that I would be playing again. "I have to accept the end, but I have no wish to move away from Tyneside. Despite all that has happened to me here, it's still a place I love."

Green would later recall that he had to console his manager Harvey on one occasion, so distraught was the Newcastle boss, while club chairman Lord Westwood immediately announced that there would be a testimonial for "a grand little fellow with a marvellous heart. It's very tragic indeed. Tony was a fabulous footballer and will be irreplaceable. No one could excite me with their skills like he could."

A hoped-for testimonial against boyhood idols Celtic failed to materialise when manager Jock Stein pulled the Hoops out through fear of crowd trouble, but Middlesbrough stepped into the breach, and Green was given the pick of all Newcastle's top players for the game despite the fact they had a league game the next day! "Joe was more interested in the testimonial than he was in the league game," recalled Green, who was staggered at the donations and gestures from a heartbroken footballing public. "Loads of people, like the doormen, came up and gave me their wages. They were saying things like: 'It's been nice watching you play. Will you take my wages?'"

More than 30,000 fans turned up to the testimonial, and many of those who could not attend, like Middlesex-based supporter Terry Pattinson, sent donations instead. "The shortage of skilled footballers is bad enough without losing men of his calibre," wrote Pattinson in a letter to the *Evening Chronicle* which included a £1 cheque for the testimonial fund. Green admitted he had been inundated with similar gestures, declaring: "Everyone has been so kind I don't know how to thank them." Other supporters, who could not bear to accept that Green would never again dance across the turf in a black and white shirt, sent special ointments passed down by grandparents, or even suggested miracle treatments to bring their idol back to full strength!

The emotional public grieving for Green's career undoubtedly helped to give him a permanent place in Tynesiders' hearts reserved for the special few. He remained in the bosom of his adoring public after training for a second career as a teacher, taking work at Gosforth East Middle School just a few miles from St James' Park. But when teaching took him to Lancashire, and his home in Poulton-le-Fylde, he still found reason to return to Tyneside, and relished the opportunity to return to his adopted home. "It's an incredible place," he declared, long after hanging up his boots. "I don't suppose there's another place like it for football. People stop you in the street, in the shops… everywhere you go you're recognised. It always was a great feeling and it still is."

Green walks around with the likes of Gallacher, Len Shackleton, Len White, Paul Gascoigne and Peter Beardsley in the United Hall of Fame – pure football technicians who elevated the game to another level. But in his blink-of-an-eye Magpies career, he left a legacy far beyond mere talent.

Throw in his determination, enthusiasm, his achievement in inspiring a club out of the doldrums of a relegation battle, his preference for club over country and his uncanny ability to find an extra gear on matchdays, before you get a true picture of what Tony Green really meant to the folk of Newcastle.

Keith Burkinshaw was quick to point out that Green's bravery on the pitch – and his determination off it, particularly in his battle against injury – helped endear him to supporters who simply longed for him to return to the fray. "Tony's character was tremendous," he said, "he rarely let it get him down. That's what makes it all the worse for him, all the hard work and suffering had just come to nothing. It takes tremendous willpower to keep going week after week and overcome setbacks like Tony did. I honestly don't think the ordinary bloke in the street realises just what it's like. Joe Harvey has said that Tony did more in the revival this club made than any other player. And he's so right. He WAS a rare individual. At times like this you can get a bit emotional, but he was unique – and I mean that literally. I have tried to think of another player in the First Division like him, and I can't."

But if the fans did not physically share the pain, they understood the stakes Green was playing for – like his supporters on the terraces, he was a football obsessive, and that devotion, while helping him to build a legendary reputation, meant the end was so much harder to stomach.

Given Green's devotion to the game, many supporters were surprised that he did not train as a coach and work towards a career in management. The man himself, whose only regular involvement in football was a long-term appointment to the pools panel, starting in 1975, explained that the pain of his early retirement as a player made this a non-starter. "It would be very hard just to sit and watch a game, knowing that I could not get physically involved," he said, in the immediate aftermath of his fateful diagnosis.

Green's lack of longevity and silverware will always, ultimately, count against him when pitched against the likes of Hughie Gallacher and Jackie Milburn – the two supreme icons in Newcastle's history. But the intensity of his ascent to idolatry suggest that, save for an awkward challenge at Selhurst Park 33 years ago, Tony Green might just have been the best player – and the biggest hero – of them all.

As it is, we have to manipulate that well-known "pound-for-pound" phrase so beloved of boxing commentators to assert his claim that, game-for-game, Tony Green was the greatest player Newcastle have ever had.

Kevin Keegan

1982-1984: 85 games, 49 goals

NEWCASTLE FANS OVER 30 must remember this:

> – A helicopter takes off from the centre circle, as a black
> and white No. 7 shirt falls to the ground…
> – A man stands on the steps of St. James' Park addressing
> an angry mob…
> – The same man, headphones on, shouts into a
> microphone: "I'd love it, just love it…"

So many of the iconic images from Newcastle United's modern history involve one man. It begs the question: Was anyone ever more popular on Tyneside than Kevin Keegan? Not in my lifetime. His achievements as a player and manager, coupled with a massive, infectious personality, sent fans and media alike scrambling to find new superlatives to portray his unique status among supporters.

Hero? Certainly. Legend? No doubt. Messiah? Not really – but still the tag stuck. Other words just did not seem big enough to capture the little man. Keegan stands alone in this book as a man whose popularity in Geordieland emanates partly – in fact, mainly – from his time as a manager. There are precious few who withstand the pressures of the United hotseat – but to do it while retaining the common touch and heroic status among supporters is totally unique.

But then, Keegan the man is a one-off.

National TV audiences, entranced by Newcastle's Premiership progress under his stewardship in the early 90s, think they know him well – and Keegan infamously laid much of his soul bare during the media revolution of that time. But those who followed his Tyneside career most closely know that there is much more to KK than an infectious attitude and a short fuse. Indeed, there are many layers to the Keegan psyche, and many reasons why he became so revered.

THE KEEGAN NEWCASTLE fans got to know was passionate, vivacious, positive, vibrant, inspirational, confident, loyal, honest, committed and determined. But at times he also seemed morose, over-sensitive, bad-tempered, naive, stubborn, foolhardy and egotistical. There were those supporters, it should be pointed out, who believed Keegan's exit was the right thing for the club when he walked out of St James' Park on 8 January 1997 – yet they too felt the grief. And even those who agreed with the man's own parting shot ("I have taken the club as far as I can") had to agree that it was a mighty long way.

Keegan had, after all:

- Scored 49 goals in 85 games as a player for Newcastle
- Skippered the side to promotion back into the top flight in 1984
- Saved the club from relegation to Division Three as a manager in 1992
- Taken United into the Premiership as record-breaking First Division Champions the following year
- Led the Magpies back into Europe 12 months after that
- Come within a whisker of the coveted Premiership title in 1996
- Broken the world record transfer by bringing Alan Shearer home for £15m in July 1996
- Won 55 per cent of his games in charge of Newcastle, the highest mark of any post-war United manager

But those facts, dramatic as they are, do not even begin to capture the excitement of two remarkable revolutions on Tyneside, brought about largely down to Keegan's sheer force of personality. And as ever with the man, it was not so much what he did, as the way that he did it.

At the risk of offending his legions of followers in the North East, it has to be pointed out that there are players elsewhere in this book who stand head and shoulders above the 5ft 8in striker when it comes to natural ability; players like Hughie Gallacher, Peter Beardsley and Paul Gascoigne. But, at least partly because of his diminutive stature, Keegan had long since turned himself into a master of positive thinking and determination. Force of personality is at the core of the Keegan legend – and even those cynics turned off by an ultra-professional, squeaky clean image had to admit that he brought tangible excitement to Tyneside.

BY THE TIME he joined Newcastle in 1982, Keegan had learned, after fashioning a spectacular playing career which brought almost every club honour imaginable, that it takes more than ability to make it to the top. The steely-eyed determination which would take United fans on a rollercoaster ride was there to see as he pumped weights in his Doncaster home as a lad, determined to prove wrong the sceptics who felt he was too slight to ever forge a successful career in the professional game. And how wrong they were. Keegan came to Tyneside as arguably the biggest name in world football, having won two European Footballer of the Year awards, one Football Writers Player of the Year award, one PFA Player of the Year award, the German Fooballer of the Year award, 63 England caps (31 as captain), three league titles, the FA Cup, the European Cup, the UEFA Cup and the Bundesliga title.

His status on Tyneside began with that momentous decision, at the age of 31, to swap a Southampton side that had just finished seventh in the top flight for a Second Division Newcastle side that looked more likely to go down than up. If many in the game regarded the move as foolish, Keegan saw it instead as a challenge to get his teeth into and, helped by the fact that United chairman Stan Seymour accepted his off-the-cuff request for 15 per cent of any increase in gate receipts, he sparked football fever in Newcastle by signing on 19 August 1982. Later, there would be Alan Shearer and Michael Owen. But the first big Newcastle signing of many a supporter's lifetime came at the Gosforth

Park Hotel (venue of the press conference to announce Keegan's arrival) that day. As word leaked out, hundreds of supporters besieged the hotel and he was given his first taste of football fever, Geordie-style.

The foundations of a legend were already in place – Keegan's popularity already burgeoning through sheer gratitude that the England skipper had agreed to join a sleeping giant of club, outside the top flight, which had been in danger of becoming a footballing backwater. But for Keegan's part, the lure of following in the footsteps of his father's heroes was too powerful to resist. Joe Keegan had been a miner in Hetton-le-Hole before moving his family to Doncaster, and KK also had a strong link to Tyneside culture through the bravery of his grandfather, Frank, a hero of the 1909 West Stanley pit disaster, who had helped to save 30 lives on a day when 198 perished.

As the astute Keegan recalled in his autobiography, he was well aware that he had a chance to become a legendary figure on Tyneside:

> "They were still talking about the events of 20 or 30 years
> before, about Hughie Gallacher, and to a lesser extent
> about Malcolm Macdonald... they were in dire need of
> a new hero, and Arthur Cox and Stan Seymour wanted
> me to fill that role."

Keegan immediately fanned the flames by declaring at that first press conference, to the delight of the uninvited fans behind the hastily-erected barriers, that "promotion is on".

It wasn't. The First Division would have to wait for another year – but supporters did not have to wait long for a goal to consummate the marriage. That came on his debut, a 1-0 win over QPR on 28 August in front of a sell-out 36,185 crowd. The fans chanted their new hero's name almost constantly in a fairy-tale atmosphere.

Keegan's arrival had ignited the natural passion for football in an area long starved of success, and his canny idea of negotiating a cut of the gate receipts – almost unheard-of at the time and certainly not reported – was about to pay off handsomely. One of the first footballers to capitalise heavily on sponsorship and marketing deals, Keegan had long since established a reputation for spotting a commercial opportunity, and he knew he was on to a winner again when 27,939 turned up to the next home game against Middlesbrough and 29,084 for Chelsea.

Overall, gates were up nearly 40 per cent to an average of over 24,000 that season – despite the fact United finished fifth and never seriously looked like going up – and Keegan later admitted: "It brought me in so much money that I was embarrassed". But the arrangement cut both ways. If the fans were keeping Kevin Keegan in the style to which he had become accustomed, he was providing football to which they certainly weren't.

He may have lost half a yard of pace since his prime – and newly-appointed England boss Bobby Robson clearly thought so, causing outrage on Tyneside by dropping him – but he was still a class ahead of most Second Division defenders, and rattled home 21 goals to prove the point. With a prodigious workrate, superb vision, courage, deadly finishing and uncanny knack of being in the right place at the right time, his arrival had a massive impact on the team and it seemed at times as if Newcastle had made two or three new signings all at once.

OFF THE FIELD, Keegan's strength of personality was about to strike a blow for the Geordie cause in the summer of 1993, when he asked for a crisis meeting with manager Arthur Cox and chairman Stan Seymour. Fifth place was not good enough for Keegan, and he wanted assurances about the club's transfer plans before committing to a new one-year contract. "I'm not holding a gun to their head, but I want to see some movement from the club," he said at the time. Full-backs Malcolm Brown and John Ryan duly arrived, along with goalkeeper Martin Thomas as Keegan agreed another 12-month deal – but his request for a new strike partner was the catalyst for the most important signing, as Peter Beardsley arrived from Vancouver Whitecaps a few weeks after the start of the season. Keegan had never heard of the 22-year-old Geordie – but soon had reason to thank Cox for the unknown's arrival, as the pair, aided and abetted by another wizard's apprentice in Chris Waddle, terrorised Division Two defences. Beardsley – who played alongside Ian Rush, Gary Lineker, Andy Cole, John Barnes, Les Ferdinand, Duncan Ferguson and Alan Shearer in his career – would later pick Keegan as his greatest ever strike partner.

Keegan (28 goals), Beardsley (20) and Waddle (18) were the three biggest reasons Newcastle won promotion that year, producing some of the best attacking football ever seen at St James' Park before or since.

But United fans desperate to see them repeat the trick in Division One were in for a massive disappointment.

Those same supporters had been eagerly awaiting their hero's return to Anfield to take on his old side Liverpool with the Magpies, when the two teams were paired together in an FA Cup tie, eagerly snapped up by BBC television for live Friday night transmission. But United were hammered 4-0 on the night, and worse still, although most of the nationwide audience will not have picked up on it, an incident in that game convinced Keegan that this had to be his last season as a player. His strength of mind – and a proud desire to quit while still near the top of his game – were in evidence when he called a press conference on his 33rd birthday, breaking hearts right across the North East on St. Valentine's Day. With typical honesty, he immediately told the media why he was quitting. The incident is vividly recounted in his autobiography:

> "The moment I realised my career had peaked came after I knocked a ball past Mark Lawrenson. When you are a top player, you have this dismissive air about you in those circumstances. You know from the second you play the ball that the defender is now out of the equation and you are already thinking about what you are going to do next. Where's the keeper? Where's the next defender? All that was going through my mind when Mark suddenly took the ball off me. Over a stretch of six or eight yards he seemed to take 10 yards out of me. That was what made up my mind."

He would not go back on that decision, but would still provide moments of magic before bowing out as a player at home to Brighton in the last match of the season. A brace in a 5-1 home win over Carlisle – with Beardsley also scoring twice and Waddle once – was particularly memorable, while his role in the after-match celebrations following a 4-0 home rout over Derby, which effectively sealed promotion with two matches to spare, provided Newcastle fans with the first iconic image of the Keegan years on Tyneside.

The club skipper had already earned respect by playing on with a head injury – after receiving on-pitch treatment for concussion – sustained in a clash with Derby keeper Steve Cherry as he headed Newcastle in front, but as the final whistle blew, Keegan was determined to live the moment, picking up and wearing as many club scarves as he could find as United fans threw them onto the pitch in adoration. Those photographs of the 5ft 8in striker almost swamped by scarves and saluting his loyal fans, are one of many enduring symbols of his time at the club.

But if that was an emotional day, Keegan wrenched every drop of pathos out of his farewell tribute game against Liverpool on 17 May – the proceeds of which he agreed to hand over to the club. Some critics of the Yorkshireman's managerial career would later complain about Keegan's emotional approach and sense of showmanship. But was ever anything as over-the-top as being whisked away by helicopter from the centre-circle at the final whistle, theatrically throwing his No.. 7 shirt down on to the turf?

That stunt was Tyneside's mid-80s equivalent of the Posh and Becks wedding, but the United fans lapped up the schmooze. British football had never seen an exit like it, and there were precious few names big enough to even try and pull it off.

IT WOULD BE 10 years before Keegan was reunited with his spiritual home, and some might say that glamour and high drama were conspicuous by their absence from the club throughout that decade. But his return, in February 1992 to succeed Ossie Ardiles as manager and take over a side struggling to stay in Division Two, was a predictably passionate reunion – on both sides.

Media critics were stunned at Newcastle's gamble on an untried manager who had never done a day's coaching in his life – but the majority of Magpies fans, banking on the charisma and determination of an inspirational figurehead, saw him as the perfect choice. They were right. Keegan's achievements in the role are now legion for the generations who followed the early years of the Premiership.

For starters, he saved United from Division Three – although only just – before taking the newly-christened First Division by storm in a record-breaking Championship-winning season. United won their first 11 games of an unforgettable campaign, and eventually finished with 96 points, eight clear of second-placed West Ham, and launched their promotion party early with a 7-1 romp over Leicester City on the final day of the season.

But Keegan was just beginning.

The following season, he would arrive on the Premiership stage as THE leading man in Sky TV's fledgling marathon production. Newcastle's new boss – passionate, eloquent, honest, and always ready with a soundbite – remained the darling of the media until his team's infamous title blow-up in 1996. The United manager's upfront approach allowed fans across the nation – many of whom had adopted the free-flowing black and whites as their second favourite team – to live with him the highs and lows of an amazing rollercoaster ride. Keegan would later admit: "We were riding a tiger I couldn't always control". His team, meanwhile, produced some of the most exciting attacking football ever seen in these shores, earning the nickname "The Entertainers" and direct praise from FIFA president Sepp Blatter for their positive approach to the game.

His achievements all helped to build an impressive legend on Tyneside, as Keegan established United as one of the elite clubs in the land, with Premiership finishes of third, sixth, second and second (the last of those four finishes coming in 1997, when Kenny Dalglish took over from Keegan in January). Newcastle fans were treated to their most exciting spell since the triple FA Cup win of the 50s – and, in terms of league placing, this was the most successful United side for more than 70 years.

This drama on the pitch was unfolding in front of sell-out crowds, as the ground began a massive transformation into one of the finest all-seater stadia in the country. Keegan – aided and abetted by chairman Sir John Hall and a board finally matching the supporters' ambition – had roused the sleeping giant that had first attracted him to Tyneside; and it was now trampling on reputations right across the country.

That there were no trophies to show for it seemed, genuinely, to hurt Keegan as much as it did the fans. Indeed, the incredible near-miss in 1996, when Newcastle imploded to throw away a 12-point lead and hand the crown to Manchester United, was the beginning of the end for the manager, who seemed burnt out by the pressure and emotion of the campaign. He admitted after leaving the club: "We could and should have won the title... losing out to Manchester United affected me greatly and undoubtedly played a major part in my ultimate decision to quit." Whispers from the dressing room from this time suggest KK had lost his legendary self-belief during the title run-in, and this nervousness quickly spread to the players.

But Keegan's all-out devotion to attacking football – the bedrock of his managerial style – was itself held in many quarters as the reason for the collapse, with the Magpies famously coming a cropper at home to Manchester United (1-0), and away to Liverpool (4-3) and Blackburn (2-1) in games that, had they been drawn, would have been enough to bring the title to Tyneside. But if that season was a failure, it was a heroic one, and some would argue that it seems churlish and almost pointless to blame for their collapse the attacking style which had got Newcastle so close in the first place.

NEVERTHELESS, IT MUST be pointed out that Keegan had his critics, and there were many supporters who wished that, having taken Newcastle so far, he had stiffened his team up to hang for a few precious draws in that title run-in. Instead, a stubborn refusal to compromise his ideals seemed to contribute to that late-season decline. Yet it was this self-same determination which had taken the club so far. Positive thinking gave Keegan the courage to capitalise absolutely on a golden age of spending at Newcastle United. Just a few years before, Magpies fans were welcoming the likes of George Reilly, Tony Cunningham and Billy Whitehurst to the club. Under the reign of millionaire chairman Hall, who underwrote massive bank loans in the successful hope that the club could afford to pay them off after a successful flotation on the stock market, some of the biggest names in football arrived on Tyneside. Keegan was like a kid in a sweet shop, and held nothing back in delivering signings he knew would make United fans drool.

Andy Cole, Les Ferdinand and Alan Shearer would be up there in any all-time top 10 of Newcastle centre-forwards – and they all arrived during the Keegan years. Tino Asprilla, David Ginola and Peter Beardsley (signed for the second time) were also captured to add magic and artistry, while Darren Peacock, David Batty, Robert Lee, Philippe Albert, John Beresford and Barry Venison all proved their worth.

It was a fantasy team played out in black and white and if many fans questioned the wisdom of playing with four or even five natural attackers, there were plenty more who admired Keegan's audacity for – more often than not – pulling it off. Supporters were gripped by the thrilling edge-of-your-seat football his teams produced, and their defensive vulnerability was almost always overshadowed by breathtaking approach play at the other end. Keegan himself would later look back on this time and claim he always felt under pressure from the supporters to concentrate on attacking play – insisting the very nature of the club demanded it. This is a debate which still rages among supporters – and there are many who would not have welcomed a George Graham-style manager determined to keep a clean sheet and grind out results.

As ever with Kevin Keegan, though, he seems to have taken the argument to extremes, insisting that the Geordie love of attacking play "tied a noose around my neck". Whatever the catalyst for it, by the time that title battle came around in 1996, Keegan had long revelled in his reputation for all-out attack. "When it came to a toss-up between a really skilful player or one who would do a job, I always went for the exciting option, whatever the risk," he said. "We bought Philippe Albert instead of a rugged defender because we wanted someone to come out of defence with the ball. The more I was told I should change things, the more stubborn I became. I decided that I wasn't prepared to compromise."

It was the bloody-minded determination which had taken KK to the top of the world game as a player – the same massive self-belief which had enabled him, as manager, to transform a North East institution in just four years. Keegan's dictatorial, almost arrogant style of leadership had picked an ailing club up by its bootstraps – and his iconic status is inextricably linked to the manner in which he dismissed a Newcastle United inferiority complex which had lasted for decades. It was almost a confidence trick – and one which he had prepared all his life for through a devotion to motivational self-help books. "I'd spent hours reading books on positive mental attitude, management skills and the advanced thinking of experts," he said. It helped to explain those almost boastful public targets – he told Alex Ferguson he was gunning for Manchester United's title even before promotion to the Premiership was achieved, and once declared that Newcastle were on target to win the treble.

A supporter's reaction to such outbursts would depend entirely on whether he was a cynic or a romantic. Was this embarrassing and unnecessary tub-thumping that made him and the club look foolish? Or reassuring soundbites that proved the man in charge was aiming high? Whatever your viewpoint, as a Newcastle fan, you had to admit that Keegan was one-off and life at the club was never dull under his stewardship.

LIKE THE SUPPORTERS, the players were thriving under his inspirational leadership. His motivational qualities were – when he was at his peak – awesome, and he helped turn players such as Robert Lee, Barry Venison and Steve Howey into England internationals. The latter's transformation from run-of-the-mill striker to cultured centre-half – a switch initiated by Ardiles, but developed by Keegan – was an inspired piece of management, and remains as proof positive that KK could turn his mind to defensive football when he wanted to. Many Newcastle players improved remarkably under Keegan's tutelage, and keen devotees like Lee and full-back John Beresford would frequently wax lyrical to the media about their manager's capacity for instilling self-belief. "I have always felt that motivation was the core, the very essence of being a manager," said Keegan. " That's what I was about: working with my players' minds, encouraging the ones who were down, spurring on those who were doing well to play even better." Lee admitted: "When Kevin Keegan bought me he brought me out of my shell. He pressured me to get involved in off-the-field stuff and he wanted my opinion about tactics. Talking more helped me as a player and, as a person."

Keegan would later claim, before resigning in January 1997, that he had lost that ability to motivate, and critics would point out his tactical armoury was never ample enough to sustain the momentum on those occasions. Yet Keegan had to be still doing sometime right – his team scored 10 goals in their last two league games before he walked out, beating Tottenham and Leeds 7-1 and 3-0 respectively. And in his pomp, it seemed the entire club – nay, the whole of Tyneside – was powered not by the National Grid, but Kevin Keegan's self-belief.

In turn, his determination would bring him – the critics argued – too much power at St James' Park, where there seemed no equivalent of the famous Anfield boot room to help him with decision-making.

It seems unthinkable, just a decade later, to recall that the manager was allowed to scrap the reserve team, rather than play two games a week on the St James' pitch, when the Pontins League refused to allow matches to be played at Gateshead Stadium. That was one of Keegan's biggest mistakes, but, during the five-year managerial career of a man who believed anything was possible, his stubborn streak would frequently come in handy. That strength of mind proved crucial as KK squared up to the Newcastle board in two stand-offs of seismic proportions in United's modern history.

The first came when he effectively resigned as manager just a month after taking over, following a 3-1 home win over Swindon, because promised transfer funds were not forthcoming from Sir John Hall. Keegan won that battle, as he did the following summer when he turned down a new managerial contract which obliged him to raise money by selling players. His stance in the latter row effectively marked the end of George Forbes' reign as chairman, and set the blueprint for United as an ambitious buying club under his successor Sir John Hall.

Keegan's role in both instances – as fans' champion, fighting with the moneymen to fulfil the supporters' ambitions – was seen as heroic on the terraces. Yet ironically, one of the most famous examples of Keegan's bravery came after he unwittingly revived the ghost of United as a selling club.

Keegan faced an angry mob of hundreds on the steps of St James' Park, after selling one of the most popular players in the club's history – striker Andy Cole – to bitter rivals Manchester United. But, single-handedly standing up to his critics, Keegan soon had the assembled hordes eating out of his hands – and the incident, played out live on TV, soon became a much-lauded example of crisis public relations work at company seminars across the country. There are precious few managers who would have dared to have pulled off the Cole deal, let alone explain it face-to-face to the fans.

Ultimately, the jury is still out on whether the Cole deal was a master-stroke. The makeweight in the deal, Keith Gillespie, failed to live up to his billing as the next George Best and Cole did go on to score 121 goals in 231 starts for Manchester United. They are impressive figures, yet for some reason Cole never quite recaptured the scintillating form which had made him a legend on Tyneside, while his replacement, Les Ferdinand, proved another superb acquisition, even if the fans did have to wait another six months for his arrival.

Looking back, if Cole had managed to continue his epic efforts in black and white, he should surely never have been sold – but that is a big 'if'. The incredible thing is that, despite the striker's huge popularity, letters to local newspapers at the time came out 2 to 1 backing Keegan – it was a massive vote of confidence in his managerial ability.

But if the Cole deal was a courageous decision, Keegan's reputation for bravery had been established long before he ever arrived in Newcastle as a player. This was the man who, as an England international, insisted on playing for his country against Yugoslavia, heading home an equaliser in the 2-2 draw just a day after being beaten up by security guards at Belgrade airport. He had also insisted on playing in a crucial World Cup qualifier away to Northern Ireland in 1975, despite death threats and against the advice of his national manager Don Revie. But, almost inevitably, there were casualties of Keegan's gung-ho approach. As a Newcastle player, he had shown his short fuse when he went for team-mate Kenny Wharton, pinning the local lad up against the wall after a pulsating home defeat to Fulham. Wharton's crime? To admit he felt privileged to have played in such a game. Ironically, many of Keegan's players would feel the same after the famous 4-3 defeat away to Anfield 13 years later.

AS A MANAGER, Keegan's didactic approach to his job, and an all-encompassing St James' Park powerbase where it seemed nobody questioned the boss, made United's manager ever more sensitive to criticism – and brought his unpredictable temperament to bear on many occasions. There was a time when Newcastle as a city seemed like Keegan's personal empire – and the media were wary not to cross him. One Newcastle-based sports journalist, The *Journal*'s Tim Taylor, wrote some of his last ever printed words on United when one of his articles offended Keegan and his No. 2 Terry McDermott, resulting in a permanent club ban. On another occasion, a young reporter working on a club-backed weekly newspaper was forced to read every word of a semi-critical piece on David Ginola to the unperturbed Frenchman.

No North East journalist saw more of him than the *Evening Chronicle*'s long-time Newcastle United reporter Alan Oliver, who said Keegan was the best – and the worst – manager he had ever dealt with, claiming he had "ruled the press with fear". The manager's massive personality certainly seemed out of control on occasion – but little wonder there was nobody at St James' Park to keep him in check, as the whole of Tyneside seemed in thrall to the man they were only half-jokingly referring to as the Messiah.

Yet his behaviour often seemed childish rather than god-like. Five times Keegan threatened to quit Newcastle as manager before the break became permanent, and the term "prima donna" was frequently used by his critics. At times, those threats achieved something – such as precious transfer funds – at other times, the suspicion remained that this nevertheless proud man simply needed to know he was loved.

He was, despite, and sometimes because of, his headstrong nature. This was the man who once pulled out of a Sky TV job as pundit on a Southampton game, because the attendant, whom Keegan remembered from his time as a player there, would not let him into the Dell car park! It seems amazing that one of the biggest names in the game, who had conquered the football world, could let such a laughable incident get to him. Yet he would later describe this tiny spat as "one of the low points of my life". Keegan had also once put his England playing career on the line by walking out of the team hotel, going home and taking his phone off the hook, after being rested for a match against Wales at Wembley. Revie forgave him and Keegan had to admit "I'm not sure I would have done the same thing in his position".

Yet this over-sensitive man would earn plaudits aplenty – and sheer adoration on Tyneside – for his brutal honesty. It showed itself with the almost religious fervour Keegan showed in exceeding his daily media obligations in the early years of his Newcastle tenure. Embracing the fans, through the media, like no other United manager him, he saw it as his duty to keep the faithful informed and he introduced an unprecedented daily press conference at the club's training ground. Through it and Keegan's desire to feed the thousands their daily bread of news from St James', Newcastle fans were given more daily insight into the goings-on at their beloved club than ever before.

But his managerial colleagues regarded this development with amused bewilderment – not dissimilar to the national reaction at Keegan's infamous Sky TV blow-up during Newcastle's 1996 title collapse. The rant – after a 1-0 United win at Leeds – was aimed at Sir Alex Ferguson after the Manchester United boss had suggested Leeds had tried harder against the Red Devils than in many of their games this season. Ferguson, in an attempt to gee up the Yorkshire side for their match with his title rivals, had publicly questioned whether they would match that effort against the black and whites. He had also, knowing that the Magpies had yet to face Nottingham Forest, publicly wondered about Forest's approach, since they would soon face Newcastle in a testimonial game. These were low blows, and Keegan's frustration was no doubt exacerbated by the fact that they brought no FA censure. Newcastle's manager was almost besides himself as he told the TV cameras: "We are still fighting for this title and I'd love it, just love it , if we beat them".

When the drama died down, Keegan was widely ridiculed for losing his cool at a time when the title race was all but run, and his words became a mocking national catchphrase. Yet however unwise and impetuous he had been (he later admitted he did regret the timing and manner of the outburst, although he stuck by every word), many United fans agreed wholeheartedly with his standpoint. If the effect was ultimately embarrassing, Keegan was at least still trying to fight their corner.

THAT HEART-ON-THE-SLEEVE APPROACH was, after all, what had first endeared the region to a bubble-permed little player 14 years previously. "They are so up-front and frank, and open-book," Keegan said of his Geordie followers. "I certainly developed a very special relationship with them. They appreciate honesty in other people because they are so honest themselves." But if honesty was a cornerstone of the Keegan legend, so too was joy. He put a smile as wide as the Tyne Bridge on Newcastle during his two years as a player, and for most of his five-year managerial reign.

Aided and abetted by his perennial sidekick Terry McDermott, Keegan's wind-ups on players and media alike were legendary, and his strictly-enforced, on-the-spot club punishment of five press-ups for any misdemeanour once resulted in a bizarre sight during an away derby at Sunderland, when Keegan and his entire bench dropped to do five during the match, having protested against the referee's decision, only to find it had gone United's way after all!

Supporters who had for so long been mired in depressing under-achievement simply wallowed in the feelgood factor during the Keegan years. The controversial nature of his departure – brought forward from the end of the 1996/97 season because he would not agree a two-year deal to preserve continuity for the club's share flotation – smacked of high drama, like so much of Keegan's tempestuous love affair with the club.

WHEN IT CAME, the split, on 8 January 1997, was arguably the biggest sports story of modern times on Tyneside; bigger than Shearer signing, bigger than Gullit being sacked, bigger than Bobby Robson's departure. It sent shockwaves throughout football. Keegan had become so entwined with the very identity of Newcastle United that, as he would later admit, even he was no longer sure where the man ended and the club began. "I felt increasingly that my whole life had become Newcastle United Football Club," he said. "I didn't blame anyone other than myself for that…"

He remains one of the most fascinating characters in Newcastle United's rich history, and he leaves as part of his legacy, a myriad tales of a complex personality, full of contradictions .

He was, after all

- the positive thinker who quit while his team were riding high in the Premiership table
- the determined tough guy with the eggshell temperament
- the motivational master who lost his own self-belief

Yet if there was one overriding quality which marked Kevin Keegan out as a bona fide cult hero on these shores, it was his passion for the game. It was a passion shared by the obsessive fanatics who form huge black and white snakes as they trek to and from St James' on match days – and a trait which allowed him to tap into the Geordie conscience like no manager before or since. Keegan bitterly regretted his failure to finish the job by winning the title for his thousands of disciples in 1996 – yet now the dust has settled on that epic and vainglorious attempt, we can put his considerable achievements into perspective. And perhaps greatest of those is the excitement he brought to this corner of the world in two turbo-charged spells as player and manager. United fans of the Keegan era lived in fascinating times.

The man was enigmatic, he was charismatic, he was hydromatic – why, he was grease lightning.

Peter Beardsley

1983-1993: 321 games, 119 goals

'PEDRO' – THE BOY-NEXT-DOOR with the magical footballing gifts – is one of the most adored players in Newcastle United's history. Kevin Keegan – who himself knew a bit about popularity on Tyneside – once described him as "a legend to the supporters of Newcastle United". For many thousands of fans, Beardsley is the greatest player ever to wear a black and white shirt, and he has earned the right to sit alongside the likes of Hughie Gallacher and Jackie Milburn at the high table.

Beardsley approached his career like a football-mad schoolkid, so obsessed with the game he would play until the sun went down – and then some. The difference was, this little rascal was doing it in World Cup semi-finals, by lifting league titles and FA Cups.

Not, sadly, with Newcastle, of course.

But his achievements with his hometown club were significant – and he took the pride and affection of the region with him wherever he went on his footballing travels.

PETER BEARDSLEY WAS as far away from being a footballing rebel as it is possible to be. A tee-total non-smoker, he was as much a gentleman on the pitch as off it, and despite a long career at the very top of British football, searching for controversial episodes is like looking for a needle in a haystack. Hughie Gallacher's hard-drinking, womanising and brawling escapades would have horrified Beardsley, while the little fella, with his crooked grin and, let's be honest, unbecoming looks, could not boast the fashionable playboy lifestyle of a SuperMac. No wideboy tales of excess to keep the fans enthralled, then. And remember, if we are honest, that Beardsley's best days were at Liverpool – a club for which he left his hometown team to win trophies.

And yet, despite his somewhat boring, puritan lifestyle and introverted personality, this 5ft 8in striker, with his unfashionable helmet haircut and awkward gait, is an idol to grown men across the North East, with memories of his sensational goals still capable of leaving bar-room nostalgics misty-eyed. United fans loved him as much as he loved the game – and Beardsley's utter, whole-hearted devotion to football is one of the secrets behind his iconic status on Tyneside. Throw in a large dose of humility, and the simple charm of a working-class kid who could not believe his luck, and you have a bona fide Geordie superstar in the making.

When a grinning Beardsley told the TV cameras at the 1986 World Cup that he was revelling in his unofficial role of "entertainments manager" to the England squad, Tynesiders everywhere just wanted to grab the little scamp, get him in a headlock and ruffle his hair.

OK then, maybe that was just me.

Entertainment, though, was what Peter Beardsley was all about. If he wasn't quite a footballing genius in the Pelé, Maradona mould, then he was mighty close – as close, some would say, as any Englishman in modern times.

> "He was little and he was very clever. He had twinkle-feet. They moved like lightning when he was on the ball. He could feint and double feint and go past people in a way that would make you think, 'How on earth did he do that?"

So said Sir Bobby Robson of the man he was fond of calling "my little gem". Robson handed Beardsley his first England cap in 1986, giving the then 25-year-old a worldwide stage on which to work his magic. But long before that, this Longbenton lad – born at the start of the swinging Sixties – had etched his own indelible mark into Geordie folklore.

Newcastle fans have a reputation for liking hard workers – players who, throughout the decades, have grafted on the pitch as the supporters do off it. But they also love a flair player – and if he happens to work hard as well, then he has got it made. Peter Beardsley was such a player. "His exuberance and skill, the things he did with the ball, stood out a mile. It was a tremendous mixture," said Kevin Keegan, who played alongside Beardsley during his first spell at the club, then, as United manager, signed him in 1993 for his second stint. Keegan added: "Nearly every day as a manager I see young lads and even older players who have one thing or the other, but rarely both. When you do, it is something special. You don't forget players like that."

And the supporters who had the privilege to watch him play in black and white will not forget it, either. Beardsley was a fantasy footballer, with a full array of tricks, superb vision and a hip swivel which bamboozled even the most accomplished of defenders. He was also a ferocious tackler – and, like a kid in the schoolyard, would take it as a personal affront if he was dispossessed, and go haring after defenders like a whirling dervish to win the ball back.

Despite his skills, he broke the mould of the "lazy genius" á la Glenn Hoddle or Matt le Tissier.

If Beardsley had one weakness – something which frustrated his managers – it was his unselfishness, and, as a consummate finisher, it seems inevitable he would have scored many more goals if he had shared the ruthless streak of an Alan Shearer or Ian Rush. As it was, he was happy to create goals for other people, although a record of 108 league strikes for Newcastle in 272 starts is still an impressive one from a player who always thrived in a deep-lying, almost midfield, role rather than as an out-and-out striker. And if Beardsley cannot match the likes of Shearer for quantity of goals, he eclipses his successor when it comes to quality. Long-range shots, mazy dribbles, dead-eye finishing and cheeky chips all figure prominently in a century of Newcastle strikes surely unmatched in the club's history.

Conversations about his best ever strikes can still provoke frenzied debate among Newcastle fans of a certain age – but two goals in particular stand out, both from his first, magical spell at the club. Witnessed by most was the strike in a 3-1 win over Brighton in the last match of that glorious 1983/84 promotion season. Beardsley showed his tenacity by retrieving the ball with a trademark sliding tackle after a wayward return pass from Kevin Keegan, before lobbing Joe Corrigan from the edge of the area to send the crowd delirious. It was an energetic, impudent goal and it is typical of the man that Beardsley, in his autobiography, neglects to mention the fact he had to work hard to retrieve that ball from his mentor, Keegan. Instead, the description becomes a barely recognisable: "We linked up in a crisp one-two passing move and when the ball came back, I chipped it over Joe Corrigan"!

Many supporters hail that Brighton strike as his best ever, but for sheer control, dribbling ability and audacity, a long mazy dribble along the byline in a 4-1 win at Portsmouth takes the biscuit – and revives memories of George Best and Maradona in their pomp. Beardsley himself, a quiet, humble man but an unashamed showman on the pitch, believes he has scored none better:

> "My great moment came a couple of minutes before half-time. I had cut inside one defender and then gone outside another and then started coming along the byline towards the goal. The ball bounced invitingly for me to take on and go around the Portsmouth keeper Alan Knight without breaking my stride. I got to within about four yards of the goal and then feinted to shoot which threw another Pompey player who came diving in and missed the ball completely. The United fans were screaming, 'Put it in; Put it in'. It must have seemed like an eternity to them, but in the end all I had to do was tap the ball into an empty net."

There were few players on the planet capable of destroying a defence single-handedlly like that. It was the sort of goal schoolboys around the world dream of scoring – and the nerve he showed to keep waiting, twisting and turning, so close to goal, was breathtaking.

ORDINARY GOALS, IT seems, were beneath Peter Beardsley – and perhaps that is why Robson's 'little gem" failed to heed the England manager's advice about getting into the penalty area more often. "He would go into the box on a dribble, but only rarely as the second striker to get the ball," said Robson. "He was always outside the box. We talked about it at length without ever fully resolving it." Beardsley's desire to be involved, to have the ball at his feet, meant he would never have been happy as a goal-poacher like Shearer, Rush or Gary Lineker – all of whom he partnered at different stages in his career. Yet his finishing was sublime, with accuracy always taking prevalence over power. If Shearer likes to burst the net, Beardsley would always pass the ball into the goal if at all possible – sidefooted nonchalantly into the corner as if he was greeting an old friend.

With such all-round talent, it has long been regarded as something of a mystery why Beardsley was 22 before he was given a proper chance in English football – compare and contrast with his one-time United team-mate Paul Gascoigne, who was already a club legend by the time he left Tyneside for Tottenham at the age of 21.

In a game so hungry for talent as special as his, Beardsley somehow slipped through the net at Newcastle (rejected by manager Bill McGarry after a spell as a teenage trialist), Gillingham, Cambridge, Burnley and Oxford before signing for former United boss Bobby Moncur at Carlisle. Leeds United great Johnny Giles, who took the youngster to Vancouver Whitecaps in 1981 from Brunton Park, believes he may have the answer to the player's series of early rejections. "At first he tried difficult things, nine out of 10 of which maybe didn't come off," said Giles. "I tried to teach him to be a little more simple and he became a better player for it." Beardsley came up against the likes of Franz Beckenbauer and George Best during his North American Soccer League adventure – grabbing a hat-trick in a victory over Best's San Jose Earthquakes side, and earning treasured praise from the Northern Irish master.

But despite impressing across the Atlantic, Beardsley's dream of making it on home turf seemed doomed when Manchester United boss Ron Atkinson decided against making a move for the player after a trial spell in 1983. Arthur Cox had other ideas, and if the then Newcastle boss – determined to assemble a team to get United out of Division Two – surprised the rest of his squad when he paid £150,000 for an unknown Geordie that September, it would not be long before the players were queuing up to thank him for it. "I wasn't over-excited by the lad's pedigree," said Keegan. "But it didn't take me long to realise that Arthur had unearthed a diamond. I remember it as if it were yesterday. After about 20 minutes or our first training session together I went over to Arthur and asked: 'Where on earth did you find him?'"

Keegan himself had signed for the club just 12 months earlier, and Beardsley was to become the missing link between a free-scoring striker, and the midfield talents of Chris Waddle and Terry McDermott.

That 1983/84 season was to prove the highlight of many a Geordie's supporting lifetime, with Beardsley (20), Keegan (28) and Waddle (18) scoring 66 goals between them – and mesmerising the crowds - let alone opponents - with their attacking football. It had been nearly 30 years since United had turned on the style like this, and history has shown how lucky the Tyneside fans were to watch three such world-class performers spurring each other on to ever greater heights.

Waddle was a master of ball control, Keegan simply could not stop scoring, but when it came to outrageous skill, little Peter Beardsley walked tallest. "Even today when he picks the ball up," said Arthur Cox, right at the end of his protégé's playing career, "I still arch forward on the seat because I know he is liable to do something special. There aren't many in the game like that."

After Keegan's retirement as a player in the summer of 1984, the pressure on Beardsley intensified to carry the goalscoring mantle in Division One – but he took the challenge in his stride, top-scoring with 17 goals the following season (Waddle pitched in with 16) to establish himself as one of the brightest talents in the game.

With bustling centre-forwards like Mark Hateley then in vogue at international level, the clamour on Tyneside for their new king to be anointed in the England side was reaching fever pitch. United had not had an England regular in their ranks since Malcolm Macdonald in the 70s, and the excitement was tangible when Robson finally threw Beardsley into the fray as a substitute against Egypt in January 1986. On the pitch for just 25 minutes, he set up Gordan Cowans to score the last goal in a 4-0 win. Peter Beardsley had arrived, and when fit, would be called up for every single England squad for the rest of Robson's reign.

Four months later, Geordie hearts would be bursting with pride as their star player gatecrashed the party to play a crucial role in turning England's World Cup campaign around in Mexico. After many years since of Newcastle players wearing England colours – Robert Lee, Alan Shearer, Kieron Dyer, Jermaine Jenas and Barry Venison – it is difficult for today's young fans to imagine the excitement generated by Beardsley's international breakthrough. And the fact he represented

United in such style at a World Cup undoubtedly helped to establish his unique legend on Tyneside.

Twelve months previously, Waddle had made his internatonal debut in a friendly just before he left for Tottenham, but Beardsley, who was to become United's most capped player ever for England with 59 appearances (until Alan Shearer eclipsed that mark with 63), is regarded as the man who well and truly buried the curse. Geordies charted the No. 8's progress proudly as if he was one of the family, and Beardsley's international glories helped to restore the North East's reputation as a hotbed of football. Yet Beardsley's breakthrough came so late in the World Cup qualifying campaign in 1986, that Newcastle fans had begun to think he would be criminally ignored. Feelings had been running high in the North East since Keegan had been overlooked for international honours on joining Newcastle, and the fans' perception, as manager Bobby Robson stuck with his preferred front two of Lineker and Hateley, was that even one of the North East's favourite managerial sons was perpetuating the bias against the region's players.

It wasn't true of course, even if Robson was a little slow to recognise a changing of the guard. Beardsley came on as sub in England's defeat to Portugal, their first game of the 1986 World Cup, then watched a double drama unfold in the 0-0 draw with Morocco – skipper Bryan Robson dislocating his shoulder and Ray Wilkins getting a red card. A reshuffle was on the cards for the third, crucial game against Poland, and Geordies across the world were glued to their TV screens as 'Pedro' replaced Hateley to partner Lineker in the starting line-up – the birth of the most high-scoring England striking partnership ever. Lineker's hat-trick – the second set up by Beardsley – secured a 3-0 win, and United's emissary earned rave reviews. A goal in the second round win over Paraguay helped to put England in the quarter-finals, and cement the Tynesider's reputation as a world-class performer.

Edged out by Argentina in the infamous 'Hand of God' game at the Azteca Stadium, England's campaign was over at the quarter-final stage, but the 25-year-old returned to St James' Park as a hero, having helped to bring passing football back into fashion in the national team.

He and Lineker would go on to spearhead England's attack through to the end of the 1990 World Cup campaign, when Robson's side came within a penalty shoot-out of victory over Germany in the semi-finals thanks to Beardsley's vision and eye-of-the-needle passing and Lineker's perfectly timed runs and deadly finishing. Lineker himself was not slow to recognise the role played by his partner in turning him into one of the most feared marksmen on the planet. "As a goalscorer, you want a fellow striker who does not get in your way and who is preferably unselfish," he said, "someone who is prepared to drop deep and confuse defenders in order to give you more space. For me, that player was Peter Beardsley. We just hit it off and became the catalyst for the team." The pair would score 33 goals in just 39 appearances together for the national side, and Beardsley, as ever, was happy to play the role of provider, with Lineker hogging 27 of those. "Some partners might get frustrated at the other person scoring all the goals, but not me," he said. "I got a buzz out of making the goals." That mark of 33 goals betters the England strike partnership of Nat Lofthouse and Tom Finney by seven (between 1951 and 1958) and the Alan Shearer/Teddy Sheringham spearhead – which mirrored Lineker/Beardsley in style – that fashioned 22 goals in 25 games.

Beardsley's man-of-the-match display in a 1-1 draw with Brazil at Wembley in May 1987 left another Newcastle United legend purring. "He was absolutely magnificent last night," said Jackie Milburn. "He looked like a Brazilian and I can pay him no higher compliment than that. I sat and watched the game on TV and I had a lump in my throat. I was proud to be a Geordie." Lineker, whose goal in that game was created by his strike partner, was equally fulsome in tribute. "It was Peter's goal, really," he said. "I just managed to get on the end of it, which happens so often with us. Peter has been magnificent every time he has played for England. He is such a good creative player and he causes so many problems. He can do things that I cannot do."

Testament to the character behind Beardsley's undoubted ability came in arguably his finest hour in an England shirt – that epic 1990 World Cup semi-final against Germany. Beardsley had to wait until the last moment before hearing he was in the team – when John Barnes failed to recover from injury – yet went on to produce one of his best-ever performances – then stepped forward to take one of three successful penalties, along with Gary Lineker and David Platt, only for his former Newcastle team-mate Chris Waddle to miss the kick which knocked England out.

Beardsley also had a nervous manager to cope with before the penalty shootout, as he revealed in his autobiography.

> "Bobby, visibly shaking and beside himself with anxiety, suddenly came up to me and whispered: 'There are 55 million people watching this at home, son – don't let them down'. Talk about pressure! Gary (Lineker) turned round to the boss in protest. 'Hey, there's no need for that, gaffer. He'll do his best and nobody can ask for any more.' But I felt good, in fact, from the moment I was chosen to take one of the penalties, I knew I would score. I had played so well in the game and I had an unshakeable confidence in my ability to knock it in."

That little episode reveals much about an underplayed aspect of the Beardsley psyche – he was a tough, resilient little player. While Paul Gascoigne reversed his original decision to take a penalty (Waddle was his stand-in) after being booked in the semi-final and realising he would miss any final appearance through suspension, his fellow Geordie stood firm even as his manager wobbled.

THAT RESILIENCE WAS to stand Beardsley in good stead throughout the first major disagreement of his Newcastle career – with fellow North Easterner Jack Charlton. And his row with the latter over a true clash of footballing styles, would place him ever more firmly at the heart of the Geordie nation. Beardsley had Jackie Milburn – Jack Charlton's uncle – to thank for the appointment of the big man to replace Arthur Cox in 1984. "Take it from me, Peter," Milburn had told Newcastle's prize asset, "he'll be the best thing that's ever happened to this club." Beardsley – like the rest of Tyneside – believed it. But what followed suggests there is more than myth to the notion that football clubs take on their own personalities.

Newcastle United had always been a club which thrived on attacking football, with vibrant players given free rein to express themselves on the field. Big Jack was having none of it - the turning point was Newcastle allowing a 4-0 lead at QPR to slip to a 5-5 draw, and soon afterwards the Beardsley/Waddle strikeforce was disbanded. Instead the team was forced to adopt a defensive, low-risk approach to the game, which left Beardsley as frustrated as the supporters.

Waddle was banished to the left wing, and Beardsley to the right as two new signings, big men George Reilly and Tony Cunningham, forged a battering ram up front. It was the long-ball blueprint which United fans came to despise.

But the crowd could not have been prepared for the way their local hero was to be treated at the final whistle of a 1-0 home win over Luton. Beardsley had been taking on the last defender, Mal Donaghy, when the match ended – only for Charlton to march on to the pitch, and hand out a huge rollicking to his star player, in front of an astonished St James' Park. Beardsley recalls:

> "Suddenly I was aware of Jack bearing down on me from the dugout. I was still about 15 yards from the touchline when he came up, grabbed my arm and, in front of an audience of nearly 24,000 people, bellowed: 'Don't *ever* do that again!' I just stood there transfixed with amazement as he continued to slag me off. 'He could have taken that ball off you, booted it upfield, they could have grabbed an equaliser and the score would have been 1-1.'"

If Beardsley was amazed and disgusted, so were the fans – and, for once, Charlton's canny knack of making the right moves had deserted him. It took a brave man to take on the local hero in such a way in front of his adoring home fans, and many of those there to witness the tirade pinpoint that moment, above any other, as the beginning of the end for the manager.

For Beardsley, though, cast in the unfamiliar role of the naughty schoolboy, worse was to follow, albeit behind closed doors, when an inch-perfect last-minute free-kick on to George Reilly's head created the third goal for United in a 3-1 home win over Watford the following week. Amazingly, another dressing-down was in store from Charlton, as Beardsley explains:

> 'What did I tell you last week?' he shouted. 'When you took that free-kick, their keeper could have caught the ball. He could have thrown it down the field to one of their players and there could have been an equaliser.'

It was enough to make many players hand in a transfer request. But frustrated though he was with life at St James' Park, Beardsley was no quitter. When Chris Waddle left for Tottenham in the summer of 1985, his little team-mate stayed put – despite being granted a reported measly £5-a-week pay rise. It was a wise choice. His nemesis, Charlton, would soon follow Waddle out of the door, resigning incensed after being greeted with a chorus of booing after a home defeat in a friendly against Sheffield United just a week before the 1985/86 season.

FOR TWO MORE years Beardsley was to weave his magic in a black and white shirt – top-scoring with 19 goals in 1985/86 without ever being given the chance to earn the medals he craved. The 1986/87 season would be his last, and least prolific, producing just five goals – but one of those, in a relatively lacklustre individual season at club level, would prove crucial in keeping an average United side afloat in the top flight. It was the superb solo winner at Aston Villa in March, which gave his side a 2-1 victory and three precious points, and so ended a miserable run of one point from 10 league games stretching back to early December.

Receiving the ball on the left wing, Beardsley acclerated, and, with a dip of the shoulder, beat his man and cut inside, creating the space to shoot past Nigel Spink. "It was," wrote North East sportswriter Alan Oliver in the *Evening Chronicle* the next day, "a goal only Beardsley and a couple of other quality strikers in the country could have scored… it proved the turning point in Newcastle's battle against relegation and consequently proved priceless to the club."

Beardsley, though, did not relish another season of struggle and his first love affair with the club was nearing a tempestuous end. A minority of fans felt betrayed when he finally turned down a new contract offer in the summer of 1987 to sign for Kenny Dalglish at Liverpool – in a British record £1.9m move which more than doubled his wages. But the majority of Newcastle fans, broken-hearted though they were, accepted that United simply weren't matching their hero's ambitions. After all, he was swapping Billy Whitehurst as a strike partner for Ian Rush. "I was desperate to sign for Liverpool," said Beardsley. "But I left Tyneside with a heavy heart. "It was a pity I had to move away to realise the ambitions which were fulfilled handsomely on Merseyside."

Beardsley's heavy heart was as nothing compared to the anger on Tyneside, where his legions of followers, without their talisman, were left to face up to the prospect of a team with little or no ambition. Newcastle's reputation as a selling club was gaining momentum, with Waddle and Beardsley both sold within two years – and their next big star, Paul Gascoigne – destined to move on within 12 months. Radio phone-ins and newspaper letters pages were besieged by frustrated supporters.

Lifelong Newcastle fan John Pack remembers:

> "We lost Beardsley at the peak of his powers and it was a bitter pill to swallow. For me, he had already shown that he was the complete player, and he went on to prove it all the more at Liverpool. He could use both feet, could pass, dribble – everything. He's an all-time great a real, genuine guy and is very close to being the best player Newcastle have ever had."

Beardsley would get another chance to build on that glowing tribute. Two league titles, an FA Cup and six years later, he would be back – returning to a very different Newcastle United, and to make yet another indelible mark on the record books. His return to St James' Park in the summer of 1993, almost a decade to the day he first joined the club, was one of the most welcomed signings Newcastle have ever made. While the respective captures of Alan Shearer and Michael Owen may have set the pulses racing faster, the second coming of a 32-year-old England international still at the peak of his powers, was like welcoming home a long-lost son.

Like Waddle and Gascoigne, Beardsley had broken hearts by leaving Tyneside, but his eagerness to return, helping to ensure one of the happiest times for the club in living memory, would turn him into a bigger club legend than either of his former team-mates. Many stars leave, but Beardsley was the one who came back.

United manager Kevin Keegan, having taken the Magpies back into the Promised Land – now newly christened the Premiership – wanted a foil for his recent capture, £1.75m man Andy Cole. And if the United board had concerns about paying £1.35m for a player the wrong side of 30, Keegan didn't, and the then irrepressible manager was proved right. Beating off interest – and a much higher offer in terms of personal terms - from his former manager Arthur Cox at Derby, and stifling protests from his own board, Keegan landed himself a proven Geordie idol who was desperate to rekindle an old romance. Even before he had discussed the move, Beardsley admitted: "I knew I would be returning to Tyneside to join Kevin Keegan's fabulous Toon Army." Keegan himself later referred to the deal as his best ever. "When you add together his talent and his example, I think he has been the buy of the century," he said. "There is not another player on earth of that age for whom I would have paid that sort of money."

Beardsley found a club transformed from that which he had left – bursting with talented players such as Cole, Robert Lee, Paul Bracewell, Lee Clark, Steve Howey, John Beresford and Barry Venison. United had taken the First Division Championship in record-breaking style the season before, and the capture of Cole just three months before Beardsley arrived had raised expectations levels again.

If Newcastle United had changed a lot in 10 years, Beardsley hadn't. Although perhaps a touch more reliant on passing rather than dribbling, the 32-year-old was still a consummate performer, who had left Everton fans desolate by agreeing to the move north. But still, even the most optimistic of United supporters could not have expected his first season back in a black and white shirt to be so successful, as their newly-promoted side took the top flight by storm to finish third.

As he had proven alongside Rush at Liverpool and Lineker with England, Beardsley's vision and passing ability proved the perfect accompaniment to a natural goalpoacher, and between them, he and Cole were to be a smash hit on Tyneside. Beardsley scored 24 goals that season – his highest ever total for United – and part of a record-breaking 65-goal partnership with Cole, whose 41 strikes eclipsed the legendary Hughie Gallacher to create a new club record. Newcastle made their mark on the Premiership in swashbuckling fashion, and Beardsley's natural ability – coupled with manager Keegan's philosophy of all-out attack – helped bring United their unforgettable tag of 'The Entertainers', and the unofficial status of many fans' second favourite team. Beardsley also revelled in the captaincy of his hometown team and played a pivotal role in the biggest football revolution Tyneside had ever seen – his popularity had never been higher. He would score another 33 goals in his last three seasons, and helped them to finish third, sixth, second and second in his final four-year spell at United – now established as one of the top clubs in the land.

Beardsley would have dearly loved to have added to his Liverpool trophy collection with a Newcastle United medal – the nearest he came was the Magpies' agonising 1996 title collapse, when Keegan's side infamously threw away a 12-point lead to Manchester United. And among many theories behind the club's latter season inconsistency during that campaign, is that Keegan lost momentum by tinkering too much with the formation – and more specifically, evoking memories of the Jack Charlton regime, by once again pushing Beardsley on to the right wing, this time to accommodate new signing Faustino Asprilla up front.

Fittingly, Beardsley's final game for his beloved Newcastle left them in the Champions League for the first time, when they beat Nottingham Forest 5-0 on the last day of the 1996/97 season to finish second on goal difference under Kenny Dalglish.

He scored 119 goals in his two spells at Newcastle – making him the club's sixth highest scorer of all. But it is the quality, not the quantity of Beardsley's goals for which he will be best remembered. A long-range matchwinner at home to Arsenal in the 1994/95 season was one of the finest he had ever scored, while he almost single-handedly rallied the troops after that epic 4-3 defeat at Liverpool in 1996 by scoring twice to beat QPR at home in the following match.

Now working as a coach with United Academy and with experience of coaching at England level under Kevin Keegan, observers are baffled as to why such an inspirational player has not been given a higher-profile role at St James'. Keegan was not slow to recognise what a valuable commodity Beardsley's infectious enthusiasm was – and it is surely one of the keys to his enduring popularity. "He can show players how to train much better than I can tell them," he once said, while then Newcastle coach Arthur Cox described the 34-year-old Beardsley as "the hardest-working player in the Newcastle team". That dedication, and boyish love of the game, shone out like a beacon across Beardsley's two playing decades – a time when rampant greed and commercialism was threatening to wipe the smile off the face of the beautiful game.

A player who laughed off the 'Quasimodo' nickname bestowed by rival fans, Beardsley's attitude was undoubtedly handsome – and appreciated as much by the Magpies faithful as it was by the managers who enjoyed working with such a model professional. While fellow United legends Keegan and Shearer – players more conscious of their status and protective of their image – have been determined to bow out at the top, Beardsley was happy playing in the lower leagues for Hartlepool, as long as he could get a game. "Peter would never walk past the skip without offering to give a hand with the kit," said former England boss Graham Taylor. "Here he was, an internationally-acclaimed player, but never too proud to muck in with the mundane jobs. There are not many who would do that." Taylor here touches upon another secret ingredient which helps to make the Beardsley mix; allied to his undeniable thirst for the game was a genuine humility – a gratitude, even, for the lucky hand fate had dealt him in allowing him to fashion a career playing the game he loved.

That unspoilt, homespun nature has made Beardo a massive hit with wannabes of all ages, as North East sports journalist Stuart Jamieson explains:

> "There are two reasons why Peter Beardsley will always remain the ultimate Geordie hero for me," he said. "His footballing ability is the most obvious, but it is persona off the pitch marks him out as one of the true greats. Despite all his spectacular goals and creative wizardry, this Longbenton lad never once allowed fame and fortune to go to his head. I'll always remember queuing for his autograph on a blustery day at United's old Benwell training ground, just weeks after Beardsley had starred for England at the Mexico World Cup. He spent hours signing hundreds of autographs – and thanked each and every one for turning up and waiting. That guy was a genius on the field, and a class act off it."

Beardsley stands out among the likes of Alan Shearer and Malcolm Macdonald as arguably the shyest cult hero in Newcastle's history. This was a man who – while at Heathrow airport, waiting to fly to Newcastle to complete his first move there in 1983, clapped eyes upon his future team-mate Kevin Keegan, yet never presumed to think he should introduce himself. And that transfer must have been one of the easiest manager Arthur Cox had ever negotiated when Beardsley made no demands on wages or length of contract whatsoever. "I remember when I first spoke to him," said Cox, he was in a kiosk at the airport and we arranged to meet the following afternoon. 'Peter, by the way,' I said, 'we have not discussed a contract'. All he replied was: 'You'll look after me, boss'."

That unselfish attitude changed little throughout a career in which Beardsley – along with John Barnes – took centre stage in Liverpool's all-conquering side of the 1980s, a team hailed by some as the finest club side ever. When Beardsley returned to Newcastle, his then manager Keegan later confirmed he took a massive 25 per cent wage cut to make the deal happen. And when Alan Shearer stated his two conditions for joining in Newcastle in 1996 - the No. 9 shirt (Les Ferdinand's) and the penalty-taking job (Beardsley's), it provoked not a murmur of objection from the latter to his manager, however much the decision may have hurt in private.

Keegan, who admitted it was not so easy consoling Ferdinand at losing the No. 9, said: "I had to sound out Peter Beardsley on the second one and all he did was give his customary answer: 'No problem'."

There are those who believe Beardsley might have been an even greater player if he had shared the single-minded ruthlessness of a Keegan or Shearer – and he could certainly have scored more goals. But that unselfish play – and his dedication to creating chances for others – is actually one of the keys to his greatness.

Keegan described Beardsley's partnership with Cole as "something remarkable" and said of the former: "One of the biggest problems I had with him at first was trying to persuade him that life was not just about making goals for Andy. I knew there were occasions when he could have helped himself, but he was unselfish and derived as much pleasure out of Andy getting all the credit." That preference to pass instead of shoot might just be the biggest problem Beardsley ever created for his managers, for, unlike many of the other cult heroes in this book, Beardsley has very few stories with any hint of malice or arrogance. Despite being in and out of the side at Liverpool, and being played out of position during both his spells at Newcastle, there were no showdowns or tantrums from a player who built up a reputation as one of the hardest trainers in the game. As Arthur Cox, the man who started the legend by signing him for Newcastle back in 1983, declared: "He is one of the nicest superstars that football has ever produced."

So much has been written to back up Cox's claim that it seems almost uncharitable to point out that has not always been a universal view.

Beardsley's first departure from Newcastle provoked controversy when, in a TV interview, he accused his fellow United players of jealousy – a claim which, although backed by dressing-room ally Albert Craig, went down like a lead balloon among the majority of players. A rift seemed to have developed when some players had dared to point out, in post-match discussions, that Beardsley had been playing better for country than club that season – and the players' wives were soon embroiled in what seemed to be a growing feud. "It got bad at times and affected my wife," Beardsley told Tyne Tees TV just after signing for Liverpool. "You can't ignore it – but I realised what the problem was – just jealousy. There were one or two players involved. It certainly didn't help matters, but it was harder for my wife than for me. She was stuck at home and didn't know what was going on. The last six months were the worst of my time at Newcastle." Craig was fined by the club after publicly claiming that his friend had been driven out of United by jealous players. But team-mates Tony Cunningham and Glenn Roeder led an angry defence from a clearly divided United dressing room. "Peter is totally out of order when he says the rest of the players were jealous," said Cunningham. "I am disgusted that he has left saying this. Whenever Peter had a bad game, he thought the other players were talking about his money. He brought it on himself… Peter's wife was in tears and this was the start of the trouble. But really I feel it was blown up out of all proportion."

Roeder was equally angry, the former skipper claiming: "As far as the players are concerned, the sooner we forget him, the better. I don't want to cheapen my name by answering these allegations. The United players have kept quiet, but privately we are all seething, because we all stand accused."

Beardsley's parting shot at the United board – although difficult to argue with – was not universally welcomed by supporters, either. He told the *Sun* newspaper:

> "I am not the first big money transfer to leave Newcastle
> United – and I won't be the last. But we all leave under
> a cloud – it's always the players' fault. Newcastle should

ask themselves why the best players leave and why they haven't won the title since 1927. The only thing big about Newcastle is the size of their crowd – their supporters really are the best in the business. It was a privilege to play for them... that's why it hurts to get hate mail form a handful who don't understand why I left. But the truth is that the club is not geared up for success."

These episodes show that Beardsley could be prickly when his credentials were questioned. Yet his success on the pitch was so great that such incidents were few and far between. There has been precious little controversy involving the player since that 1987 spat – although his wife Sandra was rumoured to be involved when Beardsley fell foul of Liverpool manager Kenny Dalglish's rotation policy at Anfield. However the player strenuously denied newspaper reports that a row between Mrs Beardsley and Mrs Dalglish – who were then near-neighbours – had even taken place, never mind influenced the manager's thinking. Instead, Beardsley put the rumours down to a throwaway remark from his exasperated manager when grilled about Beardsley's recent non-selection after the player had made a goalscoring return against Everton. Beardsley recalls in his autobiography that Dalglish said: "Right, that's it. Let Mrs Beardsley pick the team. I quit."

A stranger episode in recent years saw Beardsley temporarily relieved of his Academy coaching duties at United in 2003 – and placed in a humbling 'promotional role' – despite being cleared by the FA of bullying, after allegations were made against him and fellow coach Kenny Wharton. An FA tribunal did not uphold the complaints – made by young players Ross Gardner and James Beamont, and which followed an informal complaint from Beardsley's former team-mate Terry McDermott to the club about the alleged treatment of his son Neale before the latter left to sign for Fulham. It is testament to the high regard in which Beardsley is held on his native Tyneside that, even before the tribunal gave their verdict, it was hard to find any supporters who believed he could be guilty of these complaints. Indeed, the vast majority of the Beardsley lexicon tells of a modest approach from a popular player whose tee-total lifestyle and dedication to the game earned respect, even if he was never going to be the life and soul of the party.

It is that unassuming commitment which allowed Beardsley to pull off a rare and impressive trick – becoming equally loved on both halves of Merseyside after spending four and two years respectively wowing the Liverpool and Everton faithful. His decision to accept Everton's offer certainly surprised Graeme Souness. Beardsley claims that the then Liverpool boss told John Barnes he thought the player "didn't have the bottle to switch clubs".

BUT IT IS back home in Newcastle where Beardsley's legend looms largest. His contribution to Newcastle United was celebrated in a remarkable testimonial against Celtic in January 1999 – the last to be granted to a Magpies player. United fans were treated to an unashamed nostalgia trip as star names such as Andy Cole, Paul Gascoigne and Kevin Keegan were paraded on the turf. But, from a crowd never afraid to show their emotions where football is concerned, the tributes were longest and loudest for little 'Pedro', the man who brought majesty and magic to the citadel in two spells totalling eight years at United. Geordie toddlers are now reared to stories of his epic goals, as their fathers were once enthralled at the knee by the deeds of Milburn and Gallacher. Just as importantly Peter Beardsley would approach a backstreet kickabout with the same tireless zest as a World Cup semi-final and, in a game now plagued by self-interest and commercialism, football may not see another quite like him.

As Kevin Keegan once declared: "Some of my greatest memories with Newcastle involve Peter and his goals and the way his genius turned games for us."

Paul Gascoigne

1985-1988: 109 games, 25 goals

PAUL GASCOIGNE IS like Marmite – you either love him or hate him.

He could have been the indisputable greatest. In terms of natural ability, some Newcastle fans say he was. Yet before he had even kicked a ball for United, a teenage Gascoigne had already showed off his capacity for self-destruction. Before his 18th birthday he had:

- Been convicted of a hit-and-run
- Driven a tractor into United's training ground dressing-room
- Split his leg open in motorbike accident
- Told established star Chris Waddle to "fuck off" and clean his own boots
- Been given THREE final warnings about his future at the club

But football fans, Newcastle fans, tend to love him, and his strongest supporters will argue fervently that he WAS the most talented player ever to wear a black and white shirt. There seems, indeed, no serious rival to that claim in modern times – for sheer, prodigious, talent, Kevin Keegan, Alan Shearer, Malcolm Macdonald, Jackie Milburn and even Peter Beardsley must stand aside.

If Beardsley could make the ball talk, Gascoigne could make it sing.

No, you have to go way back in time to find possibly the only two men who can stand up to Gascoigne in this debate – with testimonies to Hughie Gallacher and, perhaps most pertinently, Len Shackleton putting them in the frame.

The latter was, of course, the original 'Clown Prince of Soccer' and, though our forefathers might not like it, Gascoigne fans know full well that a sequel can be better than the original. It seems difficult to think of any trick that SuperMac, Milburn, Beardsley or even Shackleton could pull off that would be beyond Gascoigne. Then again, it is difficult to think of any trick with a football that the Dunston lad could not master.

There is certainly no direct equivalent of Gascoigne's meteoric rise through the youth ranks at Newcastle, creating a palpable sense of excitement that United had, at last, discovered a special one.

THE INTERNATIONAL MEDIA has long since debated the merits of a man who has become arguably the most famous Geordie of modern times. Is he a footballing god to rival the likes of Pelé, Maradona and George Best? Or an overhyped, overweight loudmouth with a penchant for self-destruction?

The answer, as we all know, is a bit of both. But Gascoigne was the one bona fide footballing genius to play for Newcastle in my lifetime – and true football men recognised his class as soon as they clapped eyes on him. In the late, great Jackie Milburn's final TV interview as a pundit he told presenter Bob Wilson that the 20-year-old United starlet would become the finest player on the planet – "If he can just keep his feet on the ground". Wilson was a touch incredulous – but nobody in Newcastle was laughing – and two years later, at Italia 90, some say that prediction came true.

There are many supporters out there – fans of Tottenham, England, Lazio and Rangers – who might argue that Gascoigne did not hit the heights as a player until he left Tyneside. They are talking nonsense – confused by the fact he was merely on TV a lot more and became truly world-famous once he had left these shores. But Gascoigne did nothing at any of those clubs – or at Middlesbrough, Everton or Burnley in his premature decline – that he had not mastered in stripes.

The boy wonder, as he was then, played only three times less for Newcastle than he did for Tottenham, and had long since left his adoring fellow Geordies speechless at his full array of talents. No United fan was shocked by his performances at the 1990 World Cup – a series of displays which made him one of the hottest properties in world football – indeed, they were merely wondering 'why all the fuss?' about a player who only seemed to be in third gear! They had become used to seeing Gascoigne bossing games single-handedly for three seasons at Newcastle, and in the days before widespread TV coverage, he had become United's special, closely-guarded secret.

Yet the break-up was inevitable and it inevitably caused bitterness. On returning to St James' Park with Tottenham for his competitive debut for his new side in 1988, Gascoigne was roundly booed and pelted with Mars bars – a cruel reference to his sweet tooth and lifelong battle with his weight. Before that though, the infamously insecure Gascoigne had received adoration on his native Tyneside reserved only for the treasured few. These were the days long before the alcoholism, the violent attacks on wife Sheryl, and the well-publicised depression, although the unusual behaviour – panic attacks and nervous tics which would be later diagnosed as Obsessive Compulsive Disorder – were, privately, taking a hold.

YET IN THE early days of Gascoigne's professional career, the youngster's natural mischievousness, penchant for pranks and occasional brushes with the law only served to increase his popularity. His emergence from a poor Dunston family, and his rebellious behaviour marked him out, for many of the Toon Army rank-and-file, as "one of us". A street urchin let loose on the North East's biggest stage. Indeed, in many ways, the young Paul John Gascoigne appeared to be the very blueprint for a footballing cult hero: Locally born, solidly working-class, passionate, aggressive, determined, cheeky, and full of fun. But, important though those traits were in establishing the Gascoigne legend on Tyneside, these all paled into insignificance alongside one key fact: the boy was a genius with the ball at his feet.

One-time team-mate Peter Beardsley spotted the youngster's huge potential as early as 1985, telling the *Newcastle Journal* in August of that year: "If he harnesses his skills properly, he has a good chance of becoming one of the best the club has ever seen. He has a superb football brain and should go all the way."

Gascoigne's first manager Arthur Cox was even more direct: "If he were Brazilian or Argentinian, you would kiss his shoes", and many journalists and fans have been left wondering since if he indeed is the best Englishman ever to play the game. From such lofty claims, it is almost embarrassing to remember that the only honour Paul Gascoigne won at Newcastle was the 1985 Youth Cup, after scoring twice to help beat Watford 4-1 over two legs. He still describes that day, perhaps sadly for a player of such talent, as one of his career highlights. He wrote in his autobiography: "For me, it's still one of the most satisfying-ever games – being captain, winning the match, earning the cup. I was full of such hope for the future." But in the football village that is Newcastle, the natives had for months been whispering about the outrageous tricks attempted – and pulled off – by United's chubby youth team skipper. Indeed, he had made his first-team debut as a substitute on 13 April at home to Queen's Park Rangers, to be greeted by a massive cheer from a St James' Park crowd already aware of a reputation burgeoning to match his waistline. Thousands of Geordies had bolstered the crowd to 8,500 for the second leg of that final at Vicarage Road, many travelling the length of the country to witness the sorcerer's apprentice at close quarters. They did not have to wait long to see more of the player who was to become known around the world as 'Gazza'.

United boss Jack Charlton offered the 17-year-old a professional contract on the coach ride home from Watford, and gave him a second run-out as a substitute in the last home game of the season against Tottenham. The opposition that day was significant – future Spurs chairman Irving Scholar was mightily impressed by the teenager's display, and even before Gascoigne's Newcastle career had begun, Scholar was sowing the seeds of his departure.

But the player's effect on Scholar was typical of the bewitching spell he cast on many a hardened footballing soul – one glimpse was often enough. Not so, though, at Ipswich, Southampton and Middlesbrough, who all snubbed him as a schoolboy, before Newcastle eventually made their move.

Of course, football history is littered with tales of great players facing rejection at a string of clubs – but so gifted was this teenager, so obvious were those gifts, that any unsuccessful trial seems a shock. Gascoigne, you see, stands out among many of his rivals in this book as a complete footballer, who could stamp his massive personality on a match with consummate ease. His passing was visionary, his dribbling sublime and he had an eye for the spectacular finish. On his day – and they were many – he could destroy a defence single-handed, with a killer pass or a mazy dribble. The choice was his.

On the off days at United – and they were few – he could still turn a match with one flash of genius, a knack which would persuade later managers such as Bryan Robson and Walter Smith to take a chance on him at Middlesbrough and Everton respectively, long after his legs, and his pervasive influence, had gone.

Yet Gascoigne offered so much more than flair – he broke the traditional mould of the lazy, gifted playmaker with an aggressive, hard-working approach, and would think nothing of throwing himself into a two-footed sliding tackle in the days before such challenges were outlawed. So adept was Gascoigne in the dark arts that Manchester United boss Sir Alex Ferguson wanted the young Geordie as the natural successor to his hard-tackling warhorse Bryan Robson at Old Trafford before Gascoigne went back on a verbal promise and joined Tottenham instead. Ferguson later recalled this near-miss as one of the biggest regrets of his career, and remembered in his autobiography the day he decided to go for Gascoigne:

> "I had been determined to bring Paul to United ever since he had tortured us with a devastating performance for Newcastle at St James' Park. We sent out the powerful midfield of Moses, Robson and Whiteside that day but the 20-year-old Gascoigne outplayed them, crowning his precocious display by patting Remi Moses (seven years his senior) on the top of the head like a headmaster mildly rebuking one of his pupils... What a performance, and what a player!"

If Gascoigne had one slight weakness in his game it was a lack of genuine pace – but in his pomp, he made up for this by using his strong upper body to get in front of defenders and hold them off. This was the on-pitch demonstration of a determination which fuelled Gascoigne long before the lager and kebabs – and which greatly endeared him to a crowd that has always appreciated hard work.

And while tales of Gascoigne's excess – and perennial battle with his weight – are legion, the resolve shown by the young player to make the grade has been under-publicised. "It takes determination as well as talent, and I had plenty of that. I had worked on my natural ability," he said in his autobiography. "I realised that to be the best among the youth players, which I was determined to be, I had to be stronger... working on my upper body paid off. It helped me get physically mature more quickly."

Gascoigne also kept his eye on the prize when manager Jack Charlton, on taking over from Arthur Cox, gave him a two-week ultimatum to lose weight – or face the sack. The 17-year-old left that meeting in tears, but lost the weight and bounced back to make his first-team debut months later. Jackie Milburn recognised this resolve as a characteristic which, as much as his talent, set Gascoigne apart from the rank and file. He told the *Journal* in January 1986:

> "I can't remember a better young player coming into the game in the last 30 years. Young Gascoigne has got the lot... As soon as I saw Paul I knew I was watching something special. He has the same character – that bristling will-to-win – that makes Kevin Keegan and Peter Beardsley stand apart. Chris Waddle, though, didn't have it, even though he was an outstanding player. It's the gritty determination that goes alongside the skill."

That determination would show itself in Gascoigne's knack of using his body to shield the ball – a habit which would frustrate some of the toughest tacklers in the English top flight. The St James' Park crowd were greatly amused at one incident, played out near the corner flag during Newcastle's home match against Everton in January 1986, when Gascoigne, his back to Peter Reid, completely bamboozled the England midfielder for what seemed an age yet barely moved from the spot

His aggressive approach would later cause massive problems – that infamous lunge at Gary Charles in the FA Cup final bringing a 16-month injury lay-off – but the three red cards he picked up during his Newcastle career did his popularity on the terraces no harm. Neither did his natural capacity for playing to the gallery. A born showman, who seemed to play every game with passion and a grin on his face, the young Gascoigne was an identikit crowd-pleaser. The *Sunday Sun* captured the excitement after he scored on his comeback from injury during a Littlewoods Cup win over Blackpool back in October 1987.

> "The Ali shuffle is back at St James' Park. So are the high-five hand slaps and clenched fist salute that says Gascoigne has scored. Few players celebrate a goal with as much pizzazz as Newcastle's Paul Gascoigne, but then the 20-year-old from Dunston is a one-off in a world of conformist football… When Gazza is on song, any fan from Brazil to Byker will gladly sing the chorus."

GASCOIGNE THE PLAYER was always happy to take centre stage – a role threatened, or so it seemed at the time, when Newcastle caused a stir by signing Brazil international striker Mirandinha as Peter Beardsley's replacement in 1987. Gascoigne's love-hate relationship with the Football League's first-ever Brazilian provided a wealth of hilarious tales which reflect so many of the traits of this Jekyll and Hyde footballer. The Geordie's impish sense of humour was allowed full rein as he appointed himself Mira's unofficial English teacher – starting with the days of the week. "The lads tested him afterwards every day to see if he'd got them right," Gascoigne recalled. "When it came to Wednesday, and the players asked him what day it was, he said 'Wankday'. The lads were practically in tears." But Gascoigne's capacity for overstepping the mark from lovable rascal to trouble-maker soon kicked in – when he borrowed the Brazilian's car and wrecked it in a street race, leaving the mangled vehicle wedged in a fence for days afterwards until Mirandinha enquired as to its whereabouts.

An act of generosity – buying a dog for his team-mate's two young children – saved the day, and Mirandinha christened the animal 'Gazza' in tribute. Gascoigne was so touched he told the *Evening Chronicle*: "I've got a goldfish and I'm going to call him Mirandinha. I can sit and watch him going round in circles all day." Anyone who watched the Brazilian underachieve in black and white will recognise that description – but still, Gascoigne's on-pitch battles with the Brazilian did the club no good. It was an open secret on Tyneside that the midfielder did not trust his South American team-mate, and Gascoigne seemed to go out of his way to show him up. Gascoigne's constant refusal to pass to Mirandinha, unless the Brazilian was well-marked and likely to lose possession, soon became noticeable on the terraces. A *Journal* report from 1988 brought the long-running battle under the media spotlight.

> "Young England schemer Paul Gascoigne last night denied that he is involved in a feud with Newcastle team-mate Mirandinha. The on-field differences between the pair have been evident recently and after last Saturday's defeat, Norwich defender Shaun Elliott revealed that the Brazilian international had accused Gascoigne of not passing to him."

Later that month, manager Willie McFaul was asked to comment on the issue, when the pair almost came to blows during a home defeat to Monaco. "It's nothing to get worked up about," said McFaul. "There are at least six other players Gascoigne has had a row with this season."

Former Everton full-back John Bailey was one – branded a has-been during a training ground argument, Bailey waited for his chance and gave the cocky youngster a hiding in the dressing room afterwards. Bailey was merely following Chris Waddle's example – three years' previously, Waddle had replied with his fists after a mouthful of cheek from his chubby boot-boy. Gascoigne would respond with a typical mix of fragility and toughness – running home crying, but then bouncing back to become firm friends with one of his idols. "Waddler may have called me a fat shit," recalled Gascoigne afterwards, "but I knew he'd taken a liking to me."

THE YOUNG PRETENDER'S rebellious, cheeky nature may have been causing problems within the Magpies squad, but it was that same desire to show off that brought him such adoration from the terraces, after a series of impudent displays for the club. His capacity for playing superb football on the pitch and raising hell off it brought inevitable comparisons with George Best, a man who was, at least in the early days, a confirmed Gascoigne fan.

Back in 1988, just four months before Gascoigne left Newcastle, Best told the *Evening Chronicle*:

> "The reason Newcastle have got to hang on to him isn't only because he is going to be a fabulous player, but because he is a character. The game of football is sadly lacking in characters these days but they are the players the public want to see. Newcastle have sold good players in the past, but perhaps they weren't colourful personalities in their own right. Gascoigne is one and that makes him a valuable asset among the grey players."

Gascoigne's arrogance, allied to a prodigious natural ability, helped him elevate football from a game to something beautiful and exciting to watch. Former England boss Sir Bobby Robson was as mesmerised as the fans after a superlative show from the youngster when he came on against Albania in April 1989. "The kid went out on to the pitch with cockiness and didn't care about a thing," said Robson. "We needed one ball for him and one for the team". The excitement Gascoigne brought to the game helps to explain the astonishing affection he generated at Newcastle, Tottenham, Lazio and Rangers before his career went into decline. His Serie A adventure with Lazio was only a few weeks old when the club's supporters association presented him with a stuffed eagle – the club emblem – complete with the following inscription:

> "You're already in our hearts,
> We will soon be in yours
> Tomorrow belongs to us,
> Eagles supporters."

And while the Italian media never took to Gascoigne, the public did so whole-heartedly – shown by the fact that a national survey by football sticker company Panini marked him out as the most popular player in the country, ahead of homegrown legends Roberto Baggio and Franco Baresi.

But if Gascoigne was well loved, it is only fair to point out that he was not everyone's idea of a cult hero, even on his native Tyneside. Indeed, this complex personality probably polarises opinion like no one else in this book. There are those who feel his capacity for trouble brought shame on himself and the clubs he played for. A lifelong obsession with airguns – which would later bring police involvement and mirror that of another footballer/mental case Diego Maradona – started on Tyneside when, as an apprentice, he used the backside of best friend Jimmy 'Five Bellies' Gardner' as target practice. But if Gascoigne and his willing accomplice were happy to put that sort of incident down to horseplay, there were other tales that were harder to laugh off.

Thankfully the true and widely publicised lowpoints of a rollercoaster career came after leaving Newcastle:

- Mouthing the words "Fuck off, Norway" to the TV cameras before an England international
- Belching into the microphone when asked, on Italian TV, his feelings about being dropped by Lazio
- Stirring up sectarian hatred with his flute-playing antics at Rangers, mimicking the protestant Orange marches during an Old Firm derby with Celtic
- Being photographed looking worse for wear outside a London kebab shop days before joining an England World Cup training squad
- Trashing a Spanish hotel suite after being dropped from that 1998 squad by England manager Glenn Hoddle
- Guzzling cocktails in the 'dentist's chair' during a Far East tour 10 days before Euro 96, and breaking TV sets during an angry rampage on the flight over to Hong Kong
- And, worst of all, beating his wife Sheryl black and blue during a row at a Gleneagles hotel

At Newcastle Gascoigne's off-field image was largely that of a loveable rogue. And yet, even before he left United, at the grand old age of 21, he had made enemies. A red card at Derby brought the red mist down and an FA disrepute charge when he wrecked the visiting dressing room. That incident brought a right royal rollicking from Derby boss Arthur Cox – Gascoigne's first manager at Newcastle – which reduced the young midfielder to tears and prompted a written apology.

But for Magpies fans, Gascoigne's worst misdemeanour came when he snubbed the Newcastle United Supporters Association annual presentation evening at the end of the 1987/88 season – an event at which he was due to pick up the two major awards. Hundreds of fans were left disappointed, and his argument that he was supporting a leukaemia fund-raising event at the time cut no ice. And if Gascoigne lost friends there, he would lose the support of a close one after a night out back in his native Newcastle went wrong in September 1991. Walkers nightclub was not the most sensible choice of venue in which to relax during his long recovery from that cruciate knee ligament injury, sustained in Tottenham's FA Cup final win over Nottingham Forest. And when an attack that night seriously aggravated the same injury, it proved the final straw for Glenn Roeder, who had planned to accompany his young charge in his move to Lazio as mentor and minder. Gascoigne recalls: "When Glenn heard what happened, he said: 'That's it'. He didn't even want to hear my explanation... he cancelled all his arrangements for Rome."

Newcastle and Gateshead so often provided the backdrop for Gascoigne's trouble-making and capacity for self-destruction – and a mix of alcohol, cheek, an unpredictable temperament and jealous or over-zealous United supporters proved a dangerous cocktail. It is one of the reasons why Gascoigne has never managed to settle back in his native North East, although he has never made any secret of the fact that this is where his heart lies.

Instead, his home in 2006 is a succession of hotel rooms, and after a bitter split with wife Sheryl, the debacle of a short spell in management with non-league Kettering and a continual public refusal to submit his acceptance of his alcoholism, Gascoigne now cuts a lonely figure.

Without football to provide his means of self-expression, he seems to have lost the mischievous spark that managers, players and fans alike once found so alluring. A revealing BBC TV documentary, and the player's own autobiography have shown, in recent years, that his problems – anxiety, depression, insecurity - have been deep-rooted since childhood, and were only masked by a contagious sense of fun in his early days at Newcastle. The old 'tears of a clown' cliché seems so apt when he describes the anxious rituals he enduring while trying to make his name in the game.

He admitted, for example, that a nervous habit of kicking his trailing right leg on the ground whilst running became so severe that his bloody toe nail fell off, and revealed: "Between the ages of 16 and 21 I developed nine different nervous tics. I was still making those gulping noises, like the noises a pigeon makes."

This unique mix of nervous energy, or an early case of ADHD if you prefer – which infamously exploded on the Wembley turf with that absurd kamikaze tackle on Craig Charles years later – brought Gascoigne into trouble on the pitch many times during his United career. The pattern was set early on - he had only 12 starts under his belt at Newcastle when he received his first red card – after lashing out at Birmingham' Robert Hopkins under the referee's nose. Gascoigne left the pitch crying that day, establishing a pattern that would become increasingly familiar. If Gascoigne could get over his lack of real pace, he could never quite master his temperament – a losing battle which prevented him taking his place alongside the game's all-time gods like Pele, Maradona and Puskas.

ON A PAROCHIAL level, though, Paul Gascoigne is still a giant, despite playing only three seasons for the Magpies. *Sunday Sun* chief sportswriter Neil Farrington – who watched Gascoigne's progress at close quarters – is in no doubt how special a figure he is in the club's history . . .

> "Paul Gascoigne is simply the most talented player I have seen pull on a black and white shirt. Peter Beardsley's ability was almost comparable, and his service to Newcastle far greater, but Gazza was simply the best of his generation - a talent as stellar as a Best or even a Maradona. I first saw him running QPR ragged at St James' as an 18-year-old in September 1985. So ragged, that it was clear the hype surrounding this spotty, chubby kid from Gateshead had been hopelessly underplayed. Watching his development in a struggling team over the next three seasons was like seeing Van Gogh hone his skills at a village arts class. Unfortunately, the club at that time was undeserving of his genius.

Fans elsewhere will remember Gazza for his exploits with England, at Spurs and beyond. But I'll always be convinced his best days were at Newcastle. Life was simple for him then. Life was football. And with it he brought a blinding dazzle to a desperately dull era at the club."

In truth, Newcastle United at that stage of their lack of development were not big enough to keep him, and the biggest regret is that the club did not provide enough ambition to capitalise on a unique talent. As it was, 25 goals scored – many of them spectacular – and many more created by his boots helped at least to make Saturday afternoons more pleasurable for a generation of supporters who had never before seen one of their own blessed with such ability.

Perhaps his greatest Newcastle goal, and one of the most memorable, came in a 5-0 FA Cup rout over Crystal Palace. After receiving the ball about 40 yards out, he took only a few paces towards the opposition goal before letting fly with a rocket shot which lodged in the stanchion. "That was the best goal of my life," he told the *Sunday Sun* afterwards. "It was the most spectacular and longest range goal I've ever scored. In fact, I was celebrating before it went in."

So worshipped was Gascoigne, so unique his talent, that his eventual sale to Tottenham for a British record £2.3m in the summer of 1988 is one of the most painful partings Newcastle fans have ever had to endure. His departure was not eased – nor his return with Spurs – by the fact that it was open knowledge he was keen to leave a club that had meandered along in mid-table throughout his three full seasons as a pro. Nor by the fact that he was the third star player – following Chris Waddle and Peter Beardsley – to leave the club in three years. Gascoigne would later admit feeling restless as early as his first trip to Liverpool, in December 1985, during his first full campaign in black and white, when the infamous 'This is Anfield' sign brought home to him the difference between the two clubs in terms of success. "I was sad to be leaving Newcastle," he said of his move to Tottenham, "and in some ways I didn't want to go. They have the best fans in the world, but I could see that for the moment they were a selling not a buying club."

Whilst many United fans knew in their heads that assessment was right, Gascoigne's desire to leave still felt like a betrayal in many hearts – and he had to wait many years for his due recognition at St James'. It duly came when he pulled on the black and white shirt one final time for Peter Beardsley's testimonial on 27 January 1999, and Gascoigne received a rapturous reception from his fellow United fanatics.

Gazza was equally well received when unveiled as Newcastle's 'half-time hero' on the St James' Park pitch during Newcastle's 1-0 win over Liverpool in March 2005. As a lifelong fan, nobody will be more pleased than Gascoigne that results like that had become regular for his beloved club in the 18 years since his departure. But the 37-year-old could afford to feel a little rueful in front of the 52,000 fans and established internationals on the home side that day – if Newcastle had shown a fraction of such ambition during his days at the club, his turbulent career, and United's tortured pursuit of silverware, might have read very differently in the intervening years.

Certainly, Gascoigne would have emerged an even greater legend in black and white if he had been playing behind strikers such as Andy Cole, Les Ferdinand and Alan Shearer – instead of relative journeymen such as Billy Whitehurst and Tony Cunningham. His three-year tenure at the club coincided with one of the most unspectacular spells in United's recent history, and but for him and, for the first two of those three years, Peter Beardsley, it seems likely that the mid-80s Newcastle side would have swapped mid-table mediocrity for a relegation battle.

Former Liverpool and England midfielder Ray Kennedy, who settled in the North East and was a regular visitor to St James' Park throughout the 80s, recognised the player's frustrations in an interview with the *Evening Chronicle* in May 1988.

> "I love watching Gascoigne because he's a young player with the world at his feet. Some of the forward runs he makes are brilliant – but, with no disrespect, some Newcastle players don't read him. If he makes five of those runs in a game, he might get the correct pass played up to him once."

It is tempting to daydream about Gascoigne pulling the midfield strings for Kevin Keegan's all-star side of the early 90s. And it seems likely that Keegan – a consummate man-manager – would have done as well as anyone in taming the man's demons. Instead, United fans had to sit by – jealously or proudly, depending on your standpoint – and watch Gascoigne weave his magic elsewhere for club and country, attracting fame and adulation, trouble and derision, wherever he went.

When stories resurfaced in the Italian media about Newcastle's alleged interest in their prodigal son in November 1994, United chairman Sir John Hall's dismissive reaction was nevertheless difficult to counter – the Magpies had moved on, while Gascoigne had, if anything, gone backwards. "Newcastle United are light years away from what the club was when Gazza was here," Hall said. "We are now a multi-million pound operation and the club is probably too big for Gazza. I also believe that he is planting these stories in the hope that we are interested. We are not." By this stage, the cruciate knee ligament tear which kept him out of the game for 16 months had reduced Gascoigne's effectiveness on the pitch. Indeed, he reproduced his stunning Newcastle form only in patches – during Tottenham's run to the 1991 FA Cup final, occasionally at Lazio and certainly during Rangers' 1996 League and Cup double success.

An impressive 1990 World Cup – and those iconic tears in the semi-final against Germany when a booking ruled him out of a final which England would not reach anyway, going down on penalties – would mark him out as a huge national celebrity.

His life was played out daily in the tabloids in lurid detail for years afterwards. But Gascoigne's temperament was never strong enough to cope with such attention. The media spotlight was blinding for a vulnerable man who had to battle various addictions to alcohol, cocaine, morphine, the collapse of his marriage, and a career which petered out without reaching anything like its potential promise.

But for all his personal troubles, the greatest tragedy for Newcastle fans is that the club never capitalised on his undoubted genius. Quite simply, Gascoigne was a Newcastle great born at the wrong time. With just a modicum more ambition from the club, who had failed to build on an exciting 1983/84 promotion side, and just a few more quality players around him, he may have been able to break into the inner sanctum of Newcastle United legends – the likes of Gallacher, Milburn, Keegan, Beardsley and Shearer. As it is, Gascoigne's spell at his hometown club is a metaphor for his entire career – a tale of thrills, spills and unfulfilled potential.

Yet despite his many faults and misdemeanours, he left Newcastle having built up a huge affection from the rank-and-file supporters.

The secret to that lies more in his passion, vulnerability, talent, honesty and genius more than his childishness, his obsession, anger, depression or addiction.

Gascoigne was a simple Geordie lad made great through football, and, despite his many problems, he has always believed the game saved him from himself. Newcastle United, the fans and the club he adores, played the first, vital role in that perceived redemption and a man who has contemplated taking his own life many times has gone on record asking for his ashes to be sprinkled over the St James' Park turf when the time does come. He certainly created many special memories there – and all before his 21st birthday. For biased United fans, these displays, when Paul Gascoigne conducted games like a master puppeteer, were the highlights of a troubled life.

Despite all the downsides, he remains, for many living Geordies, the most exciting thing ever seen in black and white.

Andy Cole

1993-1995: 84 games, 68 goals

"Andy Cole, Andy Cole
Andy, Andy Cole
When he gets the ball scores a goal
Andy, Andy Cole"
(Terrace chant sung to the tune of Boney M's 'Holiday')

THAT SIMPLE CHANT reflects a simple tale of the boy from nowhere who, for a time, became the most prolific striker in Newcastle United's history. It was sung the length and breadth of the land during the 22 months Cole wore black and white – plundering 68 goals in just 84 appearances wheresoever he went. And it became more firmly embedded in the consciousness of Newcastle fans than almost any other terrace song of the modern era.

Throughout his 306 days as a Magpie, nobody flew higher than Andrew Alexander Cole – in his time, he was as big a hero on Tyneside as it is possible to be. If it was between 1993 and 1995, then the name on the back of the shirt was Cole.

But his short stay on Tyneside, his transfer to bitter rivals Manchester United and Newcastle's eventual subsequent signings of Les Ferdinand and Alan Shearer all combine, in some doubters' minds, to detract from his huge achievements at the club.

THE TRUTH IS, even the likes of Alan Shearer and Jackie Milburn cannot outshine Cole at his peak – his astonishing 41-goal haul in 1993/94 stands as a club record which may never be beaten. Admittedly, the brevity of Cole's Tyneside sojourn prevents him challenging the very elite of United legends, past and present. Yet for the time he wore black and white, this whippet-like centre-forward was as popular as any No. 9 in Magpies history. The figures go some way to explaining why Cole became an almost instant idol on North East shores.

-       He scored seven goals in seven starts
-       Make that 11 in 11
-       Then 20 in 20
-       He scored the fastest 30 goals in club history
-       And made it 50 goals in 49 games
-       He became the first Newcastle player to score a hat-trick in three different major competitions
-       Collected SEVEN hat-tricks in less than two years at the club
-       And ended his United career with an 81 per cent scoring ratio, - the second best ever behind Hughie Gallacher at 82 per cent

Cole's finest achievement was undoubtedly that 41-goal seasonal haul, from just 45 games, which broke the record of 39 held jointly by Gallacher (1927) and George Robledo (1952). Newcastle's newest sensation was voted PFA Player of the Year that season – and his achievements already had manager Kevin Keegan and chairman Sir John Hall searching for new superlatives. "Andy Cole isn't going to become one of Newcastle's striking legends… he already is," said Keegan in October, 1993. Meanwhile Hall purred: "Andy Cole is our new Jackie Milburn," before adding prophetically: "He is priceless. He belongs to Newcastle United and we are a buying club not a selling club."

All the more reason then that Cole's eventual sale just 16 months after those words were spoken would go down as one of the biggest shocks the North East sporting public had ever experienced. It was arguably worse than the sale of Gallacher some 65 years earlier as there had been plenty of rumours of unrest surrounding Hughie. No one had a clue that Cole was even up for sale.

ANDREW – AS HE would later insist on being called – Cole was in many ways an unlikely icon for Newcastle fans and his rapid emergence as one of the biggest United cult heroes of modern times remains a remarkable and unparalleled tale. At 5ft 11in and 11 stone, he was smaller and less aggressive than almost all of his famous forebears in the No. 9 shirt. He was also, at various times in his United career, referred to as surly, lazy, arrogant, shy and stand-offish. The author can testify to the latter two terms – one interview with Cole at Durham's Maiden Castle training ground was the most tortuous of my journalistic career, inevitably bringing the words blood and stone to mind. Indeed, alongside the swaggering playboys of Hughie Gallacher, and Malcolm Macdonald, or the mischievous charm of a young Paul Gascoigne, Cole's personality seems downright dull in comparison.

But more to the point, much more to the point, he was black.

But bedecked in black and white, with the ball at his feet – then, more pertinently, in the back of the net – the young Mr Cole came alive. The eyes and the flashing smile would light up St James' Park in a glorious instant.

And his goals allowed a black man to become a mainstream icon in northern Britain for the first time in history.

All strikers thrive on goals, but this was one player who *lived* for them – who judged his very happiness by them. He once responded to a question about how he was settling in Newcastle by declaring: "At the moment all I think about is carrying on scoring as I have been doing. If I do that, I'll be happy."

United fans were sharing the joy on an ever more regular basis as Cole provided the cutting edge to the most exciting team most supporters had seen in their lifetime.

MANAGER KEVIN KEEGAN, who paid a club record £1.75m to Bristol City for Cole in March 1993, proved bang-on the considerable money when he hailed the new boy as "the final piece of the jigsaw".

Although Cole was not a complete unknown at the time, having scored 19 goals in 40 games for City, Keegan's deal – and the hefty fee – were still a surprise for a team which already looked on course for the First Division title.

But United's manager – already starting the rebuilding process in anticipation of a debut Premiership campaign – would not be deterred. He told his No 2 Terry McDermott that he simply had to have the player who had so impressed in United's 2-1 away win at Bristol City two months previously.

Cole had given England defender-in-the-making Steve Howey a testing time that day and caught the eye with an impudent trick that involved him leaving the field of play and re-entering to get past his man – it nearly resulted in a goal, and it stuck in Keegan's mind . . .

"I had never seen skill like it at that level," recalled the former United boss.

Keegan was so impressed that he and McDermott, on a whim, begged to borrow director Douglas Hall's private plane to jet down the West Country just in time for kick-off to watch their target in action weeks before the deal went through.

They had already had one bid rejected when United's chief executive Freddie Fletcher decided to try again, after a chance meeting with Keegan in a Jesmond restaurant. This time, Newcastle hit lucky – Fletcher's phone call coinciding with a Bristol City board meeting, and within minutes, the principles of a record-breaking deal were done.

Keegan recalls in his autobiography: "I promised Freddie that this was going to prove to be a great day for the club".

Not that Keegan and Cole got off to the best of starts – the manager calling his prospective signing "Anth" (the name of a young player on Newcastle's books at the time) during his first phone call to the striker, and the latter insisting he could not travel up to Newcastle to sign straight away, since he had arranged a night out in London.

FIRST IMPRESSIONS ON the field were more favourable – Cole scored on his full debut, a 4-0 home win over Notts County on March 20 – and he had only four starts under his belt when he scored the first hat-trick of his Newcastle career, in a 6-0 home win over Barnsley on 7 April. In all, he would score 12 times in just 11 starts in that season, collecting a First Division Championship medal and signing off with another hat-trick – a feat matched by strike partner David Kelly – in a carnival-like 7-1 home in over Leicester on the final day of the season. Yet the personal highlight of his first few weeks on Tyneside had come a week earlier – when he produced a long-range rocket shot to seal a

2-1 home win over Oxford. It left Newcastle No. 2 Terry McDermott purring: "That was a hell of a goal. I'm calling Andy 'The Predator' after that effort. I think most fans got a glimpse of the lad's potential with that strike." Cole said simply: "It's the best goal I have ever scored."

But there would be plenty more contenders over the coming months.

The third hat-trick of Cole's spectacular Newcastle career came in his 21st appearance – a 4-1 Coca Cola Cup win over Notts County at St James's Park on 22 September. The County back four must have been praying for their nemesis to be injured in the return leg – but no such luck. Cole turned up, and repeated the dose with another hat-trick and a superb performance in a 7-1 victory. For supporters' website editor Kevin Fletcher – founder of the *TalkoftheToon* fanzine and a lifelong supporter who saw every one of Cole's games for Newcastle – this was his finest hour in a United shirt. Furthermore, it was the sort of scintillating display that persuades Fletcher to rate Cole as his number one No. 9.

> "I saw all of SuperMac's games for Newcastle and Shearer of course, and, although Shearer has given the best service overall, for me, Cole is the best centre-forward I've ever seen play for the club. Nobody has matched his level of performance in those two years. His partnership with Peter Beardsley was unbelievable. They read each other's game so well, and Cole was so fast out of the blocks to latch onto Beardsley's passes. At Notts County, in the League Cup, his performance was incredible. Even the home fans were singing "Cole for England by the end – and they knew he used to be a Forest fan! But my favourite memory of Cole was away to Oldham a few weeks later. He scored twice, and produced a superb piece of skill that I'll never forget. He beat three defenders right on the touchline and then tried to bend the ball in around the post. It would have been the best goal I'd ever seen."

By this stage, Cole had proven conclusively that he scared Premiership defenders just as he had those in Division One. Shocked by his pace, and his habit of striking the ball early, opponents were given very little time to react – and his shooting accuracy meant that any half-chance around the box could prove deadly. Blackburn's Colin Hendry said at the time: "Andy is one of the most difficult strikers to play against. He is quick and instinctive around the box" Arsenal and England striker Ian Wright was even more fulsome in his praise, insisting: "He's up there with the likes of Law and Best in my opinion".

A lean goal machine with lightning–quick reflexes, Cole did not humble himself to go in for any of that "holding the ball up" business or getting involved in physical battles with defenders. He preferred to make space for himself through movement, and speed – but would only do so if he had the scent of goal in his nostrils. Keegan remembers a player who would be out of the game for long periods, only to steal the show when his chance came along – a knack which gave the striker a legend to rival Keegan himself on Tyneside. "He was just phenomenal," said his former manager. "Everywhere I went everyone wanted to talk about Andy Cole. So what was it about him? It was his finishing. Andy lived for goals. He didn't have great stamina, but he did have electric pace – and an incredible knack for scoring. Some games he hardly seemed to get involved but he would still walk off holding the ball having scored a hat-trick."

Cole's sensational success was fuelled by an outrageous self-belief, as he became the hottest property in British football during his very first season in the top flight. A hat-trick in the 3-0 home win over Liverpool on 21 November 1993 will live long in the memory of Newcastle fans – Cole proving his class against the best in a seminal victory which proved the club was back among the elite. At this stage, he had scored an incredible 21 goals in 18 matches since the start of the season.

Another hat-trick in a 4-0 home win over Coventry in February kept his strike rate at over 100 per cent and Cole broke into uncharted waters by becoming the first Newcastle player ever to score 40 goals in a season with his goal in the 5-1 demolition of Aston Villa at St James' Park on 27 April.

The goal, United's third on the night, was typical Cole – latching on to a through-ball from Scott Sellars, outpacing the defence, tricking Villa keeper Nigel Spink with a body swerve before drilling the ball low and hard into the corner of the net.

It brought the game to a standstill as the rest of the Newcastle team mobbed their record-breaker, backed by a massive crescendo of noisy adulation from the terraces. St. James' Park provided a standing ovation almost unprecedented in its scale and duration, for a man who had taken Tyneside by storm. It was one of those emotional moments that prove football moves its followers like no other sport. It elevated Cole from mere legend to the very peak of immortality.

Cole wrapped up his astonishing campaign with a strike in the 2-0 home win over Arsenal on the final day of the season – and at this stage of his United career, before a shin splints complaint dulled his sharpness a touch in the 1994/95 season, he had scored 53 times in 57 appearances. Little wonder his striker partner Peter Beardsley had described him weeks earlier as "the most exciting prospect in the world".

COLE'S SCORING ACHIEVEMENTS are all the more amazing considering that, unlike many strikers, Cole did not take penalties – indeed he had taken his very first spot-kick at Coventry in October 1993, when regular taker Beardsley was off the field injured. But missed. It was one of the very few occasions that Cole had reason to curse his strike partner. Indeed, Beardsley's creative genius played a massive part in turning Cole into a Newcastle legend. With his knack of playing the ball in behind and between defenders and his visionary, inch-perfect passing, he was the ideal foil for a pacy predator like Cole who loved to operate on the ground.

In truth, this unconventional centre-forward was never much of a threat in the air, and Newcastle's whole passing game, with quick balls played in to feet or through the defence, suited him perfectly. Beardsley himself picked up 21 goals that season as a vital part of what many fans feel is the greatest United striking partnership of all time. The two players shared the North East Sports Council Sports Personality of the Year award in 1994, and Keegan declared:

> "Andy has made a terrific impact – not just on the football club and the fans, but on the area as a whole… he's got a lot of time for kids and they love him. He's done it in his own way. He may be quieter than some of our players, but, in his own way, his personality shines through. He's overcome a lot of barriers and a few little hiccups."

Some of the barriers his manager referred to were undoubtedly racial. Cole's story is significant in North East social history, since he emerged as the region's first genuine black sporting hero. And in an area which had suffered from racism on the terraces not too long before, his success story paved the way for others to follow in his wake as black players such as Les Ferdinand and Tino Asprilla received their due share of adulation.

Newcastle had fielded black players before Cole, of course – striker Howard Gayle joined on loan from Liverpool in 1982, while Tony Cunningham became the first black player to sign permanently three years later. Cole, though, was the first to win the hearts and minds of Newcastle's footballing public, after brushing off doubts over how a black player would be received in the North East. "Yes, I was a bit concerned," he later recalled. "A few people had mentioned it to me. But the fans have been brilliant towards me. They have been unbelievably friendly. You have to go by instincts and find out by yourself. You can't go by people's reputation."

When he signed in 1993, it was a full seven years since West Ham's Bobby Barnes had bananas thrown at him on the St James' Park pitch, and even longer since Viv Anderson – the first black player to wear England colours – had branded the ground as the most racist in the country. But there was still, in truth, an undercurrent of racism among some sections of Newcastle's support and Cole's achievements with the ball at his feet enabled the club to make massive strides in silencing that moronic minority

Sunderland's Gary Bennett – who had performed a similar feat down the road at Roker Park – declared at the time:

> "There is no doubt St James' Park used to be one of the most racist grounds in the country. Andy Cole has broken down that barrier just as I did at Sunderland. That's good for the region and it's good for black players. Cole has completely transcended the colour barrier and Newcastle's latest cult hero is rapidly heading towards the sort of personal rating enjoyed by legends such as Keegan, Malcolm Macdonald and Jackie Milburn."

The *Sunday Sun's* chief sportwriter, Brian McNally, writing in October 1993, was another who noticed the warmth of reception afforded to the shy 22-year-old. He wrote: "This intoxicating display of affection and acceptance is confirmation that a slim young footballer from Nottingham, brought up in London, has emerged as the first black hero in North East sporting history." And even anti-racism campaigners marvelled at the Cole effect – how one player could change attitudes with his joy at playing the game, and his fabulous ability at putting the ball in the back of the net. "We have absolutely no doubt about the influence the success of a black player like Andy Cole has on purging racist attitudes from the terraces," purred Chris Myant of 'Let's Kick Racism out of Football'.

However, it was not all plain sailing for Cole to settle in the North East as the region's first black superstar. If he was spared racial abuse, he told the media that his family were not always so lucky, even suggesting that they had stopped visiting St James' Park to watch him play for fear of verbal harassment. In December 1994, just weeks before his eventual shock sale to Manchester United, he declared: "This type of thing is bound to upset you. I've had no problems personally because of who I am. But if you hurt my family, you hurt me. They haven't been up to watch a game for a long time now and it's partly because of that problem. It's stupid and petty, but things like that can hurt."

For Cole himself, the biggest problem was trying to keep a low profile. A naturally laid-back and very private young man, he found the pressure of being Tyneside's new cult hero hard to bear at times. The settling-in period was not helped by his decision to make his home in the County Durham mining village of Crook – where the appearance of any black man, let alone the Premiership's highest scorer – would have created a stir. Reports of the astonished Cole being mobbed by adoring fans in the Kings Head pub soon began to surface. But if he learned to try to keep his head down, the village proved a far cry from the capital in terms of sophistication. As Crook Town FC chairman Wilf Dobinson told the *Evening Chronicle*: "I'm not surprised he finds it a bit dreary here after living in London." The club would later advise Cole to move nearer the heart of Newcastle city centre, but he could not escape the adulation that followed him throughout his United career.

Cole recalled in his autobiography: "They hailed me as their king, just like Jackie Milburn and Malcolm Macdonald... that's what I was forced to accept. Centre-forwards are the very core of Newcastle football culture."

Cole might just as well have left the word "football" out of that last sentence – and it is difficult to escape a mental image of Cole being held reluctantly aloft in oversize regal robes, complete with askance crown, by an over-zealous Geordie crowd. In truth, Newcastle's No. 9 never got to grips with the media fascination into his lifestyle and would shun as many interviews as he could – saying as little as possible in the ones he did give. No North East journalist ever formed a close working bond with the player – and very few team-mates did, with Geordie midfielder Lee Clark being an exception.

Cole guarded his privacy so jealously that the fans had to survive on tiny scraps of information – he loved soul music, came from a big, close family with one brother and six sisters, and, oh yes – he loved scoring goals. He had been in the full glare of the North East media spotlight for 20 months when, in November 1994, Cole was still taken aback at a being questioned about his impending fatherhood – news having leaked about girlfriend Shirley's pregnancy. "Yes, it's true, but I don't know why anyone should be interested in this," he responded.

But if Cole could give the slip to any journalist at 20 paces, he always had time for the young autograph hunters, and would stand patiently for hours grinning and joking around with children at the training ground.

Yet still bouts of homesickness affected his mood. Keegan – who got the very best out of Cole – once declared: "I wouldn't go so far as to say he was moody, but some mornings he was brighter and more talkative than others." His manager was slightly more critical during the biggest low of Cole's Newcastle career – when he missed an away match with Wimbledon at Selhurst Park on 27 October after a row with Keegan. The manager always insisted the argument had been caused by Cole's lack of application in training – a perennial problem – but many feel the striker was upset at the way his friend Clark had been treated. Clark had been transfer-listed – temporarily – by a furious Keegan, after he had kicked the physio's bucket in anger at being substituted during the defeat at Southampton a week earlier.

And when Keegan told Cole during a training session in the capital ahead of the Wimbledon match that he might as well go home if that was all he had to offer in training, the striker took that as an invitation to walk. After the match, Keegan famously replied to a question about his star player's whereabouts by asking the assembled press to go find him. He added: "I don't want to talk about Andy Cole. I only want to talk about players who want to play for this club, week-in, week-out." But Cole hit back: "I wanted to play at Wimbledon, but the gaffer told me I didn't want to." The ruck pitted Cole, with 27 goals in 25 games, in against the manager they called "The Messiah", and the clash of the two heavyweight icons caused shockwaves back home in the North East.

The *Journal*'s chief sportswriter Paul Nunn wrote: "When it comes to hero worship on Tyneside, it is hard to separate Kevin Keegan and Andy Cole as No. 1 idols. Seeing manager and star player at loggerheads has stretched the loyalties of legions of fans to breaking point." In the fall-out and public peacemaking that followed, Cole's agent Paul Stretford cited his client's shyness and struggle to cope with superstardom as a mitigating factor. Keegan himself declared: "Andy is a very complex character and we didn't know the extent of his problems. Maybe we have failed him a little."

DESPITE HIS TEETHING problems, there was every indication that Cole had finally settled happily in the region by the end of 1994, and had grown a touch more confident in his dealings with media and fans alike. Yet, the training ground apathy which precipitated the argument would continue throughout Cole's Newcastle career. And despite his fireworks on the pitch, it did not always go down well with team-mates. Keegan recalls: "Sometimes he wouldn't train properly. He'd just be going through the motions, something which was alien to all our players." Former England under-21 boss Lawrie McMenemy, while admitting he was excited by the player's ability also described him as "a lazy so-and-so" and cited his lack of workrate as the reason for dropping him from the squad during his Bristol City days. Cole's failure to break through at Arsenal provided a motivating force for his eventual success – he was determined to prove George Graham wrong for showing him the door at Highbury after just two senior appearances – but there were members of the Gunners squad who felt Cole had not been positive enough during his days at the club. The then PFA chairman Brian Marwood told *90 Minutes* magazine: "Andy only played to 70 per cent of his potential at Arsenal. His attitude was a problem." Perry Groves went further, insisting: "I think George Graham did both Andy and Arsenal a favour by selling him".

But one manager's difficult rebel is another's dream signing. Bristol City's Denis Smith, who saved Cole from his Highbury wilderness, found the young Cole's headstrong nature very much to his liking. He said: "A lot of people have said he has an attitude problem. He wants to be the best – I don't consider that a problem. He has an arrogance, but it's a pleasant arrogance. He knows where he wants to go. That upsets some people, but you need it in this game."

Cole's unshakeable belief in his own ability – and his desire to prove himself – would turn him into a very determined player indeed. This was, after all, the same Andy Cole who, as a 10-year-old, had refused to pick up a runners-up medal with his junior side, Parkhead Academicals, because it meant nothing to him. "Every goal I score is one in the eye for Arsenal," said Cole during his first year at Newcastle. "I want to show them they were wrong to let me go. I know I could have made the grade at Highbury, but George Graham didn't do me any favours at all. I was so down at one point that I refused to train. Graham then said I was destructive, but I wasn't."

Parkhead coach Alan McCarthy could have warned Graham et al what they were letting themselves in for. He described Cole in his formative years in Nottingham as "an awkward lad to give advice to, no matter who it came from". He added: "I was always having to shout at him, he was very stubborn. He could also be morose at times if things didn't go right."

Fortunately for Newcastle United, almost everything did go right for Cole during his Tyneside adventure – with the one exception of international honours. It was a source of almost personal torment to Newcastle fans that national manager Graham Taylor, then his successor Terry Venables, failed to anoint their king in full England colours throughout his time as a United striker. Ironically, the man who stood in his way – Alan Shearer – was seen as the scourge of Geordie dreams at the time, although you would now struggle to find anyone on Tyneside who would admit to having pushed Cole's merits ahead of Shearer at the time.

Thousands did, though – and for good reason. As the petition for Cole's call-up went national, with striker Ian Wright and Liverpool defender Phil Babb pushing his merits, the *Journal* newspaper even devoted an editorial to backing their man's claims, on 5 October 1994: "It is not just the openly prejudicial Newcastle United fans who are wondering how long it will be. There isn't a fan in the land who isn't puzzled at the continual exclusion of a man who scored 41 goals for his club last season."

Cole had proven to be a regular goalscorer at England under-21 level and he would go on to score on his England B debut, a win over the Republic of Ireland at Anfield in December 1994 – but he was distraught at his failure to break into the full squad. Two months before that England B match – which also featured Magpies Barry Venison, Robert Lee and John Beresford – Cole had survived his second row with Keegan, when the latter, without telling the player, had asked Venables not to include him in the squad for a match with Romania, since he was still carrying a shin splints injury.

In fact Cole would not make his full international debut until two months after he left Newcastle, in March 1995 – and would start only nine games, winning 15 caps in total. The sceptics argue that his one goal from those games justified his continued exclusion from the team and Cole remains in many eyes as the perfect example of a proven Premiership performer whose game was just not suited to international football. Venables, after taking the national job in January 1994, gave an early clue as to his perceived problem with the player when he declared cryptically: "Cole is an outstanding finisher – we all know that he is a specialist." The feeling seemed to be that Cole's overall game was not impressive or busy enough to keep an international back four on their toes. It can have been the only possible reason to ignore a player whose career goals-per-game ratio, in October 1994, stood head and shoulders above his rivals for an England shirt - Alan Shearer included.

As Kevin Keegan complained that "England managers don't come to St James' Park", the *Evening Chronicle* published a table to ram home its point:

	Lg apps	Gls	Ratio
Cole	115	76	0.66
Wright	333	161	0.48
Ferdinand	136	61	0.45
Sheringham	332	144	0.43
Shearer	187	76	0.41

Former Manchester City boss Malcolm Allison was in the opposite camp, and duly accepted the role of pantomime villain when he told

North East-based Century Radio, in December 1994, that he had been at least partly responsible for Cole's exclusion from England squads, in his role as advisor to Venables.

"I watched Cole last year when he was really scoring goals," said Allison. "He was tremendous around the box, but he never contributed to the rest of the team... that's why I never recommended him. I've done counts on him. He got the ball 34 times in one half and lost it or gave it away to the opposition 30 times. He passed to his own team-mates three times and scored a goal. In international football, that's not good enough. He's an individual player who gets lots of good service off Robert Lee and Peter Beardsley."

...and *relied* on it too much, was the implication.

IRONICALLY, KEEGAN WOULD unwittingly side with Allison just weeks later, when, in a bombshell meeting with the Newcastle United board, he cited the team's over-reliance on a central, quick-passing game – the Andy Cole game – as one of the reasons for his shocking decision to sell the player to Manchester United.

Keegan later recalled in his autobiography: "I felt that in playing Andy all the time we were becoming too predictable. If anything happened to put him out of action we would be in deep trouble."

Keegan had to talk his board into sanctioning the sale of the king in his pomp – and that very personal decision is still much debated on Tyneside to this day. Cole went on to prove that his Newcastle United exploits were no flash in the pan – scoring 176 goals since his departure at the time of writing in 365 appearances for Manchester United, Blackburn, Fulham and Manchester City. That marks him out as one of the most successful goalscorers in Premiership history – and yet he has never gone close to matching his record in black and white. Perhaps the reason is, as Allison and belatedly Keegan would admit, that the entire Newcastle United attacking philosophy was built around his strengths at the time and in the individual creative skills of a certain Peter Beardsley, who Cole would later describe as "a gift from the gods" while selecting him as the best striker he had ever played alongside, had the perfect creative foil. Cole played alongside superb players after leaving Newcastle, but, arguably, never another one so generous and skilful in his service.

The jury remains out then, on the wisdom of the most shocking outward transfer in Newcastle's history – but it remains testimony to the faith supporters had in Keegan that, whatever their personal misgivings, they backed their manager roughly 2:1 in letters to North East newspapers at that time. On the *Sunday Sun*'s Prize Post letters page – where the region's sporting issues are hotly debated each week – Whickham-based supporter Albert Turnbull led the pro-Keegan brigade, days after the transfer had been announced:

"Congratulations to Kevin Keegan for pulling off the biggest sting since Paul Newman's film of the same name.," he wrote. To get £6m in plus one of the country's brightest young prospects for Andy Cole, just as he was being 'rumbled' will go down in soccer history." Meanwhile, Brian Huddart, of Washington, led the criticism of a deal which still mystifies many black and white fanatics. "Has KK gone mad?" he wrote. "As a season ticket-holder and lifelong United fan I am amazed and disgusted at the sale of Andy Cole. He may have hit a bad patch, but he is a proven top striker and is irreplaceable. To sell him to a Championship rival beggars belief!"

Cole's "bad patch" was a run of nine games without a goal immediately before his transfer, leaving him with the 'meagre' return of 15 goals from 26 appearances that season – a strike-rate most frontmen would kill for. That tally also included a seventh hat-trick – in the sensational 5-2 UEFA Cup home win over Royal Antwerp on 27 September.

Nevertheless, by Cole's high standards, nine games was certainly a drought – two blank games in a row earlier in the season had prompted the *Evening Chronicle*'s chief sportswriter Alan Oliver to report, only half-jokingly: "Andy Cole goes into tonight's Coca Cola Cup tie with Barnsley looking to end his personal drought of two matches without a goal."

Regular gamblers also recognised his status when one bookmaker cut his first goalscorer odds for a home match with Southampton in January 1994 down to an unprecedented 9-4 (he failed to deliver – allowing Neil Maddison to score before Cole equalised).

Cole's excuse for the only sizeable blank spell in his entire Newcastle career was a good one – he was not match fit, having failed to recover properly from the shin injury which had forced him to miss six matches in October and November. And, with no prompting from Keegan, it allowed the conspiracy theorists to predict – erroneously – that the player had begun a permanent decline.

LOOKING BACK, THE most surprising aspect of Cole's sensational departure was that Keegan managed to sell it to a public who adored the player – standing on the steps of St James' Park to confront shouts of "Judas!" and "Traitor!" then winning an ovation from the doubters after begging them for time to reveal his hand. Would the applause have been as warm if supporters knew they would have to wait another six months before Cole's replacement, Les Ferdinand, would arrive on Tyneside? Or that United – having finished third in the table with Cole in full swing – would slip to sixth by the end of the 1994/95 season, and out of the European places?

Probably not, but perhaps the moral of that particular story is that, although Cole's star burned very brightly, it did not burn long enough on Tyneside to outshine Keegan's legend. On the whole the fans stayed loyal to a manager they had faith in – although the pain of Cole's parting was still felt keenly, not least by the player himself.

Despite problems adjusting to life in the North East, Cole had done so, and had no wish to leave the club or the area. Told initially by his agent Paul Stretford that the pair were driving to Manchester for a promotional opportunity, the news that he was moving clubs came halfway through the journey, and left Cole stunned.

He had insisted only weeks before his departure: "The people here are superb, very friendly... there are exciting times ahead for this club and I don't want to miss any of it."

Five Premiership titles, two FA Cups and a Champions League trophy probably made up for that shock – as Cole became another massive success with an altogether more successful United. But at the time, Cole felt personally aggrieved that his love affair with Newcastle had come to an end behind his back. The fans would have no trophies to make up for the split – not in the next decade, at least.

But they did have precious memories of a black and white dynamite who took the striking art to another level.

Cole became a cult hero because he traded so effortlessly in goals – a commodity which makes footballers worshipped all over the world, but nowhere more so than on Tyneside. His move to a club almost universally unpopular in these parts, coupled with that natural on-pitch swagger which is so appealing in your own team's colours but offensive from the opposition, means he has never been warmly received back at St James' Park since. But many fans wait a long, long time for their due reward from a once adoring crowd – Alan Shearer, for example, ran a gauntlet of hate back at Blackburn Rovers for years before finally being applauded off the pitch after scoring in Newcastle colours in what was almost certainly his last game at Ewood Park in September 2005.

That moment is one to look forward to for Andrew Alexander Cole.

But, when it comes, it will not match the rapture of that April night at Gallowgate, when a goal against Aston Villa created a legend – and a record that may not be beaten in our lifetime.

Alan Shearer

1996-2006: 303 games, 148 goals

ONE OF THE MOST celebrated players in the history of the game, Alan Shearer's emergence as a lethal striker coincided with a football and media revolution which catapulted him to superstardom. Shearer has lived his life in a glare of publicity brighter and fiercer than all the other major Newcastle United icons. He remains, having just hung up his boots at the end of the 2005/06 season, arguably the most successful player in the history of the Premiership, which launched in 1992 just as he was hitting top gear – and it is a strong argument. In a career in which he has captained England – scoring 30 goals in 63 games – won the 1995 Premiership title with Blackburn and in total notched 283 top-flight goals, Shearer has also become one of the most talked-about footballers in history. His huge fame and the obsessive hunger of an increasingly sports-obsessed media go some way to explaining why Shearer's legacy can also be seen as one of the more controversial among the 20 cult heroes in this book.

He is not, you see, without his detractors.

Supreme self-assurance and awesome strength of character are the attributes which helped turn Shearer into a world-beater – yet those facets have also ruffled feathers. For every critic, though, there are many more disciples – and despite his lack of silverware in a black and white shirt, there is no doubt that Shearer is one of the most worshipped players ever to wear the colours. He may never match the four-trophy haul of Edwardian legends Colin Veitch and Bill McCracken, Hughie Gallacher's almost single-handed 1927 League title, or Jackie Milburn's FA Cup treble – indeed, Shearer's 1993 title win for Blackburn remains his sole team honour, but Alan Shearer's huge personal achievements mean he has earned the right to be discussed in this sort of company.

Indeed, Shearer has rarely looked back since making his debut – and national headlines – as a hat-trick grabbing 17-year-old for Southampton back in 1988. Since then he has:

- Become the Premiership's all-time record goalscorer
- Equalled Andy Cole's top-flight record of five goals in a game
- Become only the second player, after Jimmy Greaves, to hit 100-plus goals in the top flight at two different clubs
- Won the Premiership's top goalscorer award three times, and once while at Newcastle
- Skippered his country in a World Cup
- Become England's fourth highest scorer of all time behind Bobby Charlton, Gary Lineker and Jimmy Greaves
- Won two PFA Player of the Year awards and one Football Writers Association award
- Scored four hat-tricks for United
- Become the club's record competitive scorer with 206 goals
- Received an OBE and been made a Freeman of the City of Newcastle
- Been voted the Premiership's 'Player of the Decade'

With that sort of CV, it is perhaps understandable that praise for the Geordie has reached the highest levels possible.

Former Newcastle manager Graeme Souness, for example, has described his former charge as "the greatest English centre-forward there has ever been", – yes ahead of Greaves, Gary Lineker, Tommy Lawton and Dixie Dean, adding: "Greatness is a word that's overused today – greatness in my opinion is someone who does it over a long, long period of time, not just a couple of seasons. Alan Shearer certainly comes into that category."

His achievements have been recognised around the world, with Argentine footballing god Diego Maradona hailing his impact in June 2006. "I used to love watching Alan Shearer play," he told Newcastle's official website, www.nufc.co.uk. "He was one of the world's greatest strikers, not just for one or two seasons, but all the way through his career."

SHEARER'S LONGEVITY – AND consistency – is certainly a telling factor in assessing his legend on Tyneside. He is, after all, in the top 10 when it comes to all-time career appearances in a black and white shirt with, of the legends elsewhere in this book, only Bill McCracken, Bobby Mitchell and Jackie Milburn ahead of him. But Shearer's true weight is, of course, measured in goals – the club's all-time top goalscorer in European competition (30 goals) and second in the FA Cup listings (21 to Milburn's 23) and league listings (148 to Milburn's 177), Shearer has never been less than joint top overall scorer in a season at Newcastle, despite playing 10 long campaigns and despite missing massive chunks of the 1997-98 and 2000/01 seasons through injury.

Many of those strikes have been classic poacher's goals, with Shearer using his intelligent reading of a game – and his deadly accuracy – to finish off team moves time and time again. This special knack of finding the net – making quick decisions, striking the ball hard, early and true to steal a march on defenders and goalkeepers alike – allowed Shearer, when presented with a chance, to remain a feared marksman, even when his pace slowed in his last two seasons.

Former team-mate Philippe Albert once described him as: "Someone who gets three chances and scores three goals. There's not a lot in the world can do the same", and there is little doubt that Shearer's ability as a finisher is up there with the likes of Ian Rush and Gary Lineker – the very best of modern times in the domestic game. Indeed, Shearer's overall 51 per cent goals-per-game ratio at Southampton, Blackburn and Newcastle puts him ahead of Rush (47 per cent) and behind Lineker (59 per cent) in a comparison between three of the most successful goalscorers in British football over the last quarter of a century. That conversion rate – identical to Shearer's 51 per cent United mark – also puts the modern-day Geordie a hair's breadth ahead of the man he is most frequently compared to – Jackie Milburn, who ended his United career with a 50 per cent conversion rate.

Shearer's 201st strike – to break the latter's long-held official club scoring record – came in a 2-0 home win over Portsmouth on 4 February, 2006 – and prompted a raucous standing ovation the likes of which are rarely seen at a football stadium. It also prompted an uncharacteristically passionate celebration from Shearer – and a spate of emotional interviews in which he revealed exactly how much breaking that record meant to him. "Never in my wildest dreams did I think I would do that," he said. "I know what Jackie Milburn means to the people of Newcastle and for me to be out there on my own makes me feel a very proud and honoured man . . . I knew the supporters would give me a great reception but I have to say that when I scored, and the noise was still deafening five minutes later, I did get a bit emotional, I really did. They were great to me the day I arrived on that stage at the Leazes End, but the reception I got out there on Saturday will live with me forever. It was something special, it really was."

Further links between Geordie heroes past and present were made when Jackie Milburn's widow Laura telephoned Shearer on a radio phone-in to offer her congratulations, while Milburn's son Jack told the *Northumberland Gazette*: "If my dad was on a cloud up there looking down there would be nothing like begrudgement. It's brilliant. Shearer's a Geordie, he's given great service to the club over the last ten years and I couldn't have wished it on a nicer lad." Club chairman Freddy Shepherd was also aware of the inevitable comparisons – but would not be drawn on a verdict. "It meant everything," said Shepherd, referring to Shearer's 201st strike. "At one time I thought Jackie's ghost was keeping the goals out because he had so many chances, but it's fantastic for him to break the record, especially as he is a Geordie. Jackie is held in such high esteem here, but I am sure he would have wanted Alan to have done it. I saw Jackie play but you can't compare them. They're both legends and heroes and always will be."

Local heroes with almost identical competitive goalscoring records and with lengthy spells of distinguished club service behind them, Shearer and Milburn have one other thing in common – they could both thrill the crowd with spectacular goals. Shearer's very first in black and white colours – a spectacular curling free-kick into the top corner on his home debut against Wimbledon on 21 August, 1996, was just a taste of things to come. The player himself would pick a stupendous, thunderous 25-yard first-time shot at home to Everton in December

2002 as his finest Newcastle goal. Coming in the 86th minute, with United 1-0 down and prompting an unlikely comeback for a 2-1 win, it is one of the most memorable strikes ever seen at St James'.

But there were many other contenders over the years.

A 13-minute hat-trick to turn a 3-1 home defeat to Leicester into a thrilling 4-3 victory in February 1997 is another achievement that sticks out – and there can be few better examples of one man's ability to turn a match on its head. The *Daily Mirror* report claimed that "Alan Shearer staged an astonishing one-man rescue act that had thousands of Newcastle fans punching the air."

A record-equalling five-goal blast in the 8-0 win over Sheffield Wednesday – Sir Bobby Robson's first match in charge back in September 1999 – well and truly buried the ghost of his nemesis, former United boss Ruud Gullit, in a striking performance so impressive it came straight from the pages of a Roy of the Rovers comic. It was undoubtedly one of Shearer's most sensational all-round displays in black and white – but he arguably matched it against superior opposition three and a half years later.

United's 2-2 draw against Inter Milan in the San Siro was perhaps their best European performance since the 1969 Fairs Cup-winning season. In a pulsating tie in which the Italian aristocrats were fighting to hang on, Shearer – going into the game on the back of a hat-trick against Bayer Leverkusen in his last Champions League outing – terrorised a defence containing the likes of Fabio Cannavaro and Ivan Cordoba to twice put the Magpies ahead. But Shearer's legacy contains many other magical moments.

Consider a cool side-footed volley past Peter Schmeichel in a 3-1 win over Aston Villa in November 2001 – a superb piece of craftsmanship, as he dispatched a Robert Lee cross-field pass in full stride. And, in the autumn of his career, he proved he could still hog the headlines against the very best with a pearl of a strike to produce the winner in a 2-1 home victory over Chelsea in April 2004 which effectively ended the Blues' title hopes, turning France defender Marcel Desailly before unleashing a rollicking 30-yarder.

MEMORIES, FOR NEWCASTLE United fans in recent times, are made of these – and such strikes were inevitably followed by Shearer's oh-so-familiar raised right-arm salute, probably the most enduring image of the Premiership's first decade. There were a few goals good enough, or important enough, to warrant a stock-still two-armed salute to the Toon Army – that strike against Villa, his 201st against Portsmouth and his fifth against Sheffield Wednesday, for example. But how much it would have meant to his adoring disciples for one of those epic goals to have won something for the Magpies, instead of merely stopping others lifting silverware.

He came close. Two FA Cup finals – under Kenny Dalglish and under Ruud Gullit in 1998 and 1999 respectively – were as near as Shearer got to the Holy Grail of lifting a major honour with his hometown club. But in truth, Newcastle, after lacklustre seasons in the league, were simply outclassed on both days, losing 2-0 to Arsenal and Manchester United respectively.

Shearer and his team failed to hit the heights at Wembley on either occasion and, like one of his celebrated No. 9 predecessors Malcolm Macdonald, whose 1974 Newcastle side limped to FA Cup defeat at Wembley, he experienced the pain of a woeful team performance in British football's greatest showpiece event. A second-half shot against the post in that defeat to Arsenal remains the closest Shearer got to scoring in a cup final for United – and he would later admit that the two defeats were the biggest disappointments of his career.

His critics would argue that those results remain to this day the biggest obstacle to Shearer eclipsing the likes of Milburn and Gallacher as the biggest hero in club history – although, right up until Wembley itself, he had done so much to break United's long-standing trophy drought. With five strikes to his name in each FA Cup campaign leading up to the final, Shearer also scored the semi-final goals which took the Magpies to Wembley in both years.

In 1998, he smashed home the only goal against Sheffield United at Old Trafford, converting the rebound when goalkeeper Alan Kelly failed to hang on to his own downward header. And 12 months later, at the same venue, he kept his cool to convert an extra-time penalty to put Newcastle 1-0 up against Tottenham before finishing the job with a superb curling 20-yard shot.

In those semi-finals, it was a case of cometh the hour cometh the man – and against Tottenham, a lesson in staying sharp and focused right up until the final whistle. That those FA Cup finals were as close as Shearer would get to major honours throughout his 10 years of service

– and despite a period of massive investment in the playing squad – remains a scandal.

True, the Magpies also registered a runners-up spot in the Premiership – finishing seven points behind Manchester United in 1997 – but they had never looked likely to challenge for the title that year as they had done the season before, when a pre-Shearer Newcastle, inspired by Kevin Keegan, built up and then lost a 12-point lead over their Old Trafford rivals. In 1997, two other teams joined United on 68 points in the final table – but the Magpies pipped Arsenal and Liverpool for second on goal difference after a thrilling 5-0 final day win over Nottingham Forest. And yes, Shearer scored that day too – helping to bring Champions League football to Tyneside for the first time as the competition was opened up to the Premiership's second-placed team that year.

That, in terms of Newcastle United's modern history, was certainly an achievement in itself, as the Magpies joined the elite of European competition for the first time. But it did not satisfy the ambition of a player who, despite so much ability, drive, focus and determination, seemed destined to end his career with just one major honour. And so it proved when Newcastle lost 1-0 to Chelsea in the FA Cup quarter-finals in March 2006. Shearer's chance had gone.

Graeme Souness, who won 12 major cups in just seven seasons at Liverpool, admitted: "I think he's been extremely unlucky not to have a cupboard full of medals because he is certainly a player – and has been for a long time – who should have that. "He's top-class in every aspect of being a footballer – attitude, professionalism and all of the qualities he has as a player. His personal record suggests that he should have been winning things for a long time."

Of course, as a United legend Shearer is not alone in this – Albert Stubbins, Len Shackleton, Malcolm Macdonald, Tony Green, Kevin Keegan, Peter Beardsley, Paul Gascoigne and Andy Cole all hung up their black and white boots without collecting major silverware. But none of the above played for 10 years at an ambitious club in front of sell-out 50,000-plus crowds making major investment in the playing squad, managed by some of the biggest names in the game.

The reasons for his trophy drought are complex and many – and none of them call Shearer's heroic efforts as a footballer into question.

Most of the answers are more to do with boardroom and managerial decisions, a lack of stability, a lack of astute signings and, undoubtedly, a raising of the bar from the cream of United's Premiership rivals in Manchester United, Arsenal and Chelsea.

Yet in one way United's barren run has, paradoxically, strengthened Shearer's legend on Tyneside – by highlighting the striker's loyalty to an under-achieving club. Shearer's unquestioning devotion to the Magpies – offering no realistic hint that he would quit since arriving in that world record £15m deal in 1996 – is one of the single biggest reasons why his name is so revered by the fans on Tyneside. Indeed, for some supporters, the very fact that he decided to come at all – snubbing the promised medals of Manchester United for the second time (he also turned down Old Trafford boss Sir Alex Ferguson when he moved from Southampton to Blackburn) to instead bring goals and glamour to Newcastle, marked him out as a hero, even before he had ever kicked a ball for the club.

Throw in Shearer's retirement from England duty after the 2000 European Championships – a decision motivated by his desire to stay sharp for Newcastle as he entered his 30s – and it is clear to see that the player's commitment to his hometown team is beyond dispute.

Season ticket-holder Nigel Good, of Ponteland, is one such believer, "To be a cult hero at Newcastle United you need one of three things," he said. "One is to be a great goalscorer like Jackie Milburn and Andy Cole, another is have real flair like Paul Gascoigne and David Ginola, and the third is to show real passion for the shirt like Kevin Keegan did. Shearer certainly had the goalscoring ability and passion for the shirt, and he showed that right at the start by deciding to come home when he could have gone anywhere. Therefore he falls into two of the three categories, and if he'd just had the flair as well, he'd have been up there with Pele in my book."

Shearer's decision to ignore English football's aristocrats showed a depth of feeling for the region and the club which supporters rarely see in the players they pay to watch. When he sat on a hastily-erected stage at the Leazes End for the press conference to announce his world record arrival, he had the entire Geordie world falling at his feet. The deal arguably announced the Magpies' arrival – for the first time in many supporters' lifetimes – on the world stage as a major player, signing England's finest striker in his prime. It also started a love affair between player and crowd unrivalled in its strength and duration for four decades on Tyneside.

"There is a special feeling of being a Geordie," he once said. "If you go away you always want to come back."

But if Shearer was excited at the homecoming, his feelings were as nothing to the delirium on Tyneside. Although many major stars have developed in United's history, such as Milburn, Len White, Malcolm Macdonald, Peter Beardsley and Paul Gascoigne, as far as big signings go there have been only two to rival Shearer's in the post-war years.

The first was Kevin Keegan and the second Michael Owen – all three established as England stars and world-class performers when they signed on the dotted line for the Magpies. The timing of Shearer's arrival – having scored four times in Euro 96 on England's route to the semi-finals – the fact he was a Geordie returning home, and that stunning world record £15m price tag arguably make his the most satisfying deal of all, even if, for sheer shock value, the Kevin Keegan deal takes some beating.

So what did Newcastle, having just missed out, agonisingly, on the Premiership title, get for their money? The most expensive striker in the world – who looked sure, at the time, to herald an era of golden success on Tyneside – was paradoxically not the most naturally gifted of players, certainly not in the class of a Hughie Gallacher, Len Shackleton, Beardsley or Gascoigne. Throughout Shearer career he has never been blessed with the mesmerising ball skills of other world-class strikers such as Marco van Basten, Thierry Henry, Ronaldo or Ronaldinho.

He wasn't the fastest player either – nor the biggest. But, in common with his childhood idol Keegan, he was a nevertheless talented player and an utterly determined individual who worked tirelessly to improve all aspects of his game, possessing the drive to turn himself into a world-class footballer, very much in the British mould. "You can improve on all parts of your game – no one has got anything perfect about them," he once said. "But I will get better because I work hard."

And so he did.

Former Newcastle team-mate John Barnes summed up the way Shearer maximised his talent. "Alan is not particularly quick but he usually reaches balls clipped over the top," he said. "He is not particularly tall but he scores frequently with his head. For someone who isn't particularly skilful, Alan can drop his shoulder and drill a 30-yard right-footer past a keeper."

Shearer may never have scored a goal like Barnes' famous England dribble against Brazil in the Maracana – but his ability to turn his marker and shoot from distance still ensured he produced more than his fair share of sensational finishes. He also remained one of the best crossers of the ball at Newcastle throughout his years with the club, and his legendary nerve and impressive success-rate from the penalty spot would often throw his team-mates a lifeline when they needed it most.

In the air Shearer was simply awesome – perhaps the best at United since Wyn Davies a quarter of a century earlier, outjumping and outbattling taller defenders and using his head to find the net with power and accuracy, or to bring grateful team-mates into the game. Shearer's heading ability also proved crucial when his team were defending set-pieces, and more than a few keen United-watchers felt that he may have proved a more-than-useful centre-half towards the end of his career. If Shearer could defend, he was also an impressive midfield worker at times. In the early years at St James', his all-round fitness and hunger for the ball would see him drop deep and wide in his attempts to put pressure on the opposition.

Throw in a strutting on-pitch arrogance – á la Malcolm Macdonald and Kevin Keegan – and an obsession with scoring goals, and you have a Premiership defender's walking nightmare. His only saving grace, as far as they were concerned, was that he would, like any natural poacher, try to spare their blushes by claiming any own-goal as his! Because, like Macdonald and Andy Cole before him, Alan Shearer was a striker who simply lived for goals; he never needed any coaching, as Peter Beardsley did, on being more ruthless in front of the posts.

Shearer was always ready to buy a ticket – one of the reasons why he so often won the raffle. His perennial interview line – long since perfected at Blackburn and quoted here in 1994 after he bagged 31 goals for Rovers – was "I've never been motivated by anything personal. I'm motivated by the team and if the team's winning, I'm happy." It fooled nobody, of course; Shearer was a gunslinger who, one suspects, had always fully subscribed to Macdonald's old dictum for judging a striker's worth: "Put your goals on the table!"

IN SHORT, 5FT 11in tall Alan Shearer was the complete package as a No. 9 – and he knew exactly where he wanted to go. (This was, after all, the same Shearer who, as a teenage boy, had "told us he'd be a millionaire by 25" according to his one-time Southampton landlady, Maureen Wareham.) Powering the team through his energy and will-to-win, his first season, 1996/97 was arguably his finest in black and white as he scored 28 goals (25 in the league to finish as the Premiership's top scorer), with team-mate Les Ferdinand adding an impressive 21.

United fans, having bagged their very own world-class whirling dervish, were in ecstasy – and few defenders could live with the £15m man. The fact that Shearer would never quite match, at United, his astonishing goalscoring rate at Blackburn, where he scored 34 league goals in 1995, set a Premiership record of 30-plus goals across three consecutive seasons and scored 120 goals in 153 games (an astonishing 78 per cent goals-per-game ratio), has understandably led some to suggest that Rovers got the best of him.

It is a fair point. But we are merely comparing levels of brilliance; his record at Newcastle is still up there with the very best, despite a succession of injuries and his determination to play on past his peak and past an age when most top-flight centre-forwards had long since hung up their boots. Indeed, the player's knack of bouncing back after serious injury, re-inventing his game to minimise his limitations and remain a dangerous performer at the top of the British game into his mid-30s, is one of the main reasons why he is so admired by football folk across the world.

A serious injury against Chelsea in a friendly tournament known as the Umbro Cup at Goodison Park in the summer of 1997 would have dulled the edge of most strikers – United's talisman caught his foot in the turf, breaking his lower leg, rupturing ankle ligaments and dislocating the joint. He would be out of action for six months but, showing the tenacity which was to become his trademark, he bounced back with seven goals in the second half of the season (remarkably, that figure made him joint top scorer with John Barnes), 21 in the following campaign then 30 in 1999/2000.

The following December, injury struck again, with tendonitis ruling him out of the vast majority of the second half of the 2000/01 season – yet once more he finished top scorer with seven goals, sharing the honour this time with Carl Cort and Nobby Solano. Shearer's physical resilience and ability to recover quickly from injury has impressed fans and managers alike. In total, he has undergone more than 14 operations throughout his career – the most serious, to repair a torn cruciate knee ligament injury, brought an eight-month lay-off in his Blackburn days. Throughout it all, his determination to play on, score goals and establish his reputation as the country's No 1 goalscorer has never wavered an inch.

His coach at Southampton, Dave Merrington, spotted this unusual quality early on. "Alan has the most important ingredient of all – mental toughness," he said. That determination was mirrored by an on-pitch aggression that has delighted Newcastle fans, frustrated defenders and outraged away supporters the length and breadth of the land.

Although having received 44 bookings and two red cards for United (one rescinded) Shearer has, for the most part, been clever enough not to cross the line, although an ultra-physical combative style (he seems so much bigger on the pitch than his 5ft 11in frame) has made him a favoured target of abuse at away grounds throughout his career. Newcastle fans may not care to remember – but the same was true at St James' Park in his Blackburn days, and there was a time when the Geordie boy was public enemy No 1 on Tyneside for blocking United favourite Andy Cole's path to the England team. But, like another on-pitch warrior in Mark Hughes, Shearer was always the type of player loved by home supporters and roundly abused by the opposition.

Throughout his time as England's No. 9 and afterwards, opposition fans have complained that Shearer has been given the benefit of the doubt by referees too many times, with the theory often put forward that officials have run scared of taking on one of the biggest figures in the game. His knack of going down on the turn as if fouled by his marker, then walking away like a choirboy, having won the free-kick, would annoy the hell out of opponents.

Having been canny enough to perfect the art – to the utter delight of his partisan Newcastle fans – he made decisions for referees very difficult. Backing into defenders before going down as if pushed, or using elbows and knees to make room for himself – or just simply to give defenders a dig – Shearer has been one of the most successful strikers to copy and master the defenders' own black arts, fighting fire with fire.

If his style differs greatly from on-pitch gents such as Len White and Jackie Milburn, then it mush also be pointed out that the game

– faster and arguably more physical, certainly with tighter defences to block the path to goal – has also been hugely different in Shearer's day compared to the 1950s and 60s.

There were times, though, when Shearer over-stepped the mark. A kick in Neil Lennon's face in 1998 looked anything but accidental and provoked outrage from the midfielder's then Leicester boss Martin O'Neill. "I don't care if it's Alan Shearer or the Pope, you just don't do that," said the Ulsterman. "Neil got kicked in the face and yes, it was deliberate .. video evidence proves exactly what happened. It was a very poor decision by the referee."

Yet, surprisingly, Shearer escaped FA censure over the incident, in a season in which the *Newcastle Journal* reported that a string of figures within the game had made similar complaints about the player's aggression: "Shearer has been criticised by the likes of Barnsley chairman John Dennis, Barnsley defender Arjan De Zeeuw, Leeds boss George Graham and lately Spurs star David Ginola, once a United team-mate . . ."

But Shearer could rely on 100 per cent backing from then Newcastle boss Kenny Dalglish, one of the player's staunchest ever supporters, "There is a lot of rubbish being said," claimed Dalglish, before coming over all emotional by declaring: "I would be proud to call him my son."

Dalglish, incidentally, also once insisted: "I'm lost for words when it comes to describing Alan Shearer's achievements." The old debate about Shearer's on-pitch approach even resurfaced in his final season when TV cameras appeared to show him elbowing Everton defender David Weir in the face at Goodison Park. Again, United's skipper escaped censure when referee Howard Webb took no action.

But if United's talisman has dished it out aplenty, he has, throughout his career, certainly taken it too – yet has rarely risen to the provocation and has received the vast majority of his bookings for challenges rather than dissent. Newcastle fans, meanwhile, have not only accepted Shearer's aggressive approach – they have positively gloried in it. Indeed, behind his goalscoring and club loyalty it is surely the biggest reason for his hero-worship on Tyneside.

Hailing him as the living embodiment of their own will-to-win, his tendency to play on with knocks, head bandages and strappings has been welcomed passionately on the terraces. When he declared, following a running battle with defender Justin Whittle (Shearer had to have stitches after a crude forearm smash from his marker) in the 1-0 Carling Cup win over Grimsby in October 2005, that "it would have been easy for me to stick one on him - that's what I wanted to do", the Geordie fans loved him all the more.

It was a rare example of Shearer letting his cool professional guard down and showing the fire which has always burned within – even if he had, ultimately, managed to restrain himself during the game to punish Whittle in the best possible way by scoring the goal which knocked the Mariners out of the competition.

Restraint was not exactly on the agenda during a summer tour to Dublin with Newcastle when, during the team's night out on the town, United's skipper reportedly got physical to deal with some unwanted cheek from team-mate Keith Gillespie. The *Independent* reported that Gillespie "infuriated Alan Shearer so much that the then England captain apparently made his displeasure clear with a fist."

Yet such off-field scrapes are very few and far between in the career of a player who has zealously guarded his privacy from the media – and that particular tale simply raised his stock on Tyneside all the more, since the majority of Newcastle fans felt that Gillespie, plagued by gambling problems and earning a reputation at the time as something of a loose cannon, had merely got what was coming to him.

But perhaps Shearer's most celebrated moment as a black and white warrior came in the epic 4-3 home win over Manchester United in September 2001. After an aggressive stand-off between Shearer and Roy Keane in which the former tried to delay his opponent taking a throw-in, Keane made the fatal mistake of losing his cool and, after rising to the bait by aiming his throw-in at the back of Shearer's head, earned a red card for his trouble. Keane would later admit in his autobiography that he was so disgusted by the way he fell for Shearer's provocation that he considered quitting the game. But for United fans, their captain's taunting and Keane's subsequent sending-off provided the highlight of the match and the icing on the cake of a superb result.

The St James' Park crowd had long been roused by their No. 9's win-at-all-costs approach, while the man who brought him to St James' Park, Kevin Keegan, felt that his aggression and resilience also provided a real inspiration to his team-mates. "He's the best, it's as simple as that," Keegan said. "Not because he's outrageously skilful, not because he's got tremendous flair, but because every single week when you go out there and play against Alan Shearer – it doesn't matter who you are as a defender – you know you're in for a tough afternoon."

Shearer provided, as Keegan described in his autobiography, the all-round package – so many different attributes which, when combined, marked the signing out as KK's favourite ever transfer deal. "Everything about Shearer made him worth the money," said Keegan. "His goals, his character, his stability, the fact that he is a winner. When you watch him run out with the team the whole side looks so much better. He is a leader of men, as Glenn Hoddle quickly spotted when he made him England captain, and he is so strong that he looks as if he could go on for ever. Having worked with him, I am more convinced than ever that he is a special player. I wouldn't compare him with anyone and I have never met anyone quite like him. He can see exactly where he wants to go in his career. His determination is incredible, both on the field and off it."

With that sort of testimony, it comes as a bit of a surprise to discover that United's model professional could be something of a lazy so-and-so in training! In common with 70s fans' favourite Tony Green, Shearer – according to Keegan – was no great shakes at the training ground – but on match-day he had the ability to raise his game and show his true colours. "If you were asked who the £15m player was while watching Newcastle train, you would be hard pressed to pick him out," said Keegan. "But after 10 minutes of a serious match you would know straight away . . he doesn't always impress that much in training, but then neither do the great racehorses on the gallops. The moment the match starts is a different matter."

That ability to influence a game has, until the last two seasons of his career, hardly wavered despite a string of injuries and the player's advancing years, with Shearer continually re-inventing his armoury as necessary.

IN THE SECOND half of his Newcastle tenure, that tendency to wander deep and wide for the ball disappeared, and United's No. 9 reverted more to a holding targetman approach, using his strength, anticipation and ability to lay the ball off. Yet his ability to finish off a move – with foot or head (48 of his 206 goals were headers) meant that defenders could not leave him alone for a second, even in matches where he did little else.

The FA Cup third round tie at home to Mansfield in January 2006 is a prime example. To most observers Shearer frankly looked past it that day as he struggled to get the better of Second Division markers for most of the game. But United's skipper kept his focus and belatedly found the space to drive home a flick from Albert Luque in the 80th minute, saving the Magpies' blushes after a poor team performance. It was a perfect example of the philosophy that powered the career of poacher extraordinaire Malcolm Macdonald – he always believed that strikers should conserve their energy to stay sharp in case that final last chance came by.

That goal was significant for another reason – it was his 200th, equalling the club record of competitive strikes set by Jackie Milburn. But in truth, Shearer's form as that record was gradually hunted down in the winter of his career did not go down universally well with supporters – many of whom felt that he made a mistake in reversing his original decision to retire in the summer of 2005. Indeed a survey by the *Journal* at the end of the 2004-05 season showed that 42 per cent of supporters were against his decision to play on, with 19 per cent unsure about the wisdom of his choice. (Incidentally, that same survey reflected an uncertainty among supporters about Shearer's captaincy – a role first given him by Ruud Gullit – when, with the player having already decided to play on, 42 per cent voted against him continuing as skipper. This perhaps reflected a feeling among some fans that Shearer was not the type to provide his team with constant verbal motivation.)

Halfway through his final season, a poll on supporters' website *TalkoftheTyne.com* – spurred by a hint from then manager Graeme Souness that Shearer should consider postponing his retirement yet again – showed that 69 per cent of respondents were against the idea this time. The problem? Quite simply, his declining effectiveness in the Premiership where, in his last two seasons, he scored a total of just 17 goals in 60 games, and just nine from open play.

From a man whose goals-per-game ratio had, throughout most of his career, been better than 50 per cent, that was disappointing – and yet, entirely natural since Shearer was mixing it at the top level past an age when the vast majority players had called it a day. Milburn, for example, played his last Newcastle game as a 32-year-old before ending his career in the less competitive environ of the Irish League with Linfield. Shearer was approaching his 36th birthday when he retired from top-flight competition. Ultimately, things would obviously have looked better for Shearer and his team had £16m man Michael Owen – signed on the eve of the 2005/06 season – not been missing for most of that campaign through injury.

As it was, the spotlight at times fell harshly on Newcastle's veteran warhorse. With United deprived of other quality options up front, they often struggled for pace and movement up front. A run of 17 Premiership games without a goal (including the last 12 of the 2004/05 season and the first five of the following campaign) set the alarm bells ringing. While some supporters claimed on internet message boards that "the man I used to worship as a goal scorer is way past his prime and needs to be rested" and even "his hero status is waning", Shearer simply toughed it out.

Of course, there were many who backed the decision to play Shearer week-in, week-out 100 per cent – one supporter in the same debate above declared: "He may not be able to run all day but he fights for his team and can hit the target nine times out of ten". But the very fact that the debate was occurring at all was telling in itself. Supporters' massive long-standing loyalties were being tested. Sir Bobby Robson, who had been credited by the player himself with reviving his United career and under whom Shearer scored 117 of his Newcastle goals, had warned his former charge not to play on too long.

Responding to Shearer's announcement that he had decided to postpone his retirement in April 2005, Robson declared: "I just hope it works out right for him because I love the guy so much…I just hope his play doesn't deteriorate and so that when he does go out people remember him as a fine player…I remember saying to him one day, 'Alan, we have both had illustrious careers, what is important is that you and I finish in the right way'."

Did Shearer finish in the right way by postponing his retirement? Newcastle fans may remain split on the issue, and while the statistics of that last 12 months may suggest not, another statistic – that epic 206-goal milestone – will doubtless be the one that prevails over time. And the joy that Shearer clearly felt at hitting number 201 against Portsmouth to break the record indicates that that he had no regrets about his decision.

Anyone there on that historic day to witness the player's emotional celebration – and hear a week-long round of media interviews afterwards

– could be left in no doubt that the record had been a big factor in Shearer's decision to play on. And of course, the fans revelled in it, too. Shearer's five-minute ovation heralded a glut of golden memories of the 35-year-old in his pomp; days when United's No. 9 really was, in the words of the song, "England's No. 1, England's England's No. 1..."

Indeed, the passion of that day as Shearer made history was a perfect example of United supporters' preference for romance over pragmatism. Never mind that the club was too reliant on a striker past his best – what a player he had been, and what a fantastic moment! Even those sceptics who felt that Newcastle's chances of success in a disappointing season had been partly sacrificed to Shearer's pursuit of Milburn's record were quick to acknowledge what a tremendous achievement it was.

The goal inevitably brought lively debate on newspaper pages and radio phone-ins about who was the greatest player. Old-timers' points about Milburn's war-time strikes and the fact he was never a regular penalty-taker would be countered by arguments that goals were much harder to come by in the modern game. But that goal against Portsmouth proved significant in another way, breathing new life into a goalscoring career which had been in danger of ending in a whimper rather than a bang.

Buoyed perhaps by the euphoria of that climactic moment, Shearer's form took a turn for the better in the latter stages of the season, and he would finish in a flourish with four goals – two from open play and two penalties – in his last four games. A spot-kick in a 4-1 away win over derby rivals Sunderland on April 17 was his final goal, United's skipper sustaining a knee ligament injury in that game which would rule him out of the club's final three games. It was reported by some as a tragedy, but in reality it was a heck of a way to go out – scoring in a derby win to further a little purple patch reminiscent of the goalscorer supreme in his pomp.

The following game – a 3-0 home win over West Brom – marked perhaps the most moving moment of all in Shearer's career, with the home crowd bursting spontaneously into a rousing five-minute long chorus to their hero, despite the fact he was playing no part in the victory unfolding before the Gallowgate crowd. It was a remarkable moment which even left a lump in the throat of hardened press box hacks.

With no proven top-class goalscorers to replace Shearer in those final three games (Owen was still recovering from a broken metatarsal bone in his foot, an injury sustained on New Year's Eve), the extent of United's reliance on Shearer was self-evident. Some would say it was over-reliance, because this situation was nothing new – despite the move towards squad rotation elsewhere in the Premiership, Shearer had rarely had serious competition for a striking berth throughout his 10-year tenure. Indeed, some critics have claimed that the player's huge legend on Tyneside has been overpowering; a problem for players and managers for some time.

The theories have been fuelled by the fact that Ruud Gullit and Sir Bobby Robson both lost their jobs within days of dropping Shearer, for the first time under their reigns, from a Premiership game. Gullit resigned his post – although he was almost certain to be pushed anyway – after putting his skipper (who had scored once in his last six games) on the bench for a rain-sodden 2-1 home defeat to bitter rivals Sunderland on 25 August, 1999, as the Dutchman's always-fraught relationship with the Geordie folk hero reached its nadir.

Five years and three days later, Robson was sent packing just two days after a Shearer-less United lost 4-2 at Aston Villa, where Patrick Kluivert and Craig Bellamy led the line. Although the first time Robson had dropped Shearer in the league, it was the second time he had left the No. 9 out – the first coming in a UEFA Cup tie away to Valerenga in 2004. Shearer had told the Press at the time: "I was disappointed and angry that I did not start but what can I do? That was the manager's decision." However Robson undoubtedly enjoyed a much better relationship with Shearer than did Gullit, who would later lay the blame squarely at Shearer's door for his problems with the Newcastle United dressing room.

This was a theme the Dutchman revisited in an interview with *FourFourTwo* magazine in January 2006, "It's still the same situation. I spoke to fans on the radio recently and asked if it had improved since I left. They said no, so maybe I was right. The coaches since me have tried to do the same thing and they couldn't because he (Shearer) is so beloved there. That is why I thought 'I cannot change this, it's better for me to go'. I'm sitting here now and I know I was right. It was six or seven years ago and nothing has changed."

At the height of his power struggle with the player, whose form was certainly uncharacteristically lacklustre under the Dutchman, Gullit had unsuccessfully tried to sell Shearer to Inter Milan – and was urged to do just that by playing legend-turned pundit Malcolm Macdonald, who declared five days before the manager's resignation that "Gullit has to take some action because his reputation is being eroded on a daily basis".

Meanwhile, Patrick Kluivert, whose career at Newcastle started brightly in the autumn of 2004 before petering out (he made just 15 starts and 10 substitute appearances before joining Valencia} left the club feeling that manager Graeme Souness was biased in his team selection towards Shearer. "There is only one man responsible for the fact that I did not become a big hit in Newcastle," Kluivert told Dutch magazine *Voetball International* in November 2005. "His name is Alan Shearer. That man really thinks he is God at Newcastle. Shearer is a fantastic footballer, but Graeme Souness should have played Craig Bellamy and me together in the front line all the time. But every week it was either a combination of Shearer/Kluivert or Shearer/Bellamy. Newcastle United is all about Alan Shearer. It is as simple as that. Nobody can beat him, nobody can touch him and nobody can do anything about it."

Kluivert may have just had a point. In the currency in which Shearer's greatest fans always judged his worth – goals – his return of seven in 26 starts that season does not compare well to Kluivert's six in 15 or Bellamy's seven in 21, with many of the latter's appearances made on the wing, where he was moved to accommodate his two striking rivals through the middle). Bellamy himself showed he was no member of the Alan Shearer fan club when, having been farmed out on loan to Celtic following a spat with Souness in January 2005 (the origins of which lay in the decision to play him out of position), he was reported to have sent his former skipper abusive text messages suggesting he was past it. And former Tottenham manager David Pleat entered the debate about Shearer's huge status in January 2006, after United's 2-0 defeat to Spurs. He told BBC Radio Five Live: "There is no question they (Newcastle) have got problems. I don't think Alan Shearer can do it consistently at all. He is 35, not 25, and it is unfair to expect it of him but they have this aura about Shearer where they have to play him."

Of course, with the exception of Pleat, all the above critics have an axe to grind, Gullit and Kluivert having failed to succeed at United and Bellamy having been forced out – and there is little doubt that the vast majority of Newcastle fans would square firmly with Shearer against all the above detractors. Indeed, it is possible to see most of the Shearer criticism as jealous sniping from players and managers who have failed to match his achievements or personal standing on Tyneside.

AS FOR THE theories about having too much influence at St James' Park – where United opened a bar named after him in December 2004 – the player himself tackled the issue days after breaking Milburn's scoring record. Asked on *Five Live* about Gullit's views on his influence at the club, Shearer replied: "Everyone is entitled to an opinion, but I was bought to score goals - and thankfully I've done that. Other people can say what they want. My job is to try my best on the football pitch, and that's what I've always done." Yet there seems little doubt that, goalscoring apart, Shearer has long been a big influence at St James' Park – a fact given official recognition in February 2006 when he was asked to assist caretaker boss Glenn Roeder in the wake of Graeme Souness' dismissal. And, as a hugely strong and single-minded character in his own right – much like his United predecessor Kevin Keegan – it is not difficult to imagine how Shearer might have seemed challenging to a manager not confident or successful in his own right.

Keegan himself, having managed Shearer, revealed: "Behind closed doors, Alan is one of the most brutally honest people I have met", while KK's No Arthur Cox drew the parallel between two of the most imposing personalities the British game has ever seen . . .

"WHEN I SIGNED him," remembered Keegan, "Arthur Cox remarked that if I did something wrong I should expect Shearer to tell me about it, just as I had done with Arthur when he was my manager."

There remains, however, a quantum leap between that sort of observation and some of the criticism aimed at United's famous No. 9. Yet the weight of Shearer criticism when compared to that of other United legends must also be considered against the backdrop of his huge fame and an increasingly football-obsessed media; he is also by far and away the most *praised* player in United history in terms of the amount of words published and broadcast.

Indeed, when Milburn's record was broken, the *Newcastle Evening Chronicle* published a 48-page supplement on his career at the club – there was no comparable fuss when Milburn himself broke Hughie Gallacher's 143-goal mark.

Yet the fact remains that Shearer's steely-eyed determination, unwavering pursuit of his goals, his keen awareness of his own status within the game and an expectation of high standards around him have not always gone down well with everyone. Newcastle chairman Freddy Shepherd – one of Shearer's biggest fans – admits that the player "doesn't suffer fools gladly", while Shearer managed to cause a minor stir among two of his celebrated future team-mates Les Ferdinand and Peter Beardsley with two stipulations before he even joined the club; he wanted the No. 9 shirt off the former and the penalty-taking job from the latter.

Kevin Keegan revealed in his autobiography that Ferdinand was upset about losing the shirt, although he insisted that Beardsley could not have been more professional about losing the penalties. Shearer proved he was more than up to the task too, scoring 45 of his 206 Newcastle goals from the spot. Keegan also admitted, despite his massive appreciation of Shearer the player, that the media circus which accompanied his signing did not go down universally well in the St James' Park dressing room, "I was not aware of it at the time," said the former United boss, "but looking back, the fact that it was Shearer, Shearer, Shearer had an effect on the other players, and a couple of them were feeling a bit sorry for themselves."

Such massive individual fame brought its own pressures for the player himself, too – and he deserves praise for the way in which he has handled his burgeoning celebrity. The seeds of this level-headed approach were sown in his youth; as a teenager, he showed a maturity beyond his years to resist interest from Newcastle (who infamously played him in goal in one trial game) to make the long journey to Southampton because he was more impressed by the youth set-up on the South Coast. "I just fancied Southampton," he said, "though my dad would have loved me to have worn the black and white shirt."

His thoughtful, professional approach to his career since has steered him clear of many of the pitfalls that have traditionally entrapped multi-millionaire footballers with pop star profiles. Indeed, so squeaky-clean has been his public persona that he was infamously christened 'Mary Poppins' by chairman Shepherd and vice-chairman Douglas Hall in a *News of the World* undercover expose on the pair in March 1998. His decision to keep the media at arm's length – and an obvious discomfort at being interviewed which stayed with him throughout most of his career – meant that United fans had to get used to watching a scowling Shearer, giving 'nowt' away in TV interviews.

His approach with the media has been frequently compared to that of his former Blackburn boss and close friend Kenny Dalglish, yet if Newcastle fans never warmed to the latter, Shearer's goals and on-pitch passion have always brought him much more favour.

Indeed, in the twilight of his career, as he prepared for life after playing with more regular media work and assisting caretaker Newcastle boss Glenn Roeder in the second half of the 2005/06 season, it is fair to say that Shearer was mellowing. The old truculence in front of the cameras was giving way to a smiling face and a personality experienced enough to know that he can relax a little without destroying the professional public image he has worked so zealously to create. A man once happy to describe himself as boring – Blackburn team-mate Tim Flowers called him "the Nigel Mansell of football" – seems keen now to let the world know he has moved on from his publicly-declared pastime of creosoting the fence at weekends (the very thought of it).

A few tales of madcappery have even slipped underneath the Shearer radar to back up an oft-quoted claim from team-mates that he is one of the jokers in the pack. One of the most high-profile incidents came when Shearer walked straight through a Robson press conference while singing the words to 'American Pie' at the top of his voice. An incident with a fire extinguisher and a security guard at Newcastle's training ground in 2000 was further proof of Shearer the scamp, while he once won a bet with team-mates that he would not dare work an Abba song into a post-match interview by telling the Sky cameras that "the winner takes it all in this game". OK, so those tales do not exactly put Shearer up there with colourful rebels such as Malcolm Macdonald, Len Shackleton or Hughie Gallacher, but they do at least show that the man is ready to let his hair, and his guard, down on occasion.

HITHERTO, SO MUCH of Shearer's heroic status on Tyneside has been down to what he has achieved on the pitch, and in particular, goals. He may be behind Andy Cole (81 per cent) and even Les Ferdinand (59 per cent) when it comes to goals-per-game in black and white. But the thing that puts Shearer above them both, and above almost all centre-forward rivals in the history of the club, is longevity.

Shearer has stayed amazingly consistent over a decade of service for the club, and his all-round mastery of the striking art makes him a strong contender as the most complete No. 9 in club history. An intelligent reader of the game, the club's official all-time top scorer and a thoroughly reliable centre-forward with instinctive anticipation, it has simply been a joy to watch him play – one of the few true world-class performers in Newcastle United history.

Many of his contemporaries would mark out Shearer, the Geordies' prodigal son who devoted the lion's share of his career into bringing attacking glory to Newcastle games, as the club's biggest ever hero. He is certainly up there with the elite – and a sell-out testimonial crowd at home to Celtic on 11 May 2006 showed exactly how adored he is among the rank and file.

And yet, and yet...

In the final analysis, the trophies of Hughie Gallacher and Jackie Milburn weigh heavily, while Shearer, god that he is to generations of Newcastle fanatics, cannot – yet – match the universal appeal of the latter. Milburn's legend – that of a modest man genuinely bemused by his status among the people – is a different story to that of Shearer, the modern footballer-cum-businessman who has worked tirelessy to maximise his potential as a player and a product.

When Alan Shearer declared in July 1996 "I'm just a sheet metal worker's son from Gosforth", the comment stirred echoes for some of Jackie Miburn's appreciative shock when greeted by Winston Churchill at the 1952 Cup final; Milburn could hardly believe that the Prime Minister could know "a mere pit lad from Ashington". The difference may well be that Shearer, as a world record signing and returning to the club established as the most successful goalscorer in the country, had much more self-assurance; he knew full well that he was so much more.

That sense of self-worth, an in-built confidence and a ferocious drive to be the best have helped mark out Alan Shearer as one of the most remarkable players in the history of the British game; indeed without those qualities, it is difficult to imagine a player without God-given genius achieving anything like what he has done in an increasingly competitive sport. True, he may not be able to match the warm charisma of a Milburn or Keegan (as Keegan once said: "I wear my heart on my sleeve .. whereas Alan tends to give them only as much as he has to.") But that perception is changing as Shearer enters his 37th year and a new official role as a Newcastle United ambassador. The poker face is softening, the public image is gradually changing and the feeling has been growing on Tyneside for some time that, away from prying media eyes, Al just might be a decent bloke to have a pint with.

AND, AS A Magpies legend, Shearer may not be finished yet. Many within and without St James' Park fully expect him to manage the club one day – and it is an ambition he refuses to rule out. With his legendary determination, only a fool would write him off.

Until then, we are left with memories of an iconic footballer whose star shone more brightly than all but a handful in the chequered history of this black and white club. Despite his lack of silverware, there are only a few who have ever earned the sort of worship Shearer has enjoyed on North East shores; bring Milburn, Gallacher, Keegan, and Beardsley to the debate, and then forget it. This adulation was reinforced in that epic testimonial against Celtic, and if the 3-2 result (injury victim Shearer coming on in the last minute to score a stage-managed winning penalty) was a bit false, the emotion pouring down from the terraces was anything but.

The intensity of the devotion afforded to the retiring No. 9, a direct descendant of that noble lineage of Veitch, Gallacher, Milburn, White, Davies, Macdonald, Keegan, Cole, even Ferdinand for a while, has rarely been matched in the chequered history of this black and white striped club.

There are, as we have seen, many reasons behind the adoration, but any analysis of this enigmatic legend has to come back to one, simple, thing…This stone cold Geordie killer got his high the same way United fans do – watching the ball bulging in the back of the net. "Don't tell the wife," he once quipped, "but I have always said that the best feeling in the world is scoring a goal. When that ball hits the back of the net, it is fantastic."

His stunning club goals record may indeed, never be broken. Mind you, they said that about Milburn's 200-goal mark, so you never know. But until such another hallowed day, those honoured enough to watch that oh-so-regular famous right-arm salute – an image burned into the consciousness of all living Newcastle fans – have plenty to look back on. As the man who bought him, Kevin Keegan, once said: "What a player! What a man! What a signing!"